BLACK POWER AND PALESTINE

Stanford Studies in
COMPARATIVE RACE AND ETHNICITY

BLACK POWER AND PALESTINE

Transnational Countries of Color

Michael R. Fischbach

Stanford University Press
Stanford, California

STANFORD UNIVERSITY PRESS
Stanford, California

Printed in the United States of America on acid-free, archival-quality paper

Library of Congress Cataloging-in-Publication Data
Names: Fischbach, Michael R., author.
Title: Black power and Palestine : transnational countries of color / Michael R. Fischbach.
Description: Stanford, California : Stanford University Press, 2018. | Series: Stanford studies in comparative race and ethnicity | Includes bibliographical references and index.
Identifiers: LCCN 2018013070 (print) | LCCN 2018022580 (ebook) | ISBN 9781503607392 (e-book) | ISBN 9781503605459 | ISBN 9781503605459(cloth:alk. paper) | ISBN 9781503607385(pbk. :alk. paper)
Subjects: LCSH: Civil rights movements—United States—History—20th century. | Arab-Israeli conflict—1967-1973—Influence. | Black power—United States—History—20th century. | African American civil rights workers—Attitudes. | Arab-Israeli conflict—Foreign public opinion, American. | Public opinion—United States—History—20th century.
Classification: LCC E185.615 (ebook) | LCC E185.615 .F527 2018 (print) | DDC 323.1196/073—dc 3
LC record available at https://lccn.loc.gov/2018013070

Cover design: Christian Fünfhausen
Typeset by Bruce Lundquist in 10.5/15 Adobe Garamond

To Lisa, Tara and Adnan, Grace, and Sophia

CONTENTS

ACRONYMS

ACOA	American Committee on Africa
ADL	Anti-Defamation League of B'nai B'rith
AIPAC	American Israel Public Affairs Committee
AJC	American Jewish Committee
BASIC	Black Americans to Support Israel Committee
BLA	Black Liberation Army
BPP	Black Panther Party
CBC	Congressional Black Caucus
COBATAME	Committee of Black Americans for Truth About the Middle East
COINTELPRO	Counter Intelligence Program
CORE	Congress of Racial Equality
CPUSA	Communist Party USA
LRBW	League of Revolutionary Black Workers
NAACP	National Association for the Advancement of Colored People
NAARPR	National Alliance Against Racist and Political Repression
NBPC	National Black Political Convention
NCNP	National Conference for New Politics
NNPA	National Newspaper Publishers Association
OAS	Organization of Arab Students
PFLP	Popular Front for the Liberation of Palestine

PLO	Palestine Liberation Organization
PUSH	People United to Save Humanity
SCLC	Southern Christian Leadership Conference
SDS	Students for a Democratic Society
SLA	Symbionese Liberation Army
SNCC	Student Nonviolent Coordinating Committee
SWP	Socialist Workers Party
UNRWA	United Nations Relief and Works Agency
YOBU	Youth Organization for Black Unity

BLACK POWER AND PALESTINE

PROLOGUE

SEVERAL MONTHS after the June 1967 Arab-Israeli war, left-wing writer Paul Jacobs invited his friend Israeli diplomat Ephraim Evron to meet with some Black Power militants in the Watts section of Los Angeles. Evron was a minister at the Israeli embassy in Washington and earlier had asked Jacobs why black nationalists had supported the Arabs instead of Israel during the war. Jacobs used his connections to find a group of about twenty blacks willing to talk to Evron. He and Jacobs then met with the men at a private vocational training school called Operation Bootstrap on Central Avenue in Watts in early 1968.

The Israeli received an earful. The men criticized Israel's invasion of Egypt in collusion with Britain and France in the 1956 Suez war, and they told Evron approvingly that the Arabs supported peoples of color around the world. Yet most of their comments were complaints directed at the Jewish community of Los Angeles. They first complained that the money raised by Los Angeles Jews to plant trees in Israel came from profits skimmed from the city's black consumers. It therefore should be *their* names inscribed on the trees, they groused. One man lashed out at the diplomat by noting that when the Jewish community staged the Rally for Israel's Survival at the Hollywood Bowl on June 11, 1967, they invited none other than arch conservative California governor Ronald Reagan—no friend to the black community of Los Angeles—to speak.

The Israeli diplomat endured another nationalist's rant that the funds raised by the local Jewish community to help pay for Israeli arms were funds once again taken from the local black community. Continuing on the theme of guns, another man complained that while liberal Jews helped the Israelis obtain guns, they refused to help local blacks themselves acquire guns, telling Evron that this was hypocritical and would only encourage violence. When the flustered Evron finally asked why he, and therefore Israel, should be blamed for the actions of Southern California Jews, one black replied with a classic Zionist argument: "You're one people, aren't you?"[1]

The story of the Israeli diplomat's encounter with the Black Power activists in Watts is instructive inasmuch as it sheds light on the fact that African Americans were keen observers of the Arab-Israeli conflict in the 1960s and 1970s and interpreted it in ways that related to their own lives and priorities at home. Much has been written about the black freedom struggle, yet black Americans' connection to the Middle East conflict, and the ways it affected them and their conceptualization of identity and agency, have been largely overlooked. Who today remembers that famous black activists like Martin Luther King Jr., Malcolm X, and Jesse Jackson visited parts of Arab Palestine and issued public pronouncements on the Arab-Israeli conflict? Militants from the Black Panther Party (BPP), ministers from various Christian denominations, black congressional representatives, and even the boxer Muhammad Ali all visited the Middle East during that tumultuous period, where they met with Palestinians from all walks of life, including Palestine Liberation Organization (PLO) chair Yasir Arafat. Important black political conferences issued statements on Israel and the Palestinians, and men and women of the arts and letters like those in the Black Arts Movement highlighted Israel and the Palestinians in their poetry and prose.

Given the high-profile nature of the Arab-Israeli conflict after the June 1967 war in the Middle East, it should come as no surprise that militant and mainstream blacks alike found themselves drawn into taking stands on that distant conflict during the turbulent years thereafter. This was not simply because this particular foreign policy issue was in the headlines so much but also because it had such tremendous resonance with regard to their respective agendas and understandings of how black identity and black political activity should be expressed in America. The truth is that black arguments over whether to support Israel or the Palestinians mirrored much deeper intrablack debates about race, identity, and political action in the 1960s and 1970s and ended up symbiotically affecting both them and people in the faraway Middle East. How to approach the Arab-Israeli conflict became much more than just a tertiary sideshow to more important matters facing black Americans, with the result that black advocacy for one side or the other in the conflict ended up deeply affecting not just them but wider American politics and society.

For example, it was the Black Power movement in the 1960s that issued the first significant pro-Palestinian, anti-Israel viewpoints ever to reach a large American audience outside the hard Left. Stemming from their internationalist anti-imperialism, black militants latched on to the Palestinian cause as another liberation struggle waged by a people of color deserving their support. They saw themselves and the Palestinians as kindred peoples of color waging a revolution against a global system of oppression. Yet in issuing strident statements of solidarity with the Palestinians as a people fighting to be free just as they were doing, these activists also were intertwining their own identity and vision of place in America with the Palestinians' struggle.

Given that the Black Power movement threatened their vision of the multiracial beloved community of Christians and Jews united for justice, it comes as no surprise that most mainstream civil rights advocates quickly countered by lining up solidly behind Israel during and after the 1967 war. That was a safer, more traditional "inside-the-system" attitude that reflected their more conservative visions of black identity and their wider politics: change the system; don't overthrow it. This is why one's stance on the Arab-Israeli conflict rose to such importance within the two wings of the black freedom struggle. It was not merely because blacks held different perspectives on that issue but also because it became a crucial reference point by which they created and articulated their respective visions of identity, place, and struggle in America.

Black Power and Palestine explores how the Arab-Israeli conflict became connected with the way the black freedom struggle in America evolved during the 1960s and 1970s. By 1967, the rising Black Power movement saw itself as part of a global revolutionary struggle and not merely a domestic-reform campaign. Black Power activists believed fervently that they were part of a wider battle against imperialism and white settler colonialism directed against fellow peoples of color like the Palestinians. Israel's preemptive attack on several of its Arab neighbors in June of 1967, therefore, pushed them into embracing the Arab cause openly and passionately. The Palestinians were not the only Third World guerrillas they supported, but Palestine's proximity to Africa, the fact that Palestinians were Muslims as some American blacks were, and the fact that they were struggling against a country aided by the United States all served to make the Palestinians' cause near and dear to the hearts of many Black Power advocates.

Their championing of the Palestinians also said much about how black militants viewed themselves. Siding with the Palestinian national resistance became a sine qua non for radicals in the 1960s and early 1970s who perceived themselves as revolutionaries. The Palestinians also mirrored their image of themselves, the concept of identity they were creating: militant warriors, colonized people of color getting off their knees and fighting back against alien oppression. In so doing, they wanted to overturn the existing structures of power that enslaved them. Stokely Carmichael and Charles V. Hamilton noted in their classic 1967 book *Black Power: The Politics of Liberation in America* that Black Power advocates wanted the same thing that their comrades of color overseas wanted: "We see independent politics as a crucial vehicle in our liberation. But at no time must this development be viewed in isolation from similar demands heard around the world. Black and colored peoples are saying in a clear voice that they intend to determine for themselves the kinds of political, social and economic systems they will live under. Of necessity, this means that the existing systems of the dominant, oppressive group—the entire spectrum of values, beliefs, traditions and institutions—will have to be challenged and changed."[2]

Black Power groups also keenly resented what they considered white paternalism. They sought to create vibrant, independent organizations and cultural fora controlled by themselves. They also demanded the right to speak out on matters of American foreign policy, something that historically had been the domain of well-educated white elites, and cared little if coming to the defense of the Palestinians angered white supporters of Israel, notably American Jews, who traditionally had been allies of the black freedom struggle.

For their part traditional civil rights groups also took sides in the Arab-Israeli conflict in the 1960s and 1970s in ways that reflected their own respective conceptualization of identity and political action in America. Mainstream black leaders saw themselves as prying open the door to civic equality in America, not as trying to overthrow the system. They also echoed the attitudes held by many Americans that Israel was a kindred bastion of multiethnic democracy fighting against reactionary, Soviet-backed Arab anti-Semites who also threatened American Cold War interests. Part of the civil rights struggle involved coalitions with whites, notably Jews, whose financial support and opinions mattered. Supporting causes near and dear to those allies, therefore, was a vital concern.

Traditional black organizations had other priorities, too. They wanted both to preserve their focus on working against racism and avoid engendering unnecessary criticism that could dilute their effectiveness in dealing with racial matters by speaking out on foreign policy questions. Yet when it came to the Middle East, these groups believed they were forced to release statements on the Arab-Israeli conflict in order to distance themselves from Black Power groups that were attacking Israel. These voices represented an ideological and practical challenge of the first order for civil rights groups, and the Arab-Israeli conflict became a veritable fault line separating the two approaches to securing a just future for black Americans.

In part the difference in attitude between these two approaches was generational: older, established, bourgeois civil rights leaders in coats and ties versus younger, more revolutionary Black Power militants sporting dashikis or black berets. Traditional black organizations had worked long and hard for racial justice within the very liberal, capitalist American system that was now under attack by Black Power radicals. The National Association for the Advancement of Colored People (NAACP) had been doing painstaking legal spadework since 1909, the National Urban League since 1910. Activists in these organizations were integrationists working nonviolently to crack open the doors of opportunity and full equality for people of color. What they were *not* advocating was the revolutionary overthrow of the American government as called for by Black Power groups like the Black Panther Party. Nor did they view African Americans as a domestic colony that needed to break free and form its own nation as some of these other groups did. Their more cautious approach to the race question was also reflected in their choice of allies: labor unions, religious organizations, and fellow minorities.

With major issues like the war in Vietnam and violent inner-city disturbances casting such huge shadows over the period, what first brought the Arab-Israeli conflict to prominence in American racial and identity politics in the 1960s? The event that did so more than any other was the short Arab-Israeli war that broke out on June 5, 1967. After weeks of mounting tension in the Middle East, Israeli forces shattered the Egyptian, Syrian, and Jordanian armies in six days of fighting, capturing a huge amount of Arab territory in the process. In many ways the real losers in the war were the Palestinian Arabs. Palestinians had already suffered as a result of the first Arab-Israeli war of 1948, when Israel was born and nearly three quarters of a million Palestinian refugees were displaced. The 1967 war triggered another huge exodus of Palestinians in the wake of the fighting and the resultant Israeli military occupation of the West Bank and Gaza.

The defeat of 1967 proved to Palestinians that the Arab states could never liberate Palestine for them; they would have to wage that struggle themselves. Palestinian guerrilla groups like al-Fateh and the Popular Front for the Liberation of Palestine (PFLP) that emerged in the world's spotlight after the war claimed that they would liberate their homeland from the Israelis through a people's war, much as Algerian, Cuban, and Vietnamese revolutionaries had done and were still doing. The perceived impotence of the Arab states only accentuated their bravado.

The Palestinian national struggle after 1967 fit within the overall revolutionary fervor of the Global 1960s. Their faces wrapped in checkered keffiyehs and their hands gripping AK-47 assault rifles, enthusiastic Palestinian guerrillas began capturing not only the imagination of other Third World independence movements but also the global media. It was not long before they caught the imagination of the Black Power movement in the United States, setting in motion an important chapter in African American history during a period of great change in American life.

This book delves into this history by telling the story of the organizations and individuals who played key roles in the drama of black identification with the Arab-Israeli conflict during the 1960s and 1970s. In so doing, it charts how support for the Palestinians changed within a relatively short time from something expressed solely by radicals to something that became embedded within mainstream black politics. In chronicling this saga, I quote extensively from the words used and documents written during that tumultuous period in order to allow those black voices to be heard today, decades later. All the passion and conviction of that time is on full display here and tells us much about the intensity not only of that era but of the people who made it memorable.

This book is the result of many years of deep research in many states and the District of Columbia, as well as in Israel, Jordan, and Lebanon. I examined documents housed in public and university archives in addition to those available online and on microfilm. I supplemented this with research into printed primary and secondary sources and with requests, via the Freedom of Information Act, to view documents from US governmental agencies such as the United States Department of Justice's Foreign Agents Registration Unit, the Federal Bureau of Investigation, and the Central Intelligence Agency. Finally, I also utilized a number of interviews with American (and other) activists from the period of the 1960s and 1970s. Some of these interviews were conducted in the past and are available online; others I myself conducted in person, on the telephone, or through personal correspondence via mail and email. The interviews were crucial not only to fill in the historical narrative but also to capture the feelings and words of key players in this drama. Biographies of many of the figures mentioned in the book are available on my website: https://folios.rmc.edu/michaelfischbach/biographies/.

The 1960s and 1970s are over. Yet the shadow they cast continues to affect the United States in deep, structural ways. The fact that the drama of the Arab-Israeli conflict continues to this day is an important reason why the story of black Americans' passionate commitment toward one side or the other in that struggle is a story needing to be told because in that story we saw African Americans doing more than just expressing their feelings about another foreign policy issue during a turbulent time, like the Vietnam War or the Cold War. In that story they also were telling the world what they thought about themselves, their identity, their place in American society, and the ways they were going about seeking change.

In his famous "Message to the Grass Roots" speech that he delivered in Detroit on November 10, 1963, Malcolm X said, "Of all our studies, history is best qualified to reward our research."[3] Studying history indeed can tell us much about not just the past but how and where we stand in the present and how we can chart the future. I have written this book in just such a hope.

CHAPTER I

BLACK INTERNATIONALISM

Malcolm X and the Rise of Global Solidarity

ON SEPTEMBER 4, 1964, an Egyptian government car departed Cairo and headed east, crossing the Suez Canal and continuing across the hot desert of the Sinai Peninsula before finally arriving in the town of Khan Yunis in the Gaza Strip. Gaza was crammed full of Palestinian refugees, hundreds of thousands of exiles who had fled or been expelled from their homes by Israeli forces during the first Arab-Israeli war of 1948. One of the passengers in the car was keenly aware of what it meant to be an exile from one's original homeland: Malcolm X, who passionately fought for the freedom of blacks in America who lived hundreds of years and thousands of miles from their ancestral homelands in Africa.[1]

Malcolm X took aim at the structural issues that undergirded racism throughout the United States, and he demanded political and economic power, cultural independence, and identity, even the revolutionary transformation of capitalist America. Famous Black Power advocate Stokely Carmichael noted this was what set "revolutionaries" apart from mere "militants" in the 1960s: "This differentiates the black militant from the black revolutionary. The black militant is one who yells and screams about the evils of the American system, himself trying to become a part of that system. The black revolutionary's cry is not that he is excluded, but that he wants to destroy, overturn, and completely demolish the American system and start with a new one that allows humanity to flow."[2] Malcolm X also was one of the most prominent early voices in the 1960s to connect the black struggle in America with a wider global revolution being waged by peoples of color, a revolution seeking freedom, justice, and independence.

In this context of situating their own movement within the wider antico-lonial struggles of the Global 1960s, Black Power activists such as Malcolm X found themselves drawn to the Palestinian cause. It was not only an abstract ideological identification. Indeed, support for the Palestinians in their struggle against Israel became a vital part of the programs and worldviews of several important groups and individuals within the Black Power movement and, in so doing, reflected and deepened their attitudes toward race, identity, and po-litical action at home.

MALCOLM X, GLOBAL BLACK SOLIDARITY, AND PALESTINE

Malcolm X was a towering figure in the emergence of the Black Power move-ment during the 1960s, and his solidly pro-Palestinian stance on the Arab-Israeli conflict was the culmination both of his Islamic beliefs and of his keen sense of global black solidarity with liberation struggles being waged by kindred peoples of color. While imprisoned in the late 1940s, Malcolm X converted to a black American religious organization, the Nation of Islam (sometimes called the Black Muslims). Under the leadership of Elijah Muhammad, whom its adherents regarded as a prophet, the Nation of Islam was instrumental in prompting blacks like Malcolm X to connect with their African heritage and identity. It also called their attention to events in Africa and elsewhere in the Third World. Afrocentricity certainly was not new to blacks in the United States by the mid-twentieth century, nor was black transnationalism: oppres-sion against blacks abroad had affected black identity in the United States for a long time.[3] Coming, as it did, during the era of decolonization in Africa and Asia in the 1950s, however, the Nation of Islam's internationalist emphasis did much to pave the way for Black Power internationalism and support for the Palestinians later in the 1960s.

Malcolm X was well aware of the Palestinian struggle as he ascended into a leadership role in the Nation of Islam. Muslims of various nationalities, including Palestinians, maintained contacts with the Nation. Jamil Shakir Diab was one such Palestinian. Diab immigrated to the United States in 1948, the year of the massive Palestinian refugee exodus, and thereafter served as principal and instructor of Arabic at the University of Islam, a school in Chicago run by the Nation of Islam's Temple Number 2.[4] Another Arab who maintained contacts with the Nation to promote relationships between black American Muslims and the wider Arab and Islamic worlds was Mohammed Taki ("M. T.") Mehdi, an Iraqi working for the Arab League's Arab Information Office in San Francisco. Mehdi first met Malcolm X in San Francisco on February 15, 1958, and two months later worked with him to put together the Third Pakistan Republic Day conference in Hollywood, California, on April 7, 1958.

At this event Malcolm X made some of his first public comments about the Arab-Israeli conflict when he spoke at a press conference held at the Roosevelt Hotel. He forcefully revealed his growing ideas about the interconnectedness between Arabs and American blacks. After all, he stated, they were peoples of color related by blood and shared an identity. "The Arabs, as a colored people," he noted, "should and must make more effort to reach the millions of colored people in America who are related to the Arabs by blood." Were the Arabs to do this, he continued, "these millions of colored peoples would be completely in sympathy with the Arab cause." He also underscored his hostility toward Zionism. Any Arab effort to reach black Americans must not rely on the white media, Malcolm continued, because "it is asinine to expect fair treatment from the white press since they are all controlled by Zionists." Moreover, he was clear about who was to blame for the problems between Israel and the Arabs: "aggressive Zionists," just as he blamed the American government for "subsidiz[ing]" Israel.[5]

A little more than a year later, Malcolm X actually visited the Middle East. His trip came after the Nation of Islam cabled greetings to the Afro-Asian Solidarity Conference, which opened in late December of 1957 in Cairo under the patronage of Egyptian president Gamal Abdel Nasser. By then Nasser was at the height of his power and influence and was without question the Arab world's most important leader. He also was a major figure in the neutralist Third World movement that saw formerly colonized nations band together in their refusal to join either the American-dominated First World bloc or the Soviet-dominated Second World bloc. In March of 1959 Nasser reciprocated by sending greetings to Elijah Muhammad on the occasion of the Nation of Islam's convention in Chicago. Nasser then followed up three months later with a formal invitation for him to visit the Arab world. Because of problems obtaining an American passport, Muhammad deputized Malcolm X to travel in his place.

Malcolm's first trip to the Arab world proved immensely significant for his religious and political development. During the July 1959 trip he visited Egypt, meeting with Nasser's deputy for Islamic affairs, Vice President Anwar al-Sadat, and other officials before traveling onward to Saudi Arabia. He also traveled briefly to Jordanian-controlled East Jerusalem, in the Palestinians' homeland.[6] Muhammad himself traveled to the Middle East a few months later, in November of 1959, where he too visited East Jerusalem briefly, arriving on November 28 and departing the next day for Cairo.[7]

Malcolm's trip deepened his belief that a white imperialist world was locked in a struggle with a larger black world combating racism and foreign domination. In using the word *black*, he said, "I mean non-white—black, brown, red or yellow" people: "The dark masses of Africa and Asia and Latin America are already seething with bitterness, animosity, hostility, unrest, and impatience with the racial intolerance that they themselves have experienced at the hands of the white West."[8] Palestine was such a country, a country of color. A few years later Malcolm X stated clearly that black Americans were part and parcel of the revolution being waged by peoples of color because they, too, had been subjected to that same white racism: "What happens to a black man in America today happens to the black man in Africa. What happens to a black man in America and Africa happens to the black man in Asia and to the man down in Latin America. What happens to one of us today happens to all of us. . . . The Negro revolt [will] evolve and merge into the world-wide black revolution that has been taking place on this earth since 1945."[9]

For Malcolm X, the solution for the racism experienced by American blacks lay not in trying to desegregate the United States but in waging a nationalist struggle for independence much like Third World peoples were doing. On November 10, 1963, he delivered his famous "Message to the Grass Roots" speech, in which he articulated clearly his view of a global revolution by peoples of color against imperialism and racism. He spelled out the need for American blacks to identify with this global revolution, start their own nationalist struggle at home, and thereby achieve their aims of nationhood: "In Bandung [Indonesia] back in, I think, 1954, was the first unity meeting in centuries of black people. And once you study what happened at the Bandung conference, and the results of the Bandung conference, it actually serves as a model for the same procedure you and I can use to get our problems solved. . . . When you want a nation, that's called nationalism. . . . All the revolutions that are going on in Asia and Africa today are based on what?—black nationalism. A revolutionary is a black nationalist. He wants a nation."[10] In his famous "The Ballot or the Bullet" speech a few months later, in April of 1964, Malcolm X stated that "the dark people are waking up. They're losing their fear of the white man. No place where he's fighting right now is he winning. Everywhere he's fighting, he's fighting someone your and my complexion."[11]

As part of this internationalist worldview, Malcolm X continued to connect the plight of American blacks with that of Arabs. He once noted the particular color bond between Arabs and American blacks by remarking acidly, "The people of Arabia are just like our people in America. . . . None are white. It is safe to say that 99 per cent of them would be jim-crowed in the United States of America."[12] He also began linking the specific victimization of the Palestinians in the Middle East with the exploitation of blacks in America—in both instances, he claimed, by Jews. In an interview with C. Eric Lincoln, Malcolm noted: "The Jews, with the help of Christians in America and Europe, drove our Muslim brothers [i.e., the Arabs] out of their homeland, where they had settled for centuries, and took over the land for themselves. This every Muslim resents. In America, the Jews sap the very life-blood of the so-called Negroes to maintain the state of Israel, its armies and its continued aggression against our brothers in the East. This every Black Man resents. . . . Israel is just an international poor house which is maintained by money sucked from the poor suckers in America."[13]

Given that Malcolm X connected Jews with the exploitation of blacks in America, the Jewish nature of Israel probably played a role in his support for the Palestinians. On occasion he pointedly criticized Jews, whom he claimed were exploiting blacks as Jews, not just as white people. In a 1963 interview, for example, he laid into Jews and accused them of having pursued one agenda for dealing with their own oppression but advising blacks, by virtue of Jews' important roles in civil rights groups, to adopt another, more passive solution for dealing with theirs. Jews, he said, used economic power to improve their lot in America but then told blacks to employ sit-ins and other tactics that would not transform blacks and place them in a position of power or otherwise threaten them. Because they owned so many businesses in the ghettos, Malcolm also complained that Jews took the profits they made there with them when they went home at night, ensuring that the inner cities stayed poor by failing to reinvest those profits in the neighborhoods.[14] Yet despite his attitudes toward Jews in America or in Israel, Malcolm X's support for the Arabs in their struggle against Israel was deeply embedded in his Black Power internationalism.

Malcolm X visited the Arab world a second time in April and May of 1964, and the trip deepened his knowledge of the Palestinians and their struggle against Zionism. He gave a talk at the American University of Beirut, an intellectual center of secular political thought in the eastern Arab world that attracted a number of Palestinians. Malcolm X also met with one of the twentieth century's most important Palestinian leaders: al-Hajj Amin al-Husayni, the preeminent Palestinian political and religious leader from the 1920s through the 1950s. The two met in Jeddah, Saudi Arabia, when they both were undertaking the Islamic pilgrimage, the hajj, and were staying as guests at the Jeddah Palace Hotel. Their lengthy discussions included talk about Jewish political influence in the United States.[15]

It was during his third trip to the Middle East, a few months later, that Malcolm X visited Gaza, the second time he had set foot in the Palestinians' homeland. Like his 1959 trip to East Jerusalem, it was a short visit. He left the United States in early July of 1964 for what turned out to be a four-month sojourn throughout the Middle East and Africa. The first stop was Cairo, where he attended a summit meeting of the Organization of African Unity from July 17 to July 21. During a speech he gave to the summit, Malcolm X hailed the fact that many African leaders had for the first time denounced Israel and "supported the right of the Arab refugees to return to their Palestine homeland."[16]

After the summit ended, Malcolm embarked on a two-day trip to Gaza on September 4, 1964.[17] After checking in to the Kuwait Hotel along the Mediterranean Sea, he spent some time shopping in town inasmuch as the Egyptians had declared Gaza a duty free zone and many products were available in the markets there that could not be found back in Egypt. The next day, he met with the Egyptian assistant military governor of Gaza, Colonel Mustafa Khafaja, and visited several Palestinian refugee camps, a hospital, and the area along the cease-fire lines with Israel. He also lunched with some Islamic religious leaders and heard about Israel's brief 1956–57 invasion and occupation of Gaza from an eyewitness, a man named Harun Hashim Rashid. Malcolm also held a press conference at the Palestinian Legislative Council building in Gaza City. Topping off a long day, he performed evening prayers at a mosque along with the mayor of Gaza City, Munir al-Rayyis. He returned to Cairo the following day, September 6.[18]

Back in the Egyptian capital, Malcolm publicly showcased his embrace of the Palestinian cause. First he attended a September 15, 1964, press conference given by Ahmad Shuqayri, chair of the newly founded Palestine Liberation Organization (PLO). Afterward, he met with Shuqayri and posed for pictures with him and other PLO officials. Two days later, he published a major statement about Zionism and the Palestinians in the *Egyptian Gazette*, an English-language Egyptian newspaper. A confidant of his, Maxwell Stanford Jr. (later known as Muhammad Ahmad), claimed that it was President Nasser himself who had asked him to write the piece.[19]

The article, "Zionist Logic," offered a hard-hitting attack on Zionism and Israel. Malcolm argued that while Zionism was tinged with messianic religiosity, it was essentially only a new form of colonialism in disguise that threatened not only the Arabs but also the newly independent black African countries that accepted Israeli development aid and expertise:

These Israeli Zionists religiously believe their Jewish god has chosen them to replace the outdated European colonialism with a new form of colonialism, so well disguised that it will enable them to deceive the African masses into submitting willingly to their "divine" authority and guidance without the African masses being aware that they are still colonised. . . . Their colonialism appears to be more "benevolent," more "philanthropic," a system with which they rule simply by getting their potential "victims" to accept their friendly offers of economic "aid," and other tempting "gifts," that they dangle in front of the newly-independent African nations, whose economies are experiencing great difficulties. . . . The modern, 20th century weapons of neo-imperialism is Dollarism! The Zionists have mastered the science of dollarism.[20]

Malcolm also focused on the plight of the Palestinians, dismissing Zionism's logic of returning the Jewish people to their ancestral homeland (at the Palestinian's expense) after thousands of years of exile:

Did the Zionists have the legal or moral right to invade Arab Palestine, uproot its Arab citizens from their homes and seize all Arab property for themselves? Just bassed [*sic*] on the "religious" claim that their forefathers lived there thousands of years ago? Only a thousand years ago the Moors lived in Spain. Would this give the Moors of today the legal and moral right to invade the Iberian Peninsula, drive out its Spanish citizens, and then set up a "new Moroccan nation" . . . where Spain "used to be" . . . as the Zionists have done to our Arab brothers and sisters in Palestine?[21]

He went on to question whether it would be legal and moral for blacks in the Western hemisphere to do likewise and return to Africa, dispossess the Africans currently living there, and establish a nation for themselves, or for Native Americans to retake their lands and evict white settlers. He ended the article by saying, "In short the Zionist argument to justify Israel's present occupation of Arab Palestine has no intelligent or legal basis in history . . . not even in their own religion!"[22]

By the time of his murder a few months later in February of 1965, Malcolm X was fully convinced that the black freedom struggle in the United States was part of a larger global, black anti-imperialist revolution. The struggle at home had to be part of this wider revolution if for no other reason than that there was strength in numbers: through global unity American blacks could count on the support of oppressed peoples overseas and force white America to recognize the power and determination behind the black struggle. Three months after visiting Gaza, he noted as much in November of 1964: "But the point and thing that I would like to impress upon every Afro-American leader is that there is no kind of action in this country ever going to bear fruit unless that action is tied with the over-all international struggle. You waste your time when you talk to this man just you and him. So when you talk to him, let him know your brother is behind you, and you've got some brothers behind that brother. That's the only way to talk to him, that's the only language he knows."[23] An important cornerstone of this international solidarity was the Arab world, including the Palestinians: "The African representatives, coupled with the Asians and Arabs, form a bloc that's almost impossible for anybody to contend with.

The African-Asian-Arab bloc was the bloc that started the real independence movement among the oppressed peoples of the world."[24]

Malcolm X did not live long enough to draw further attention to the Palestinians. Yet pro-Palestinian sentiments such as his would surface time and time again among other African Americans, particularly after the June 1967 Arab-Israeli war. This process started when a little-known friend and follower of his published an article about Israel and the Palestinians a few weeks after that war ended.

SNCC'S SUPPORT FOR THE PALESTINIANS

Twenty-eight-year-old Ethel Minor surely had no idea that she was making history when, in August of 1967, she published an article in the newsletter of the Student Nonviolent Coordinating Committee (SNCC; pronounced "Snick") that strongly criticized Israel and championed the Palestinians. Yet that was the event that first rocketed the Black Power movement into the American public's view in terms of black support for the Palestinians and the mixing of domestic racial identity with Middle Eastern politics.

SNCC was established in 1960 as a student-based civil rights organization that became famous for its grassroots organizing among working-class southern blacks. From its inception SNCC sought to do more than just integrate the South and push for black rights as traditional, middle-class civil rights organizations had been doing. The group increasingly "sought structural changes in American society itself" as it matured, and this included foreign policy.[25] Malcolm X's internationalization of the black freedom struggle was one of several factors that helped propel SNCC in new and broader directions beginning about 1964. SNCC activists who traveled outside the United States began to find themselves being asked about Malcolm X and what their respective stances on global issues were, too.

This development became abundantly clear to John Lewis and Donald Harris when they traveled to Guinea in September of 1964 as part of an SNCC delegation and thereafter as they spent a month traveling elsewhere in Africa. On their return to the United States, Lewis and Harris informed their SNCC colleagues that they had been bombarded with questions in Ghana and elsewhere about their group's relationship with Malcolm X. In a December 1964 report they wrote for SNCC, the two men told their comrades that SNCC immediately should begin explaining where the group stood on important world issues like the Cuban revolution, the Congo crisis, and the widening war in Vietnam.[26]

SNCC did, in fact, devote increasing attention to global issues. In January of 1966 it famously became the first civil rights organization to come out in public opposition to the Vietnam War, receiving tremendous criticism for that stance. Later, the group moved even further away from its hitherto exclusive focus on domestic issues by issuing a press release in May of 1967 stating that it had changed from a civil rights group to a human rights organization. Among other things, the statement noted: "We assert that we encourage and support the liberation struggles of all people against racism, exploitation, and oppression. We see our struggle here in America as an integral part of the world-wide movement of all oppressed people."[27] In the late 1960s, SNCC's rising profile as a militant Black Power group was exemplified by some of its leaders, such as Stokely Carmichael and H. Rap Brown, who became some of the most prominent public figures associated with the Black Power movement. It was Carmichael, for example, who garnered national attention by using the phrase "black power" for the first time in public in June of 1966.

Ethel Minor, by contrast, was a relative newcomer to SNCC in 1967 and stayed out of the limelight. While studying elementary education at the University of Illinois at Urbana, she became acquainted with some Palestinian students and thereby learned of the history of their people. In 1962 she first encountered Malcolm X speaking on television. Impressed by what she saw and heard, Minor became involved with the Nation of Islam and worked as a teacher at its University of Islam in Chicago.[28] She later worked for the Organization of Afro-American Unity, which Malcolm X formed in 1964, and joined SNCC after his assassination.

Having worked with Malcolm X, and having met and interacted with Palestinians while in college, Minor was in a good position to merge her own interest in their cause with Malcolm X's concern for the Palestinians and transmit the connection between their plight and that of American blacks to her staff colleagues at SNCC. Longtime SNCC activist Courtland Cox remembered that Minor was passionate about the Palestinians and often talked about their plight. "Ethel would talk to everybody! Ethel was dogged on this question. She was very focused on this question. [For her] it was not something peripheral."[29]

Minor's good friend Stokely Carmichael recalled, for example, that Minor organized a Middle East study group among SNCC staff members in the mid-1960s in Lowndes County, Alabama, where SNCC was active. Members of this group, which included Carmichael and H. Rap Brown, used to read one book a month and discuss it together. Carmichael also recalled that the group had spent two years reading about Zionism, the Palestinians, and the Arab-Israeli conflict by the time he assumed the chair in May of 1966. As a result of these discussions, Carmichael was dismayed by what he learned about Israel's relationship with South Africa: "I have to say, discovering that the government of Israel was maintaining such a long, cozy, and warm relationship with the worst enemy of black people came as a real shock. A kind of betrayal. And, hey, we weren't supposed to even *talk* about this? C'mon."[30]

SNCC activists were also familiar with Frantz Fanon's *The Wretched of the Earth*, a widely read book in the 1960s that described the Algerian struggle for independence from France and spoke of "Negroes and Arabs" together as one when discussing the colonized peoples of Africa. Algeria's bloody war of independence proved quite influential in SNCC's thinking, and the fact that Algeria was both African and Arab helped solidify the bond between blacks and Arabs in their minds. This no doubt deepened SNCC's growing interest in Palestine and the rest of the Arab world.

One day in May of 1967, Carmichael and Brown were in Alabama chatting with Donald Jelinek, a lawyer who worked with SNCC. Jelinek, who was Jewish, expressed his positive feelings about Israel and his concerns about the Jewish state's situation in that tension-filled month as war clouds were on the horizon in the Middle East. "So it was a shock to me," Jelinek later recounted, "when my SNCC friends mildly indicated support for the Arabs." Mildly stated or not, their sentiments prompted Jelinek to reply, "But they may wipe out and destroy Israel." Carmichael adroitly changed the subject with some humor, and the men began laughing. Jelinek thereafter overheard Brown quietly singing to himself, "arms for the Arabs, sneakers for the Jews." When Jelinek asked him what that song meant, an embarrassed Brown explained that he had learned the song as a student in Louisiana. It implied that the Israelis would need sneakers (tennis shoes) to run from the Arabs, who were armed with weapons from abroad. Brown then apologized.[31] It was just one example of how Israel and Palestine were clearly on the minds of SNCC activists as the world focused on the situation in the Middle East. Another occurred later that same month, on May 31, when SNCC picketers participated in a pro-Arab demonstration in front of the White House staged by the Organization of Arab Students.[32]

SNCC headquarters in Atlanta was also focusing attention on the Middle East that spring of 1967. As tension between Israel and the Arab states rose in the Middle East, leading to considerable press coverage in the United States, several SNCC staff members were at work writing background papers on Israel and the Arab-Israeli conflict in order to educate SNCC activists about what was happening. One staffer was Robert Moore of SNCC's research department. On June 5, 1967, the day that Israel broke the tension and launched a war against the Arabs, Moore and two others, Karen Edmonds and Warcell "Tex" Williams, issued a news summary for their colleagues in Atlanta. The three authors noted that the news summary was designed to enlighten SNCC staffers who may have missed the stories coming out in the press or who did not have enough background information to make sense of the news. Because of the large amount of press coverage of Middle Eastern events, a full four pages of the document included a "History of Zionism and the Isreali-Arab [sic] Conflict."

The section on the Arab-Israeli conflict discussed in detail subjects like the rise of Zionism and the British government's November 1917 Balfour Declaration; the growth of the Jewish population of Palestine during the interwar period; the Holocaust and its effect of generating global sympathy for the Jewish people; the 1947 United Nations partition plan for Palestine and the Arab response to that plan; the April 1948 massacre of Palestinians by Zionist forces in the village of Dayr Yasin during the first Arab-Israeli war; the exodus of Palestinian refugees during the war; and the rise of Palestinian guerrilla groups like al-Fateh in the 1960s. Perhaps realizing that they were treading on potentially hazardous political ground, the three writers also told the staff, in a memorandum attached to the news summary, "We welcome all constructive criticisms of the research department with open minds and open hearts, and without malice. If any of you have comments on the news summary, it would especially be appreciated. PLEASE READ."[33]

By the time that SNCC's central committee met that month to discuss the group's position on Palestine, most committee members apparently supported the Palestinians. They could not agree, however, on whether this position should be articulated publicly because of the likelihood that it would affect fund-raising negatively—a reference to the fact that Jews in the North provided a good percentage of SNCC's budget and were not likely to take kindly to a pro-Palestinian position. When the committee asked for more information on the Arab-Israeli conflict, it was Ethel Minor who apparently responded.[34]

Minor was at that time working as SNCC's communications director in Atlanta, where she was described as "very efficient and we could not ask for a better worker."[35] She began researching the history of Israel and the Palestinians. Carmichael later claimed that in his last act as outgoing SNCC chair, he and Minor cowrote a "hard-hitting position paper, much of it in the form of sharp questions against a background of incontestable facts." The paper, which was written in a question-and-answer format, was intended to generate discussion within SNCC and was only "possibly for distribution in the SNCC newsletter."[36]

Minor in the communications department and the three staff members in the research department were not the only ones at SNCC who conducted research on the Arab-Israeli conflict. So had Jack Minnis, a legendary researcher who directed the research department until 1966. Several SNCC staff members recalled that his research on the Middle East also played a role in developing SNCC's eventual policy on the Arab-Israeli conflict.[37] Edmonds noted decades later that these various efforts were really all part of the same process of educating SNCC members about the issue. Her office abutted Minor's, and she was in frequent daily contact with her about this and other issues. She recalled once overhearing Minor discussing the idea of actually publishing her piece with SNCC project director Ralph Featherstone: "I can remember Ethel discussing it ahead of time with 'Feather.' I remember him saying to her, 'This is going to raise a real barnstorm.' I think that was the term he used. And she said 'Well, do you think we publish it?' And he said 'Yes.'"[38]

The topic therefore was not a secret around the office by the time that Minor decided to publish an article on the Arab-Israeli conflict in the *SNCC Newsletter*. "The publication was reviewed," Edmonds recalled. "She [Minor] circulated it. There were discussions about it. She didn't spring it on anybody. The sign-offs were done."[39] Years later, former SNCC staffer Charles Cobb Jr. remembered the document as it circulated within the office in the spring of 1967: "This was when we were beginning to look more seriously at the liberation struggles, particularly in Africa. But the 1967 Arab-Israeli War was very much in the air. What I recall about that position paper was a very general ongoing conversation in the Atlanta office. Folks would stop by, read it, make comments or suggestions. It was all very casual. On the level of 'Hey, these folks [Palestinians] once had a country. Now they don't, they're all scattered and displaced. There's something very wrong about that.' "[40]

Some of SNCC's national leaders outside Atlanta knew about the pro-Palestinian feelings among SNCC staff members and worried about the domestic political repercussions of issuing any kind of statement critical of Israel during or shortly after the war, a war that many American Jews viewed as a war of survival forced on Israel by its Arab neighbors. James Forman was one of them. Forman was a major figure in SNCC and the growing Black Power movement. He served as SNCC's executive secretary from 1961 to 1966, after which he became the head of the group's newly created International Affairs Commission in May of 1967. The outbreak of war found him traveling overseas as part of his new assignment. A concerned Forman wrote in detail about the political ramifications of the issue to SNCC Executive Secretary Stanley Wise on June 7, 1967, the third day of the war.

From the outset in his letter Forman noted that public opinion in the United States was pro-Israeli, especially among Jews. The challenge was that there were many Jews in the "liberal-labor leadership circle" that had proven so supportive of SNCC in the past. Therefore, Forman wrote, "any black person of national stature who speaks against Israel must expect a certain isolation from the press—all white controlled and so forth." He added, "I am trying to make an analysis and I am not saying that we should be worried about these matters, but we do need to analyze them." He was careful to tell Wise that "if by chance or by design we were to take a position on the Arab-Israeli war such as we took on the war in Vietnam, the reaction would be fantastic against us. . . . I am not personally sure we can take a position at this moment."[41]

Forman's letter indicated how ambivalent he was personally about SNCC coming out with a pro-Palestinian stance at that time. On the one hand, he offered Wise a cautionary note. Yet later in the same letter, Forman pointed out that "the 'gut' reaction in many [black] people is against Israel and for the Arabs, reflecting black-white tension, the hardening of racism, and the particular circumstances in which we find ourselves in this country." He also believed that if the war continued, the "class struggle in the black community will become sharper." Forman wrote, "Actually Israel represents an extension of United States foreign policy as well as an attempt by the Zionists to create a homeland for the Jews." In this regard he was careful to note that SNCC "must have 'clarity' about the real essence of the Arab-Israeli struggle: class and not merely racial analysis." Despite his caution and desire for more "clarity," Forman's letter also revealed an activist's frustration with play-it-safe politics and a desire to speak out on Palestine, no matter what the consequences: "Is it not sheer opportunism to keep silent for the sake of trying to please the crowd? Is the role of leadership always to think that it is enough to know what people are thinking, and only to say those things we know will be acceptable? How are we going to lead people within the United States and relate them to international forces, when we ourselves are afraid to say those things which we know are true?"[42]

A few days later, with the war winding down and Israel poised to complete a massive victory over Arab forces, Forman again wrote to Wise about the issue. Setting aside his activist's inclinations, he again cautioned SNCC to be extremely cautious about taking a public stance against Israel. Three issues were of particular concern to him. The first was that SNCC needed to call a special meeting to educate its staff about this issue before going public, so that staff members would understand more about the issue and why SNCC was taking such a position. Second, Forman remained very worried about the hostile reaction that was sure to come should the group come out publicly in favor of the Palestinians and other Arabs. "I know that we would be united internally, but the external pressures would be fantastic, especially in New York," where SNCC maintained a fund-raising office. Finally, he was concerned that the situation in the Middle East was "very muddy," and he believed that SNCC should wait to see what transpired. In this regard Forman seemed to be concerned *about the wording of any position, for that is a very delicate question given the nature of the governments of some countries.*"[43]

At some point in midsummer of 1967, after Israel's six-day victory in the war, Minor and the SNCC staff in Atlanta reached the fateful decision to publish an article on the Arab-Israeli conflict in the *SNCC Newsletter*. The publication was done as a local initiative for educating SNCC activists; Minor never claimed that the piece she published represented SNCC policy or an official stance reached by the group's leadership. On the contrary, she made it clear that it was presented simply to help readers understand the Arab-Israeli conflict better and to explain "how it relates to our struggle here." The reasons readers should become more familiar with overseas events, Minor wrote in the piece, echoed the Black Power internationalist sentiments of Malcolm X and the growing consensus within SNCC: black Americans were "an integral part of the Third World (Africa, Asia, Latin America, American Indians and all persons of African descent)" and therefore needed to know what "our brothers are doing in their homelands."[44] It was a question of revolutionary black identity. Minor's article stated bluntly why *SNCC Newsletter* staff members were taking it on themselves to provide such information on the conflict: "Since we know that the white American press seldom, if ever, gives the true story about world events in which America is involved, then we are taking this opportunity to present the following documented facts on this problem [Palestine Problem]. These facts not only affect the lives of our brothers in the Middle East, Africa, and Asia, but also pertain to our struggle here."[45]

The article that Minor published in the June-July 1967 *SNCC Newsletter* was titled "The Palestine Problem: Test Your Knowledge" and consisted of thirty-two statements about Israel and the Palestinians that were answers to the question "Do you know?" All were strongly critical of Zionism and Israel, which it called an "illegal" state. Such sentiments were apparent from the very first statement:

[Do you know] THAT Zionism, which is a worldwide nationalistic Jewish movement, organized, planned and created the "State of Isreal [*sic*]" by sending Jewish immigrants from Europe into Palestine (the heart of the Arab world) to take over land and homes belonging to the Arabs?

Some of the statements merely stated facts that, while perhaps not widely known in America, were fairly straightforward:

THAT this [Israeli] conquest of Arab land took place, for the most part, before May 15, 1948, before the formal end of British rule, before the Arab armies entered to protect Palestinain [*sic*] Arabs, and before the Arab Israeli War?

Others, while based on the historical record, were presented in hard-hitting, polemical fashion:

THAT the Zionist terror gangs (Haganah, Irgun, and Stern gangs) deliberately slaughtered and mutilated women, children and men, thereby causing the unarmed Arabs to panic, flee and leave their homes in the hands of the Zionist-Israel forces.[46]

Other statements underscored SNCC's growing identification with African liberation struggles and the racial prism through which it increasingly viewed international issues. One asked readers if they knew that the Rothschild family of Jews not only conspired with the British to create Israel but also "THAT THE ROTHSCHILDS ALSO CONTROL MUCH OF AFRICA'S MINERAL WEALTH?" Another asked if they knew that "dark skinned Jews from the Middle East and North Africa are also second-class citizens in Israel, and that the color line puts them in inferior position to the white, European Jews?"[47]

The article featured three photographs and two cartoons. Two of the photographs carried the caption "Gaza Massacres, 1956. Zionists lined up Arab victims and shot them in the back in cold blood. This is the Gaza Strip, Palestine, not Dachau, Germany." The cartoons in particular proved to be immensely controversial, perhaps even more so than the article and photographs. They were the work of Herman "Kofi" Bailey, who drew cartoons for SNCC publications although he was not actually a member of the staff. The cartoons he drew for the article gave visual depth to Minor's themes. The first one featured the face of retired Israeli general Moshe Dayan, easily recognizable by his trademark eye patch, who as Israel's defense minister had overseen its victory in the recent war. In addition to a Star of David on Dayan's uniform, there were dollar signs on each of the two epaulettes on his shoulders. The other cartoon featured the American boxer Muhammad Ali along with Egyptian president Gamal Abdel Nasser, each with a noose around his neck. The nooses were at opposite ends of a rope that was grasped by a hand emblazoned with a dollar sign within a Star of David. Another, scimitar-carrying arm labeled "Third World liberation movement," was preparing to cut the rope and free the two men.[48]

The issue of the *SNCC Newsletter* containing the article was dated June-July 1967 but was actually published in mid-August. The public reaction was immediate. Some reacted quite hostilely, others more positively. SNCC activist Phil Hutchings recalls how anxious people were to read the issue. He showed up at an event in New York City in August of 1967 with a number of copies of the newsletter to distribute shortly after it came out. Decades later Hutchings recalled how people thronged to get a copy: "And I got there at the very end of the meeting, and people were walking out the door and I went up to the person who was chairing the meeting and said, 'Can I make an announcement?' And I said, 'I have the new newspaper of SNCC with the article on Israel and Zionism.'

People literally turned around who had walked outside. I got mobbed. I mean not physically mobbed, but I mean, these people, everybody wanted that paper because that was the issue, and I was sold out in probably about five minutes."[49]

As attested to by the positive reception Hutchings experienced that day, SNCC activists clearly were not alone in their attitudes about the Arab-Israeli conflict in the summer of 1967. Supporting and identifying with the Palestinians in their struggle with Israel came naturally, easily, and sincerely to Black Power militants. For them it was a question of identity. Global anticolonial movements deeply affected the development of Black Power consciousness in the United States. African American solidarity with colonial peoples overseas helped these activists redefine *blackness*.[50] Transnational oppression abroad affected black identity in the United States in symbiotic fashion: blacks viewed racism, imperialism, and oppression around the world as extensions of the American racism they faced at home, and in turn they considered it their duty to fight oppression overseas.[51] Nigerian scholar E. U. Essien-Udom had written five years earlier, in 1962, that African independence struggles already had had a transformative effect on the self-consciousness and conceptualization of identity—what he called a "new psychology"—among American blacks.[52]

SNCC's stance on Palestine therefore served as an important example of its attempts to build a revolutionary identity and culture for black Americans. Fanon was clear in *The Wretched of the Earth* when he wrote that people of color needed to destroy the vestiges of mental colonialism and instead foster a culture of "negritude." He also consciously compared the need for blacks in America to decolonize their minds with the need for Arabs to do the same: "The poets of negritude will not stop at the continent. . . . From America black voices will take up the hymn with fuller union. . . . The example of the Arab world might equally well be quoted here."[53] Black Power had fired its first major shot in its battle to include support for the Palestinians in its definition of negritude in the United States.

BLACK DEMANDS AT THE NATIONAL CONFERENCE FOR NEW POLITICS

By August 1967, young Harvard professor Martin Peretz had been at work on his plan for months. Peretz was one of a number of left-wing activists who believed that the time had come for the various sections of the black freedom struggle, the white New Left, and their respective sympathizers to come together and discuss joint political action. Such action to create a "third force" in American politics might even include running candidates as an electoral alternative to the Democratic Party in the upcoming November 1968 presidential elections. Peretz and his colleagues therefore decided to plan a conference around the "new politics" that had emerged in the 1960s, and he became one of the main organizers and financial backers of the conference. Little did he realize that the meeting that eventually was held in the late summer of 1967 once again would showcase Black Power criticism of Israel, much to his chagrin.

There was considerable momentum behind the idea of a new politics conference. The idea for the conference emerged out of meetings among civil rights advocates, the student New Left, and anti–Vietnam War groups that had begun to emerge in mid-1965, conversations that led to the eventual establishment of the National Conference for New Politics (NCNP). Its cochairs were Julian Bond, an SNCC activist and member of the Georgia House of Representatives, and reformist Democratic Party activist Simon Casady. A number of nationally recognized figures, both blacks and whites, served on the NCNP national council, including Peretz, Stokely Carmichael, Martin Luther King Jr., and several dozen others. The NCNP was seen by many on both the liberal Left and radical Left as a major opportunity to discuss united action to change America. Indeed, preconference publicity stated, "We want to talk about **1968 and Beyond**. We start with one committment [*sic*]! **Don't mourn for America—ORGANIZE!**"[54]

More than twelve hundred delegates from some two hundred organizations arrived for the opening of the NCNP on August 31, 1967, at the Palmer House Hotel in Chicago. More than two thousand others also attended the gathering as observers before it closed on September 4. Expectations were high. Martin Luther King Jr. delivered the keynote address at an opening rally held at the Chicago Coliseum. But the NCNP was immediately beset with black-white tensions, which quickly led to conflict over what position to take vis-à-vis the Arab-Israeli conflict.

The mostly white NCNP organizers had worked hard during the summer of 1967 to ensure black participation in the conference, months that included not only the June war in the Middle East but the bloody black insurrections in July in Newark, New Jersey, and Detroit, Michigan, as well. Their efforts did lead to several hundred African Americans showing up, but the politics of

Black Power, combined with the angry mood in black America after Newark and Detroit, quickly created an atmosphere of tension. Some 350 blacks immediately staged a walkout to form their own separate conference, while approximately 400 others remained and formed a black caucus within the NCNP that presented a thirteen-point policy statement to the other conference delegates. They demanded that it be adopted lest they, too, abandon the meeting. Anxious to support black aspirations and worried that disunity could tear apart the meeting, whites voted three-to-one to adopt the statement.[55]

One part of the policy statement that caused long-lasting controversy even after the conference ended was a condemnation of Israel's attack on Arab states three months earlier. A group called the Ad Hoc Committee on the Middle East later claimed that one of its members, a black American who had embraced Islam named Ali Anwar, introduced the statement on Israel in the black caucus.[56] Beyond Anwar, SNCC's H. Rap Brown and James Forman reportedly were among those who had lobbied for inclusion of the statement.[57] The policy statement condemned "the imperialistic Zionist war" and added that "this condemnation does not imply anti-Semitism."

Many delegates were surprised and outraged by this particular part of the black policy statement. The fact that SNCC had just issued its own blistering attack on Israel earlier that month exacerbated the situation. Some white liberals and leftists saw Israel as a beleaguered little country that had acted in self-defense in the recent war to prevent another Holocaust and that the Arab territories it now controlled were merely the fruits of a war it was forced to fight. Debate immediately broke out after the statement was presented for a vote. NCNP official Robert Scheer proposed changing the wording of the statement to call for an Israeli withdrawal to the 1967 borders and Arab recognition of Israel. Despite his high position in the NCNP, the assembled delegates voted to deny even giving him the floor to speak.[58] Martin Luther King Jr. later claimed that the director of voter registration for the Southern Christian Leadership Conference (SCLC), Hosea Williams, raised "spirited opposition" to the black caucus's Israel plank from the floor.[59] Militants within the black caucus even pulled a gun on SCLC's James Bevel and threatened to kill him when he tried to speak out against the Israel resolution.[60]

In the end the uproar partially succeeded in forcing the black caucus to back down. Caucus members agreed to remove specific references to Zionism in the policy statement and to refer the final wording of the document to the conference's executive board. On September 4, 1967, the day the NCNP concluded, a spokesman for the caucus said that the condemnation of the "imperialist Zionist war" in the statement had been changed to a condemnation of "the Israeli government" for starting the war.[61] Critics were hardly mollified.

The NCNP highlighted several growing fissures among the black freedom struggle, the Left, and the antiwar movement. First, it became clear that the divide between traditional civil rights groups like King's SCLC and Black Power militants was widening, with significant implications for their respective understandings of black identity, activism, and relations with white groups. Second, it was becoming more obvious that liberals and even moderate white leftists were following different trajectories than were Black Power advocates in their assessments of international affairs and the United States' role in the Third World. Finally, with the antiwar movement adopting the new strategy "from protest to resistance" in 1967, both liberals and the moderate Left were coming face-to-face with a radical black nationalism that was not merely content to challenge American society and foreign policy but to revolutionize it. It also had become clear that support for the Palestinians was part and parcel of that revolution.

The public attacks on Israel mounted by SNCC and blacks at the NCNP in the summer of 1967 stunned many in America and indicated that the Black Power movement was interested in more than just domestic race relations and the war in Vietnam. These attacks set in motion the drama of different black views on the Arab-Israeli conflict, views that competed with one another throughout the rest of the 1960s and 1970s. How African Americans understood the Arab-Israeli conflict was becoming a major component of how they understood their country and their world during that period.

CHAPTER 2

THE FIRE THIS TIME

SNCC, Jews, and the Demise
of the Beloved Community

ON AUGUST 14, 1967, Irving Shulman, the southeastern director of the Anti-Defamation League (ADL) of B'nai B'rith, publicly laid into SNCC for what its recent newsletter article had said about Israel. He accused SNCC of anti-Semitism and of having followed "the pro-Arab, Soviet and racist lines" on the Arab-Israeli conflict. Arnold Forster, the ADL's general counsel, commented the same day that "it is a tragedy that the civil rights movement is being degraded by the injection of hatred and racism in reverse."[1] At least four other national Jewish groups issued statements denouncing SNCC two days later. Morris Abram, president of the American Jewish Committee (AJC), summed up their outrage: "Anti-Semitism is anti-Semitism whether it comes from the Ku Klux Klan or from extremist Negro groups, 'Snick' included." Abram was also careful to echo what the ADL had said: that SNCC's article put it in the same anti-Israeli trench as the Arab world and the Soviet Union.[2] Clearly the article had touched a nerve, and Black Power voices in support of the Palestinians immediately found themselves in the national spotlight in the late summer of 1967.

Jews and Jewish organizations, particularly those who had supported SNCC financially and morally in the past, were outraged by SNCC's article on the Arab-Israeli conflict. For them, Israel's victory over the Arabs just two months earlier was nothing short of miraculous. They firmly believed that Israel was a progressive democracy eminently worthy of Americans' support. The thought that fellow Americans not only would question that view, but actually champion the Arabs, criticize Israel, and compare Israelis to Nazis, came as nothing short of a thunderbolt. The fact that those particular fellow Americans were blacks, whose cause Jews had supported, added to the sense of betrayal.

THE JEWISH BACKLASH AGAINST SNCC

Jews had long advocated for black liberation by, for example, playing a role in the foundation of the National Association for the Advancement of Colored People (NAACP) in 1909. Jewish support for blacks was well known; as early as February of 1942, the American Jewish Committee published a study titled "Jewish Contribution to Negro Welfare."[3] Having experienced the sting of anti-Semitism, many Jews believed they were fighting in the same trench against discrimination alongside African Americans. When the civil rights struggle grew to become a mass movement in the 1950s and early 1960s, Jewish moral and financial support was crucial, and Jews were disproportionately well-represented among those whites who lent their support to the cause. Jewish financial contributions to civil rights groups were also significant. Jews even were the subject of criticism from some southern whites for the high-profile role they played in helping blacks win their freedom. All this compounded a sense of betrayal by SNCC that was felt by many Jewish Americans.

But the fiercely hostile Jewish reaction to the SNCC newsletter came in the context of years of deteriorating relations between blacks and Jews that were the subject of much public discussion by the early and mid-1960s. Several factors help explain this communal tension. One was the question of alleged "black anti-Semitism." Blacks had attacked Jews for years about how they treated them; black writers Kenneth Clark and James Baldwin aired such grievances against Jews as far back as the mid to late 1940s.[4] Some black claims of exploitative inner-city Jewish landlords and shopkeepers who took advantage of them used language speaking of "Jewish" landlords (not just "white" landlords or "greedy" landlords), which Jews interpreted as anti-Semitic.[5]

Another common black refrain was that Jews were taking the money they made exploiting blacks back to their own neighborhoods, neither putting anything back into the community nor hiring local black employees. In his 1961 classic *The Black Muslims in America*, C. Eric Lincoln quoted an unnamed source in the Nation of Islam (NOI) who described his or her attitudes toward Jewish businessmen: "'The Jew comes in and brings his family. He opens a business and hires his wife, his mother-in-law, all his brothers-in-law, and then he sends to the old country to get his father and mother, sisters and brothers—even his uncles—and he hires them all. Meanwhile, the so-called Negroes are footing the bill, but there isn't a black face behind a single counter in the store. . . . But the Jew doesn't live above the business any more. He's moved on out to the suburbs and is living in the best house black money can buy.'"[6]

Yet another source of communal tension was blacks' complaints that the Jews they regularly encountered as schoolteachers, social workers, employers, and even civil rights volunteers interacted with them in patronizing fashion. As for Jewish financial contributions to the cause of civil rights, some blacks dismissed these as mere "conscience money" given to "keep the Negro happy in his place, and out of white neighborhoods."[7]

The rise of Black Power only sharpened such complaints, as blacks and black organizations moved to take control over their own neighborhoods and organizations, sometimes to the direct exclusion of Jews and other whites. An example of this was when SNCC asked all white members to leave in late 1966 and go organize among white communities, leaving blacks to control SNCC's destiny.

Some African Americans tried to put these criticisms of Jews in context, pointing out, for example, that many of the whites with whom blacks had contact in the inner cities happened to be Jewish: black anger at Jews therefore really meant anger at whites. Municipal school districts like some in New York City did have a high percentage of Jews among their teaching and administrative staffs, which meant, as with shopkeepers and landlords, the whites that many urban blacks most encountered there were Jewish. In April of 1967 James Baldwin stated this famously in his opinion piece in the *New York Times Magazine* titled "Negroes Are Anti-Semitic Because They're Anti-White." A 1967 report on anti-Semitism issued by the American Jewish Committee agreed, noting that "among many Negroes, anti-Jewish feeling appears to be simply an expression of general anti-white feeling, for the Jew is often the white man they know the best."[8]

Compounding Jewish anger at complaints from blacks in the poverty-stricken inner cities were remarks emanating from noted black leaders and writers that unnerved many Jews in the early and mid-1960s. Malcolm X openly criticized Jews. Black Arts Movement poet LeRoi Jones, later known as Amiri Baraka, incensed Jews with his anti-Semitic poetry.[9] Black cultural nationalist writer Harold Cruse created a stir in 1967 when he published *The Crisis of the Negro Intellectual: A Historical Analysis of the Failure of Black Leadership*, which contained harsh comments on what he perceived as the negative influence on blacks by Jewish intellectuals. Jews, Cruse alleged, had deigned to understand blacks and their needs from their own perspective. Their prominence in the civil rights struggle meant that Jews had passed along this perspective to blacks themselves, who needed to break free of such constraints and develop their own culture and leadership.

Cruse also leveled another criticism of Jews: their claim to be fellow sufferers along with blacks. He dismissed such talk, stating that Jews had not suffered in America and could not seriously expect blacks to believe that they stood on the same level in this regard. Noted writer James Baldwin agreed with Cruse on that point. "One does not wish, in short," Baldwin wrote that same year, "to be told by an American Jew that his suffering is as great as the American Negro's suffering. It isn't, and one knows that it isn't from the very tone in which he assures you that it is." He continued by noting that whatever suffering Jews may have experienced, it occurred overseas; black suffering occurred here at home.[10]

Moreover, Baldwin said that in the end Jews were still white in an America founded on a racial fault line and therefore had benefited from white-skin privilege: "The Jew profits from his status in America, and he must expect Negroes to distrust him for it. . . . He is white and values his color and uses it." Baldwin also argued that Jews' white-skin privilege led them to lecture blacks about the need for nonviolence in their search for justice: "The Jew is a white man, and when white men rise up against oppression, they are heroes: when black men rise, they have reverted to their native savagery. The uprising in the Warsaw ghetto was not described as a riot, nor were the participants maligned as hoodlums. . . . While America loves white heroes, armed to the teeth, it cannot abide bad niggers."[11]

Jews began firing back publicly in their defense, which added to the friction. One of the most noteworthy early examples was Norman Podhoretz. Using his position as editor of *Commentary* magazine starting in 1960, Podhoretz began writing about the growing problems between Jews and blacks in America. In

February of 1963 Podhoretz published a landmark article titled "My Negro Problem—and Ours" in *Commentary*. He used the article to discuss his youth as a
Jewish boy growing up in Brooklyn, New York, during the 1930s and how, from
his perspective, blacks were not oppressed but rather were the oppressors—of
him personally.[12] Six years later sociologist Seymour Martin Lipset wrote that
the tension between the two minority groups stemmed from the fact that Jews
were disproportionately well-represented among those whites who were involved
with the civil rights movement. So when SNCC demanded that whites leave
the group so that blacks could run their own groups and set their own agendas,
he argued, this in effect meant that *Jews* should leave.[13] Lipset also argued that
black attacks on Israel in the 1960s actually had nothing to do with Israel itself
but were simply a way that blacks could express their anti-Semitism by attacking a surrogate: "They [blacks] attack Israel and Zionism as an expedient way
of voicing their anti-Semitism. In essence, therefore, the attack on Israel on
the part of some sections of the Negro community reflects tensions in the local
American scene, not in the Middle East."[14]

Against this background of communal tension came SNCC's passionately
pro-Arab, anti-Israeli newsletter and the controversy about Israel at the National Conference for New Politics in Chicago, both in the late summer of
1967. In the context of these increasingly embittered black-Jewish relations,
Jews and Jewish organizations were livid. Two particular themes emerged from
the sharp Jewish criticism of SNCC in the months after the newsletter came
out. The first dealt with Jews and black anti-Semitism: blacks and Jews had
worked together in defense of civil rights in the United States, and therefore
SNCC's article represented an anti-Semitic blot on that record of bicommu-
nal cooperation. The other theme focused on Israel and international affairs:
SNCC had now sided with Arab and communist nations, thus representing a threat not only to Israel but to America as well. Faced with the uproar,
SNCC fought back.

SNCC ON THE DEFENSIVE

SNCC staffers in Atlanta quickly mobilized to deal with the brouhaha over
the newsletter. After all, they knew ahead of time that there would probably
be a negative reaction. Decades later, several former SNCC staff members

remembered those tense times. Karen Edmonds recalled: "It didn't catch us by surprise. We made it happen. . . . The Palestinian question was one of many struggles for independence or against colonialism, so to take a position on the Palestinian struggle with the Zionists was not anything out of character for us. We took positions on just about every struggle against oppression. . . . We all knew it was coming."[15] Her colleague Charles Cobb felt similarly: "By this time we weren't really surprised by any negative reaction to anything we were doing. It was a little surprising in the sense that the piece on Palestine was not an advocacy piece as much as an informational piece. . . . We had learned by this time that any piece of our thinking that was outside the mainstream box would be denounced."[16] Courtland Cox agreed: "It wasn't a hard sell in SNCC. We were very clear about what was going on. We had taken our position on Vietnam. I was at the Russell Tribunal. Charlie [Cobb] had been to North Vietnam. What Ethel [Minor] did was focus and give us some facts about what was going on. . . . Palestine was another example of what was happening to us. It was happening to us, and it was the same people involved in our oppression who were involved in their oppression over there. People saw people in like situations."[17] The resultant hostility leveled at SNCC by whites only deepened SNCC's determined to speak out on the Arab-Israeli conflict.

SNCC activists knew they were likely to be attacked harshly for the newsletter article but went ahead with its publication because their stance on the Arab-Israeli conflict stemmed from their worldview and their sense of black identity and struggle. SNCC truly believed that American blacks needed to fight more than Jim Crow laws in the South and conditions of racism and poverty both there and in the North; they also needed to take part in the worldwide struggle against imperialism and capitalism—the structural underpinnings that held back the progress of oppressed people of color both in America and across the globe.

Moreover, perhaps more than any other foreign policy issue except Vietnam, the Arab-Israeli conflict was recognized by SNCC activists as an example where their own government was playing a leading role in supporting the side that they considered to be the aggressors, the local client of American imperialism. Israel's ties with racist South Africa also enraged them. It was for these reasons that supporting the Palestinians in their struggle against Israel was not simply an abstract issue of revolutionary solidarity with another oppressed people of color but part and parcel of SNCC's deeply held belief that America was the enemy both of its black citizens and of the Palestinians. This belief introduced a new discourse into American political life: open support for the Palestinians.

To explain this and defend their position on Israel and the Palestinians, staff members from the Atlanta office called a press conference on August 14, 1967. Ethel Minor joined Program Director Ralph Featherstone and Executive Secretary Stanley Wise in explaining the article to the assembled journalists. Featherstone ended up bearing the brunt of media attention at this and subsequent press conferences. Featherstone had taken part in Minor's Arab-Israeli conflict book group in the mid-1960s. In May of 1966 he joined SNCC's central committee and was elected program secretary one year later in May of 1967. The *New York Times* quoted Featherstone as saying at the press conference that SNCC sought a "third world alliance of oppressed people all over the world—Africa, Asia and Latin America," adding that Arabs were oppressed, too. More controversially, the *Times* also claimed that Featherstone linked Israeli oppression of Palestinians to Jews' oppression of blacks in the United States by saying that SNCC was not against Jews as a whole but "only Jewish oppressors" in Israel and "those Jews in the little Jew shops in the [American] ghettos."[18]

The attribution to Featherstone of the phrases "Jewish oppressors" and "little Jew shops in the ghettos" drew additional opprobrium from Jewish organizations. In their minds SNCC's attack on Zionism and Israel seemed linked to the group's own anti-Semitic views of Jews in America. Those words put SNCC generally and Featherstone personally on the defensive. But did he actually utter them? The historical record is not clear. In an internal document written in the fall of 1967, an SNCC staff member denied that Featherstone had used such language at the August 14 press conference and claimed that the *New York Times* had misquoted him. Based on conversations the document's author had with Featherstone, the writer stated "that the term Jew shop and some of the other formulations were foreign to his [Featherstone's] thinking." The author also claimed to have researched other newspapers and press agencies that covered the press conference and found that none of them quoted Featherstone as having said anything like that.[19]

The *Chicago Defender*, however, a noted black newspaper, *did* quote Featherstone as saying something similar: "Some people might interpret what we're saying as Anti-Semitic. But they can't deny it is the Jews who are exploiting black people in the ghettos. And there is a parallel between this and the oppression of the Arabs by the Israelis."[20] Whether or not Featherstone actually used phrases like "Jew shops in the ghettos," the *New York Times* story, appearing as it did in the most prestigious newspaper of record in the United States, became the official public record of what transpired at the Atlanta press conference and did little to dampen the mounting hostility against SNCC.

The day after the press conference, the Atlanta office issued a press release titled "The Middle-East Crisis." Perhaps trying to address the charges of anti-Semitism that were being leveled against SNCC, the first sentences of the document mentioned the Holocaust and noted, "SNCC understands this tragedy of what happened to the Jews and sympathizes with them since we black people possibly face the same fate here in the United States. . . . We recognize Hitler's massacre of the Jews as one of the worst crimes against humanity." It then connected this with Israeli behavior toward the Palestinians: "By the same token, we do not see how the Jewish refugees and survivors could ever use this tragedy as an excuse to imitate their Nazi oppressors—to take over Palestine, to commit some of the same atrocities against the native Arab inhabitants, and to completely dispossess the Arabs of their homes, land and livelihood."[21]

The press release then went on to reiterate, sometimes verbatim, the points raised in the newsletter article, points that the statement claimed "have been completely hushed up in the United States press and T.V. news media." Connecting Middle Eastern events with the United States government, it boldly noted: "Gentlemen, the facts are that Israel is and always has been the tool and foot-hold for American and British exploitation in the Middle-East and Africa. . . . In the Middle-East, America has worked with and used the powerful organized Zionist movement to take over another people's home and to replace these people with a partner who has well served America's purpose, a partner that can help the United States and other white western countries to exploit and control the nations of Africa, the Middle-East and Africa!"[22] The hard-hitting press release probably did little to assuage SNCC's critics, but it did clarify SNCC activists' thinking about why they were taking the Palestinian side.

Bob Smith and John A. "Johnny" Miller of SNCC's fund-raising office in New York also quickly held a press conference on August 15 amid the uproar. Miller, who was head of the office, used the opportunity to state that staff members in his office had been caught unawares by the article, and he further stated that it did not represent any official SNCC position.[23] Three days later, Featherstone joined SNCC's new chair, H. Rap Brown, in New York at yet another press conference, where they rebutted charges of anti-Semitism and stood by the group's criticism of Israel and Zionism. Featherstone stated, "Our position was clearly anti-Zionist, not anti-Semitic. It was a bit disconcerting to us, the reaction from the Jewish community, in that anything that is not pro-Jewish is interpreted as anti-Jewish."[24]

Brown chimed in as well. He went on to become one of the most visible figures associated with the Black Power movement in the 1960s, once famously writing that "violence is as American as cherry pie."[25] Resenting the focus on alleged black anti-Semitism, Brown stated at the press conference that "white America has a longer history of anti-Semitism than black America." He continued: "We are not anti-Jewish and we are not anti-Semitic. We just don't think Zionist leaders in Israel have a right to that land." Finally, Brown also denied that SNCC obtained money from Arab sources but did state that SNCC had obtained the information on which the newsletter article was based from information obtained from research conducted in Atlanta libraries, as well as material obtained from Arab embassies.[26]

Critics of SNCC quickly made political hay out of this last point: that SNCC had used Arab public relations/propaganda material as the basis for the newsletter article. Several Jewish groups had claimed right away that the SNCC article, in the words of American Zionist Council chair Israel Miller, sounded like "propaganda statements, which pattern those of the Communist and Arab extremists."[27] Several months after the article came out, the ADL issued a publication in October of 1967 claiming that the article in fact had cited almost verbatim from two texts written by Palestinian authors.[28] The first source was a pamphlet published in May of 1965 by the PLO's Research Center in Beirut titled *Do You Know? Twenty Basic Questions About the Palestine Problem*.[29] The pamphlet had been written by Fayez Sayegh, a leading Palestinian-Syrian scholar, public relations/propaganda official, and member of the PLO executive committee. The other source was *The Enraging Story of Palestine and Its People*,[30] published in 1965 by the head of the PLO's office in New York, Izzat Tannous. The ADL offered no reason why using these sources should cast doubt on the validity of the facts contained in SNCC's article; no doubt the ADL thought that the public would consider that use of Arab-produced material somehow had a sinister ring to it and therefore would make SNCC seem to be hapless dupes of Arab propagandists.

Behind the scenes SNCC staff members were concerned enough about the newsletter controversy that they prepared internal guidelines and explanations for how they should deal with the ongoing queries about the group's stance on the Arab-Israeli conflict. It was apparent from a draft document written by SNCC's New York office that the organization decided publicly to distance the group's leadership from the newsletter article. The unsigned, undated, hand-written document declared that the *SNCC Newsletter* did not represent the official position of SNCC, of its international affairs commission in the New York office, or of its central committee. It stated that SNCC's central committee "has no policy for or against the Arabics [*sic*], or for or against the Jews." As for the newsletter, the document suggested that staff members say that the group sought to print the viewpoints of all sides to the conflict, although "it so happens that we printed the Arabic side first."[31]

Another internal document, titled "Suggested Response to Questions Dealing with SNCC and Israel," was probably produced in the Atlanta office to help staff members deal with media inquiries. It stated, "Our opposition is political opposition to the state of Israel, not to Jews." If some Jews equated Jewishness with Zionism, and thus felt attacked, that was their "error," not SNCC's. Pressing on a sensitive nerve in black history, the document suggested that the hostile reaction to SNCC's position was tantamount to a lynching. The document argued that this was the case because no one yet had refuted any of the actual facts printed in the newsletter, facts that hitherto had been suppressed by the American media. The document then waxed bitter: "It is also evident that there has been no honest discussion of the Middle East Crisis among Jewish liberals, whose liberality suddenly has become strangely like facism [*sic*]. It is unfortunate that Jewish liberals have allowed their often times acute political perceptions to have dissolved under the power of emotion."[32]

The two Kofi Bailey cartoons that appeared in the newsletter were singled out for particular attack because many perceived them as anti-Semitic, pandering to vicious stereotypes of Jewish money controlling the world. SNCC denied that Bailey's drawings were anti-Semitic, explaining in a subsequent newsletter what the cartoons really had been about. The Stars of David and dollar signs had not been making a statement about Jews at all, SNCC claimed, but rather were symbols of Israel and the United States, respectively. An editor's note in the September-October issue of the *SNCC Newsletter* explained: "In the Cartoon with Nasser and Muhammad Ali, the Star of David on the hand holding rope symbolized ZIONISM strangling the Arabor [*sic*] Muslim World. The dollar sign was used to show the United States strangling Muhammad Ali, and also the Arabas [*sic*] through using Israel. Both signs were placed on the hand to indicate the close relationship of the United States with ZIONISM and U.S. support of the Zionist State—Israel."[33]

Throughout the late summer and fall of 1967 SNCC continued to fight back against its critics and uncompromisingly state its support of the Palestinians against Israel. This was more than just defending a stance; it was SNCC defending its very identity and vision of principled activism. Two weeks after the brouhaha over the newsletter article first broke, H. Rap Brown spoke at an event titled "Vietnam and Black America," which drew three thousand people at the Village Theater in New York City on August 29, 1967. Brown criticized the white antiwar movement, calling it "hypocritical" for protesting against the war in Vietnam but remaining silent when Israel attacked the Arabs. "When the shit hit the fan in the Middle East," Brown intoned, "you dug in your pockets and supported it [Israel's war]."[34] An opinion piece in the September 1967 issue of *The Movement*, a San Francisco publication associated with SNCC, continued this questioning of SNCC's erstwhile white allies. The article bluntly questioned the motives of those who opposed US president Lyndon B. Johnson but hailed Israeli defense minister Moshe Dayan, as well as those who opposed dropping napalm bombs on Vietnamese people but supported the napalming of Arabs as "necessary." It also acidly claimed that whites who denounced SNCC did so out of fear that blacks were starting to make foreign policy statements opposing those of the elites in the country.[35]

This last point was significant in that it reflected the fact that SNCC's specific stance on Israel and the Palestinians reflected deeper existential issues bubbling below the surface—an indication of how the group's attitude toward the Arab-Israeli conflict was central to its identity and evolving sense of self as a black organization. SNCC's charge that white critics were actually afraid of militant blacks daring to speak out on foreign policy issues reflected the attitudes that some blacks already had been feeling for some time: that their voices were not welcome in the realm of foreign policy and other elite fields traditionally dominated by well-educated whites. Thus, for SNCC it was not merely a question of a Black Power group siding with the Palestinians out of Third World solidarity but one that also reflected a deeper black complaint about the patronizing nature of the liberal white elite that claimed to support black aspirations. One of the earliest manifestations of Black Power to have emerged within SNCC in 1966 was the desire for blacks to run the organization themselves and not cede leadership to well-intentioned white liberals. SNCC activists insisted on attacking the perceived enemies of people of color both at home and abroad regardless of what whites or even establishment blacks thought.

Subsequent SNCC publications picked up on the theme of black autonomy. The September–October 1967 *SNCC Newsletter* claimed that the hostile reaction to the article on the Middle East in the previous issue was rooted in American racism, in the unspoken question, "How dare blacks comment on foreign affairs?" An article in the newsletter written by Junebug Jabo Jones (a pseudonym) seems to have been based on internal "talking points" documents drawn up by SNCC staff members as the controversy broke. The article challenged Jewish liberals to examine the Arab-Israeli conflict without emotion. Black radicals "have no emotional hang-ups about criticizing reactionary African governments" or "Uncle Tom leaders in this country," Jones wrote, so by that logic, why should American Jews be reticent to criticize Israel? The article also conceded that SNCC's liberal Jewish allies could not be expected to back SNCC's ongoing efforts to support Third World revolutionary movements such as that being waged by the Arab world: "perhaps we have taken the liberal Jewish community or certain segments of it as far as it can go. . . . Our message to conscious people everywhere is 'Don't get caught on the wrong side of the revolution.'" Jones continued by noting that Arabs are Semites, too, like Jews, and that "our position is that it is anti-Semitic to napalm a Semitic people, as Israel did to the Syrian Arabs in June."[36]

The same issue of *The Movement* also challenged Jews to reread the original newsletter article "in good faith, quietly and without malice aforethought" rather than resorting to "hysterical" attacks on SNCC that amount to "slander." This, the writers suggested to SNCC's critics, indicates that "you have lost you [*sic*] cool: you are afraid." The opinion piece stated that SNCC knew all too well that a people must not be judged as a group. It took care to point out that SNCC's position on the Arab-Israeli conflict required it to examine the actions of Israel as a state, not Jews as a people. If such an examination determined that the actions of that state were wrong and require it to be condemned, then "SNCC has never flinched from speaking its mind."[37] SNCC argued that true progressives were those who were consistent in their advocacy for justice and their condemnation of oppression—regardless of who or what country was the aggrieved or who the oppressor was. If SNCC's Jewish critics were aghast that the group had dared to position Israel as an aggressor, SNCC activists were equally vehement in their denunciation of what they considered pseudo-progressives who hypocritically were willing to criticize everyone except their own people.

By the end of 1967, SNCC was still not apologizing and was taking no prisoners in its public pronouncements about the Arab-Israeli conflict. The December issue of the *SNCC Newsletter* proudly proclaimed that the organization "reaffirms its political opposition to Zionism."[38] Internal SNCC documents also reflect a stiffening of the back in the face of the withering criticism the group had received. An article that seems to have been written in SNCC's New York office derided the claims that SNCC was anti-Semitic as a "big lie" propagated by a "wolf pack" consisting of "establishment Jewish organizations" and even many progressive Jews. Again referencing the image of lynching, the article asserted that these people were "out to get SNCC's blood." Furthermore, the document noted that many Jews considered criticism of Israel anti-Semitic. If this is the case, then, "SNCC qualifies as such. It admittedly is 'guilty' of charging Israel with aggression and with acting as the imperialist's catspaw against the Arabs."[39] A September 1967 editorial in *The Movement* had put these same sentiments bluntly a few months earlier: SNCC is "partisan" and "political." As such, "SNCC clearly supports the revolutionary aspirations of the Third World: and Israel, as characterized by the actions of its statesmen and military men, is opposed to these aspirations."[40]

THE LONG-TERM IMPACT ON SNCC

SNCC's fortunes changed forever after the newsletter controversy in 1967. First, it helped seal the financial fate of the old civil rights SNCC, leaving the new, revolutionary Black Power SNCC without the budgetary wherewithal to grow. Donations to SNCC had already dropped off dramatically in 1967 for a number of reasons. Decades later, SNCC worker Dorothy Zellner noted that while much of the group's financial support was already gone by mid-1967, the newsletter issue "was the death blow" to SNCC.[41] Cleveland Sellers had served as the organization's program director since 1965. He agreed with Zellner's assessment that while SNCC was only receiving a "little money" by August of 1967, even most of that evaporated thereafter.[42] The FBI also concurred. It claimed in a classified internal report that by December 1, 1967, SNCC had to close its Chicago office for lack of funds, had its telephone service at its Atlanta headquarters turned off for lack of payment of a $2,200 bill, and also had electricity service in Atlanta turned off for failure to pay a $400 bill.[43]

At the same time, Cleveland Sellers also pointed out a second impact that the controversy had on SNCC: it stiffened the group's resolve and solidified its determination to take stances against American foreign policy and in favor of armed Third World liberation movements. The negative reaction to their stance on the Middle East convinced SNCC cadre that whites cynically thought that blacks were welcome to talk about domestic race relations at home but not to take stances on foreign policy issues. For some black SNCC activists, the vitriolic backlash against the organization also showed that many white critics were simply racists: they would encourage blacks to be nonviolent but then criticize them and withdraw their support if blacks condemned American violence in Vietnam or Israeli violence against Arabs. Sellers later recalled: "Rather than breaking our will, this made us more convinced than ever that we were correct when we accused the majority of America's whites of being racists."[44] SNCC support for the Palestinians clearly was an exercise in the forging of a revolutionary identity: African Americans would support Third World liberation regardless of what whites wanted.

Two of the most influential and nationally recognized SNCC figures, James Forman and Stokely Carmichael, nonetheless later admitted that SNCC should have handled the issue differently. In his memoirs Carmichael (by then known as Kwame Ture) discussed the flaws he saw both in the content of the newsletter and the way it had been issued without a more systematic discussion within SNCC, although he insisted that support for the Palestinians on a "moral level" was the right stance to have taken. He claimed that the majority of SNCC staff members in Atlanta would have supported justice for the Palestinians had they sat together and formally talked about the issue.

Carmichael believed that despite such pro-Palestinian sentiment, SNCC should have had such a formal discussion first to debate the political wisdom of issuing a public statement at that time. Should SNCC even have a foreign policy at all? If so, why adopt a stance on the Arab-Israeli conflict? Other civil rights groups had not done so, for an important reason: "A good deal of their financial support came from mainstream liberals, quite often from the progressive elements of the Jewish community." Among such supporters, he noted, "anything other than unquestioning support of Zionist policies was unthinkable, taboo." Given the amount of criticism already directed at SNCC because of its opposition to the war in Vietnam and its drift toward Black Power, was it worth it to generate another political controversy? Moreover, Carmichael also believed that a public statement should have been more "nuanced," written in "properly diplomatic language," lest SNCC "offend or alienate our Jewish friends on a personal level."[45]

James Forman also had opposed SNCC's coming out with a statement on the Arab-Israeli conflict when the 1967 war broke out. After the article was published, he was disappointed that his advice to Stanley Wise had been ignored and that, as SNCC's international affairs director, he was not consulted. Forman also believed that the article itself was not written properly. He wrote that the thirty-two questions had been "hastily edited" and were "not framed to make the kind of educational presentation desirable—especially for the black movement." Forman also believed that while the article did not represent an official SNCC position, it was interpreted as such by the public. But he wrote in his memoirs that regardless of how "raggedy" the arguments in the article had been stated, "I knew we had to support the people of the Arab world in their fight to restore justice to the Palestinian people."[46]

Despite their respective beliefs that the newsletter issue should have been addressed differently, both Carmichael and Forman continued to support the Palestinians. In this way they are emblematic of the way that the SNCC's stance on Israel and the Palestinians helped change the political attitudes both of SNCC and other Black Power activists. It was now not only a matter of defending a cause they supported but also a matter of racial politics and identity: defending the principle that blacks could form and articulate their own stances independently of liberal white interference.

Carmichael's continued focus on the Middle East was part and parcel of his wider worldview that situated blacks within a global struggle against imperialism and racism, and his ongoing support for the Palestinians specifically reflected the beginning of a growing trend among Black Power advocates to see the black struggle linked with that of the Palestinians. Carmichael would repeat his contention in the years after 1967 that the same colonialism against which blacks were struggling in Africa had harmed Palestine. "My brothers and sisters," he said in 1970, "Israel is a settler colony. European Jews leave Europe, go to Palestine, change the name to Israel, expel the original inhabitants, the Palestinian Arabs, and dominate the land."[47]

At the time the newsletter issue erupted, in August of 1967, Carmichael was traveling overseas, and he quickly spoke up from abroad in SNCC's defense despite his misgivings about how and why SNCC published the article. In fact, while he was in Cuba, Carmichael gave a statement about Israel and the 1967 war shortly *before* the newsletter story had broken in the United States. On August 2, 1967, a journalist sent a dispatch to the Algerian Press Service that included comments Carmichael made during an interview in Havana. According to the Central Intelligence Agency, which was monitoring his trip, he reportedly said, "Israel represents an enclave of imperialism in the Middle East and North Africa." He also compared the fate of Africans and the descendants of African slaves with that of the Palestinians:

Suppose I own a house and someone takes possession of one of its rooms, and then 20 years later comes to discuss the matter. I tell him: First I shall take back my room. We'll discuss it later. It is true that the Jewish people lost 6 million dead in World War II, but the Africans have been abused everywhere throughout the world. They lost their lands and 100 million persons in the time of slavery, but we do not weep over it. We shall take the land back from the hands of those who stole it. The Zionists must get out of Israel.[48]

Carmichael continued on his lengthy trip, which took him to a number of countries in Europe, Africa, and the Middle East. In early September of 1967 he sent a letter from Moscow to an unnamed SNCC colleague in which he noted that he was traveling onward to the Arab world: "So SNCC can get ready for the anti-semitic Blast. You know I'm going to denounce the Jews as a pocket of U.S. Imperialism and compare the aggression [the 1967 war] to that of the U.S. in Vietnam. So bro get ready to go DEEP, DEEP into the Black Community."[49] From the Soviet Union Carmichael traveled to North Vietnam and then to the Middle East and North Africa. While in Algeria, he spoke publicly about the controversy when he granted an interview with the Algerian Press Service in Algiers on September 7, 1967. Pulling no punches, he addressed the charges of anti-Semitism being leveled against SNCC: "The persecution of the Jews came from the white man. There is no need for the Jews to turn around because the white man persecuted them, and persecute the Africans and especially the Arabs." Carmichael also stated that if the Jews wanted a state, they should have created one in Germany when it was divided into occupation zones following the Nazi defeat in 1945, rather than unjustly taking land from the Arabs. As for the Palestinians, "the only solution to the Palestine question lies in taking up arms."[50]

Carmichael then traveled to Egypt on September 16, 1967, and arrived in Syria three days later, where he visited Palestinian refugee camps and even apparently pledged that American blacks would provide military support to the Arabs in their struggle against Israel.[51] He was escorted in Syria by Randa Khalidi al-Fattal, a thirty-two-year-old Palestinian-Lebanese scholar and writer who worked with the Arab League's Arab Information Office in New York. Expanding on his belief in black-white global racial conflict and that Arabs were a fellow people of color, Carmichael jokingly told al-Fattal—whose complexion was very fair—"Sister Randa, you don't know it, but you are blacker than I am."[52] If the Arabs were black in Carmichael's mind, Israel certainly was part of the white world. He later said, in December of 1968, "It is important because the so-called State of Israel was set up by white people who took it from the Arabs."[53]

Carmichael continued to correspond with his SNCC colleagues back in the United States during his trip, offering ongoing advice about how to deal with the question of SNCC's stance on the Arab-Israeli conflict. He wrote several times to his old friend Ethel Minor. In one letter Carmichael urged that SNCC go on the offensive against the Zionists and "hit them hard! Don't give them any slack!" He ended that particular letter with a little ditty: "Guns for the Arabs, sneakers for the Jews."[54] In another letter, Carmichael told Minor that they should generate black support by stressing that Israel was not just fighting the Arabs but that in occupying part of Arab Egypt, it also was attacking Africa: "We must step up our propaganda against Zionism—we should include in the propaganda the fact that the Zionists have invaded Egypt [i.e., Sinai]—that Egypt is in Africa and Africa is our motherland and an aggression against the motherland is an aggression against us—This is very important because every time we get a chance to hook-up with Africa *WE MUST*![55]

After his return to the United States, Carmichael continued to hammer on the theme of black American support for the Arabs in their struggle against Israel and to link that struggle with black solidarity with Africa. At a February 17, 1968, Black Panther Party rally in Oakland, California, Carmichael delivered a speech that included a long section on Israel and the Palestinians. He noted: "We must declare on whose side we stand! We can be for no one but the Arabs. There can be no doubt in our mind! No doubt in our mind! No doubt in our mind! We can be for no one but the Arabs because Israel belonged to the Arabs in 1917. The British gave it to a group of Zionists, who went to Israel, ran . . . the Palestinian Arabs out with terrorist groups. . . . That country belongs to the Palestinians." Continuing to emphasize the need for blacks to back the Arabs, especially an African state like Egypt, Carmichael chided his audience: "Not only that: they're [Zionists] moving to take over Egypt. Egypt is our Motherland—it's in Africa! Africa! We [blacks] do not understand the concept of love. Here are a group of Zionists who come anywhere they want to and organize love and feeling for a place called Israel, which was created in 1948, where their youth are willing to go and fight for Israel. Egypt belongs to us. Four thousand years ago, and we sit here supporting the Zionists. We got to be for the Arabs. Period! Period!"[56]

For several years thereafter, the themes of the Africanness of Egypt, Israel's threat to the African Motherland, and the need for American black support for the Arabs featured regularly in Carmichael's speeches around the world. Yet despite his Black Power–inspired emphasis on the wider Arab world and the particular African Arab state of Egypt, Carmichael never lost sight of the particular problems and struggles of the Palestinians. In an August 1968 speech to the convention of the Organization of Arab Students Carmichael stated, "We feel very close to the commandos in Palestine. We feel they are the group that will get most of our support." Waxing sentimental, he also told the assembled students, "Now there are two dreams I have in my life. My dreams are rooted in reality, not imagery. I dream, number one, of having coffee with my [South African] wife in South Africa; and number two, of having mint tea in Palestine."[57]

SNCC's other leader who maintained a great interest in foreign policy, James Forman, did not address the Palestinians and the Arab-Israeli conflict after 1967 nearly as much as Carmichael did. Unlike Carmichael, Forman insisted that other factors besides race were involved with the Arab-Israeli conflict as the 1967 war broke out. He continued to preach that blacks must understand this and all political issues in class terms, not merely in black vs. white racial terms. When Forman wrote to Stanley Wise from overseas earlier in June of 1967 to caution him about SNCC issuing a formal statement on the war, Forman affirmed his opposition to the "race war theory," carefully noting that SNCC "must have 'clarity' about the real essence of the Arab-Israeli struggle: class and not merely racial analysis."[58] Israel was, for Forman, a "powerful conservative state in the Middle East." It was its role as a conservative, pro-American client that concerned him, not the fact that it was, as seen by other black militants, a "white" state fighting people of color.[59]

Forman believed that American blacks must take part in the worldwide struggle against imperialism, racism, and capitalism and not just support Palestinians because they were a people of color. He understood that one of the roles that blacks could play in this international revolutionary upsurge was to keep United States imperialism tied down, struggling against black militants at home and therefore unable to intervene against other peoples' struggles overseas.[60] Forman also believed that supporting the Palestinians served to propel SNCC toward greater involvement in the global anti-imperialist struggle—an important part of its identity as a Black Power group. As he noted in his memoirs: "Our position against Israel, as I saw it, took us one step further along the road to revolution. For SNCC to see the struggle against racism, capitalism, and imperialism as being indivisible made it inevitable for SNCC to take a position against the greatest imperialist power in the Middle East, and in favor of liberation and dignity for the Arab people."[61]

Forman's statement underscored the centrality of Black Power's support for the Palestinians in its overall vision of the revolutionary transformation of America and the world. It was not an incidental chapter of SNCC's history. The Palestinian cause had become a very important dimension of the Black Power movement's agenda, as well as its self-conceptualization, and was something that would transform many aspects of American political life in the 1960s, far beyond what SNCC could possibly have imagined when it published its newsletter article in 1967.

Black Power's pro-Palestinianism revealed its truly revolutionary nature, a force for what Frantz Fanon called "complete disorder."[62] Threatening enough in terms of what it called for in the way of domestic change, the Black Power movement's embrace of the Palestinian struggle revealed itself to be a real threat to the establishment: the white, liberal, capitalist order that controlled their lives and the lives of people of color overseas. Opposing America's war in Vietnam was hardly revolutionary by 1967; even Martin Luther King Jr. and famed pediatrician Benjamin Spock had turned against the war by that time. Going after Israel, however, was another matter, one that struck at the heart of the very establishment Black Power was challenging. Vietnam was important to American Cold War interests, but the Middle East contained the world's largest reserves of oil. Challenging America's unofficial ally Israel represented a serious challenge to longer term American interests, not to mention a challenge to American Jews.

The domestic political fallout of Black Power's embrace of the Palestinian cause in 1967 proved to be immense. Indeed, black militants' attacks on Israel and open embrace of the Palestinians had a dramatic impact on the American political landscape in the late 1960s. It started an earthquake in terms of attitudes in the United States toward the Arab-Israeli conflict. The pro-Arab publications and speeches of black militants were mightily unpopular among white liberals, and particularly among Jews of all political stripes, and provoked a viscerally harsh reaction. The fact that the anti-Israel chorus started by black militants also was quickly echoed by white New Left activists and partisans of Old Left Marxist parties starting in 1967 and 1968 only heightened the importance of this new discourse on foreign policy in the country.

Of particular note is how mainstream civil rights organizations responded to the pro-Arab rhetoric of black militants. Caught between their desire to work within the system alongside Jews and other white liberals and their need to remain relevant to young African Americans in an era of increasingly shrill black militancy, these groups were far from united in how they responded to blacks who openly championed the Palestinians and demonized Israel. The idea of Palestine as a country of color was proving immensely divisive among African Americans in the late 1960s.

CHAPTER 3

REFORMERS,
NOT REVOLUTIONARIES
The NAACP, Bayard Rustin, and Israel

JUST AFTER war broke out in the Middle East on June 5, 1967, the Conference of Presidents of Major American Jewish Organizations began planning a large pro-Israel rally in Washington that was to be held on June 8. The group asked Roy Wilkins, executive director of the National Association for the Advancement of Colored People (NAACP), to issue a statement of support. Wilkins then sent a telegram on June 6 to each member of the NAACP's board of directors asking whether he should release a statement for the rally. Wilkins pointed out that he had received numerous requests that the NAACP issue a statement supporting Israel but noted that the group had not taken a stance on the Vietnam War, and therefore he was reluctant on his own to issue something on this foreign policy issue without consulting the board.

Wilkins had maintained a policy of silence on the situation in the Middle East for several weeks: when Moshe Decter of the Conference on the Status of Soviet Jews wrote to Wilkins on May 31, for example, asking him to endorse a statement on the growing tension in the region, Wilkins responded that the NAACP was "not signing any statement at this time having to do with the Israeli-Arab situation."[1] Wilkins soon sent a memorandum to NAACP staff members reiterating this: "The NAACP is making at this time no official statement on the dispute between Israel and the Arab countries. As you know, we have made no official statement on Vietnam." Wilkins told NAACP employees that they were free to make comments as individuals as long as they did not identify themselves as having a connection with the NAACP.[2]

Wilkins needed a clear response to his telegrams quickly, but board members' opinions varied. Some wanted to continue adhering to the policy of avoiding statements on subjects not related to civil rights. At least one of them recognized, though, the political difficulty in refusing to issue a statement of support for Israel given the past financial generosity of Jews: "It is difficult to refuse," read a return telegram from board member Charles R. "C. R." Darden, "a request from our great benefactors." Others left it up to Wilkins to decide or did not make their wishes clear. In the end twenty board members ended up approving issuing a statement, compared to fourteen against and three who were not clear in saying one way or the other. But by June 7, when Wilkins apparently needed an answer, the vote stood at eleven for, and eleven either against or uncertain. It appears that given the tie vote, Wilkins did not release a statement for the June 8 rally.[3] Yet for Wilkins this was not the answer for how to deal with the Arab-Israeli conflict. Like other mainstream civil rights leaders, he was being drawn into the politics of the conflict, like it or not.

The Black Power movement's increasingly vocal support of the Palestinian national liberation movement starting in mid-1967 did not just engender public controversy among Jews and others who were accustomed to widespread American support for Israel. These pro-Palestinian sentiments also made traditional black civil rights leaders uneasy and put them on the defensive for a number of reasons. By the time of the 1967 war, mainstream black groups were already feeling marginalized by the Black Power movement. They struggled to maintain the initiative at a time when the "classic" civil rights struggle in the South was generally over and when Black Power advocates were confronting institutional racism in the North along more aggressive lines. While traditional civil rights groups worked within interracial coalitions to change the system, Black Power militants spoke openly of revolution against the system on their own without white allies. They stressed a new, revolutionary black identity that understood blacks in America as constituting an internal colony to be liberated, whereas civil rights activists saw blacks as Americans, albeit second-class ones, but fully capable of fighting for inclusion in the American system as equals. Combined with the violent urban rebellions that rocked various inner cities from 1964 to 1968, Black Power was posing a powerful threat to the strategies and nonviolent tactics of traditional civil rights organizations and their vision of black identity in America. These attitudes were reflected in the differing stances the two sets of black activists adopted toward the Arab-Israeli conflict.

Civil Rights activists not only believed that their own approaches and leadership styles were being threatened by black militants' attacks on Israel; they also thought that their own efforts to maintain forward movement on civil rights were put in jeopardy as a result. Many mainstream black leaders therefore felt a tremendous need to reassure whites in the face of militant black assaults on mainstream sensitivities. Traditional African American leaders were particularly anxious in 1967 to assure Jewish allies of their commitment to reciprocating the Jewish support they had received in their struggle by taking up a cause near and dear to the hearts of many Jewish Americans—Israel.

There had long been bad blood between Black Power and civil rights groups. Malcolm X derided mainstream civil rights leaders for their cautious, safe-and-sane approach, sometimes calling them "house negroes" wishing to maintain the system as opposed to more militant "field negroes" working to overthrow it. In 1964 he described mainstream civil rights groups' vision of black identity: "As a rule the civil rights groups, those who believe in civil rights, spend most of their time trying to prove they are Americans. Their thinking is usually domestic, confined to the boundaries of America, and they always look upon themselves as a minority. When they look upon themselves on the American stage, the American stage is a white stage. So a black man standing on that stage in America automatically is in the minority. He is the underdog, and in his struggle he always uses an approach that's a begging, hat-in-hand, compromising approach."[4]

Malcolm X was right: civil rights organizations certainly were not on board ideologically with Black Power approaches and criticisms. Their outlooks and worldviews were completely different; moreover, they were loath to do something that might fracture their carefully constructed coalitions with Jews and other whites. So when matters relating to the Arab-Israeli conflict emerged within the national discourse in the 1960s and 1970s, these groups generally went out of their way to stay on the mainstream path by supporting Israel wholeheartedly. The venerable NAACP was noteworthy in this regard, for its stance, too, reflected its own sense of identity and place in America, as well as its belief in working together with white allies on behalf of civil rights.

THE NAACP

Roy Wilkins had been around racial politics for a long time. He began working for the NAACP in 1931, and by the 1960s he had risen to the top of the group and was one of the so-called Big Four of the civil rights movement, a term used to describe the heads of the four main civil rights groups in the 1960s: the NAACP, the Congress of Racial Equality (CORE), the Southern Christian Leadership Conference (SCLC), and the National Urban League. All these organizations ended up dealing with the Arab-Israeli conflict during the 1960s and 1970s, particularly because the media and the public often demanded to know what their positions were. As the historical record shows, traditional civil rights organizations were far from unanimous or consistent in how they handled this controversy and what it meant for identity politics.

The NAACP was the nation's oldest civil rights group, having been founded in 1909 with support from the Jewish community. It comes as no surprise, then, that from its inception the NAACP prized mutual black-Jewish cooperation in the service of racial justice. In 1951 Roy Wilkins continued this heritage by joining with Arnold Aronson of the National Jewish Community Relations Council and A. Philip Randolph of the Brotherhood of Sleeping Car Porters union to form the Leadership Conference on civil rights. Moreover, the NAACP had a long tradition of supporting Israel stretching back to the Jewish state's formation when the NAACP saluted the brand-new Jewish state at its thirty-ninth annual convention in Kansas City in June of 1948.

The Middle East war in June of 1967 presented Wilkins and the NAACP with a political problem. Having avoided taking a position on the war in Vietnam and other foreign policy questions, Wilkins was extremely reluctant to do so now, even though Jewish organizations were calling in favors from groups that they had supported in the past. While he waited to hear from the NAACP board about issuing a statement, Wilkins went ahead and wrote a draft statement on June 7, 1967, and showed it to a few confidants for comment. Even though he decided in the end not to release a statement in the NAACP's name, the draft document sheds light on Wilkins's own thinking about the Arab-Israeli conflict.

Considering both his personal aversion to revolutionary Black Power politics
and the NAACP's long record of supporting Israel, Wilkins was nothing if not
totally supportive of the Jewish state in his draft and completely antagonistic
to the Arabs. Wilkins was unwilling or unable to understand Arab grievances
as emanating from anything other than a "fanatic" hatred of Jews and Israel:

A people persecuted down through the centuries has been returned to its motherland
and through sacrifice, industry, knowledge and ingenuity has made a land bloom and
has built a bastion of democracy. . . . The hateful and chilling cry that she must be
destroyed must never be raised again, even as it is unthinkable that it be raised today
against Chile or Iceland or India or Ethiopia. Never again must it be possible for 14
nations, united only in a common and fanatic hatred of a people and its religion, to
surround, militarily, another nation and announce brazenly to a stunned world that
their concerted mission is one of extermination.[5]

Wilkins went on to offer his personal comments on the conflict in letters
and articles after the war ended. All of them expressed total support for Israel, a
position that reflected his mainstream view of the slow-and-steady struggle for
black equality. He wrote that a peaceful resolution of the Arab-Israeli conflict
would only come when the Arabs let bygones be bygones and recognized Israel;
peace for him had nothing to do with movement on the Palestinian refugee issue
or any other matter dear to the Arabs. "Peace with justice and honor," Wilkins
wrote in a June 17, 1967, letter, "will come only with the recognition of the
fact of Israel as a nation."[6] He did not explain how this would bring "honor"
to the Arabs. Wilkins also wrote an article entitled "Israel's Time of Trial Also
America's," which appeared in the June 24, 1967, edition of the Philadelphia
Afro-American. Yet by the month after the war, the NAACP's board made it
clear that it did not want Wilkins signing statements any longer that did not
originate from the NAACP itself. Meeting in Boston on July 12, the board instructed him not to sign any such statements "for an indefinite period of time."[7]

The SNCC newsletter controversy that exploded a few weeks later in mid-
August of 1967 gave Wilkins the chance to defend Israel publicly by attacking
SNCC, particularly because the controversy had raised the question publicly of
black anti-Semitism. There certainly was no love lost between Wilkins and the
younger generation of SNCC activists such as Stokely Carmichael and H. Rap
Brown. The NAACP had struggled patiently for years on behalf of black rights

by building coalitions, courting officials in Washington, and filing lawsuits. It was working within the system to crack open that system so that blacks could participate fully within it. SNCC represented students, young people committed to obtaining their rights as soon as possible through direct action, grassroots activism, and increasingly militant-sounding politics. Wilkins and the NAACP in return had little patience for SNCC's growing Black Power attitudes or rhetoric, which they not only did not share but believed drove away sympathetic whites and their financial support.

The time had come for Wilkins to let loose at SNCC, and the newsletter controversy provided him the pretext. He was quick to condemn SNCC, even though he had not read the article. In a press release he issued on August 17, 1967, he not only faulted SNCC but even suggested that it was becoming un-American and anti-Semitic. "If the text is as reported," Wilkins intoned, "S.N.C.C. is openly following the Soviet line in the Arab-Israeli matter. In addition, by its reported attacks upon Jews, it is following the age-old hate line." He lamented: "It is a sad development that young Negroes, seeking to overcome the injustices suffered by their race, should employ against the Jews the same hateful distortions and lies that have been used for 350 years against their own kind."[8]

Ever the insider and politician, Wilkins also worked hard to let Jews know of his position in contrast to Black Power advocates, probably because he feared the Jewish backlash against SNCC might hurt the NAACP's fund-raising. He had reason to worry: the NAACP did in fact begin receiving angry letters and even hate mail from disgruntled Jews announcing that they would no longer donate to black causes because of what they had heard about SNCC and the National Conference for New Politics (NCNP). Wilkins needed to distance the NAACP from black radicals inasmuch as some whites could not or would not always differentiate among civil rights groups.

Touting his pro-Israeli credentials was a remedy. On November 10, 1967, Wilkins addressed the convention of the Jewish Labor Committee at the Commodore Hotel in New York City. The speech afforded him another opportunity to attack Black Power criticisms of Israel as "anti-Semitism" in front of a supportive audience. Wilkins accused "some of the new emerging Negro militants" of using anti-Semitism "as an organizational cement, as a scapegoat."[9] A major Jewish organization decided to reward him for his long years of civil rights work and perhaps for his strong pro-Israeli orientation: the American

Jewish Committee bestowed its highest honor, the American Liberties Medal, on Wilkins at its annual meeting on May 14, 1970—twenty-two years to the day after Israel declared its independence.

Wilkins's position on the Middle East offered a clear example of the conflict between the views of racial identity and place in America held by the Black Power and civil rights movements. Wilkins proved so unhesitant in his denunciation of SNCC for its hostility toward Israel because it had violated "the rules" about groups involved with the black freedom struggle speaking out on other issues such as Vietnam or, now, the Middle East. What stance to adopt on the Arab-Israeli conflict had become a litmus test for black groups' wider conceptualizations of themselves and their respective missions.

THE NATIONAL URBAN LEAGUE AND CORE

The National Urban League was another important civil rights group that never wavered in its pro-Israeli attitudes in the face of Black Power challenges. It was led by Whitney M. Young Jr. at the time of the 1967 war. Young began his association with the League in 1949 and eventually was appointed the group's executive director in 1961. Another of the "Big Four" civil rights leaders, Young rose to become one of the movement's most important Washington insiders. Like Roy Wilkins, Young had no sympathy with the Black Power movement or its stances on the Arab-Israeli conflict. Black Power advocates reciprocated the ill feeling, frequently deriding him as "*Whitey* Young."

When the 1967 war broke out, Young made it clear that he was solidly supportive of Israel. He signed a pro-Israeli statement in the *New York Times* on June 7, 1967, and later offered one of the most stinging rebukes of SNCC delivered by any party during the newsletter crisis in 1967. Young remarked that the SNCC newsletter resembled the Nazi Party's attitudes toward the Arab-Israeli conflict.[10] He later visited Israel, in April of 1969, to attend the "International Conference on Technological Change and Human Development" held at The Hebrew University of Jerusalem. After his visit he wrote a glowing article for a liberal American Zionist publication expressing his admiration of the Jewish state.[11]

Continuing to support Israel whenever he could, Young wrote a letter on October 7, 1970, blasting an unnamed critic who had objected to Young's signature on a strongly pro-Israeli statement published in the *New York Times* the previous June. In it, Young defended his decision to add his name to the advertisement: "I would continue to favor providing Israel with the weapons she needs to defend herself against those who have sworn to destroy her." Yet he went further. In a clear swipe at Black Power's embrace of both Africa and the Palestinians, Young also took the opportunity to criticize the Arab world: "If the Arab nations had really been concerned with improving 'the social, economic and political existences' of their people, they would long ago have ceased threatening to push Israel into the sea and concentrated their energies on improving the lives of their people." Young went further, to expose what he called the "the myth of Arab-black friendship," a theme that had been developed by pro-Israeli propagandists as a public relations tool to combat Black Power criticisms of Israel as a "white" country in league with imperialism.[12]

The position on the Arab-Israeli conflict taken by CORE, by contrast, was more difficult to judge than that of the NAACP and the National Urban League because it fluctuated over time as CORE negotiated with the changing times by flirting with Black Power. Established in 1942, CORE became a major interracial group committed to waging the black freedom struggle nonviolently under its leader, James Farmer. Farmer was another establishment black leader who had a good opinion of Israel. The Histadrut, Israel's labor federation, hosted Farmer on a five-day visit to Israel in January of 1965. He not only met with Israeli leaders like Prime Minister Levi Eshkol and former Chief-of-Staff Moshe Dayan but visited Jewish farming communities and came away feeling they offered a good model for rural American blacks.

Yet by 1966 CORE was moving in the direction of Black Power, a process that accelerated under the leadership of Floyd McKissick, who became CORE's national director in early 1966. The SNCC newsletter controversy forced him to deal with the issue of the Arab-Israeli conflict. At an August 17, 1967, press conference at the YMCA in Harlem, he declined to address the issue directly when asked because he had not studied the newsletter. When reporters pressed him by asking CORE's stance on anti-Semitism, McKissick demurred by referring them to the group's position paper on the subject, which had been issued in April of 1966 and had stated that there is "no room in CORE for persons with anti-Semitic sentiments."[13]

A few weeks later McKissick found that his attendance at the National Conference for New Politics in Chicago in September of 1967 drew attention from

Jewish groups. The Commission on Social Action of the Union of American Hebrew Congregations and the Central Conference of American Rabbis soon contacted him inasmuch as he had attended the conference as an observer and inquired about his position on the Israel resolution adopted there. On September 6, 1967, he responded by saying that he had attended the gathering a few days earlier only as an observer and had not voted on any resolutions. Furthermore, he noted, "Zionism is a form of nationalism. CORE supports nationalism and is now studying various national-state theories. Thus CORE cannot support a position against Zionism."[14] Supporter of Black Power or not, McKissick was not about to jump onto that bandwagon.

CORE's stance on the Arab-Israeli conflict soon became more solidly aligned with the Palestinians and against Israel during the period from 1968 to 1970 but not unreservedly so. CORE elected Wilfred Ussery as its national chairman in 1968. Ussery was an activist from San Francisco who firmly allied himself with the Palestinians and their cause. He attended the Second International Conference in Support of the Arab Peoples in Cairo from January 25 to January 28, 1969. On his return to San Francisco Ussery called a press conference on February 13 and stated, among other things, that "Israel exists in its present perimeter as the result of one aggression after another and in each case having that aggression condemned by the United Nations." Ussery also said that Israel never once had voted against South Africa in the United Nations. "This is of great concern to the black people in this country."[15] One year later, Ussery, who at that point was no longer CORE's national chairman, lent his name to a telegram that the World Peace Council sent to the UN Security Council denouncing an Israeli air attack on civilian areas near Cairo.[16]

In contrast, Ussery's replacement backed away from the Palestinians. Roy Innis rose through the CORE ranks to become national chairman in 1968, after which the organization began moving to the political right. Not surprisingly, Innis came out in support of Israel. He spoke out strongly when the Popular Front for the Liberation of Palestine (PFLP) separated Jews from among the other hostages it took during the dramatic hijackings of Western aircraft several months later in Jordan in September of 1970. Innis published an editorial titled "The Jews Must Not Stand Alone" in the September 19, 1970, issue of the *Manhattan Tribune* in which he wrote that this action belied the PFLP's statements that it was anti-Zionist and not anti-Semitic.

Innis's attacks on the PFLP were enough to cause others in CORE to worry about how the black public might react. A CORE spokesperson noted thereafter that Innis's comments were "not pro-Jewish or anti-Arab." Continuing, the spokesperson said that CORE "was in favor of the Arabs doing things in a fashion which everybody should subscribe to, be he black, white, Jewish, green or purple."[17] Fluctuating between traditional and more radical positions on other issues, CORE leaders could not seem to arrive at a consistent position on the Arab-Israeli conflict.

The varied and sometimes confused stances adopted by the NAACP, the National Urban League, and CORE illustrate several dilemmas these groups faced, as well as their envisioning of black identity and politics in America. All of them remained committed to improving the lot of African Americans by working with white allies within the American socioeconomic and political systems in nonviolent ways. As the 1960s wore on, their vision and their allies began to slip away. These groups struggled to remain relevant in a post–civil rights era. They also faced increasingly vocal Black Power critiques that called for drastically changing the American system, not working within it, and identifying with Third World peoples. Finally, they suffered from the growing white—particularly, Jewish—backlash as the black freedom struggle moved to the North, replete with violent urban insurrections and sharp denunciations of everything from American capitalism and foreign policy to Israel and Zionism.

For all the expressions of support emanating from the NAACP and the National Urban League, the traditional civil rights personage who mounted the most public and vigorous defense of Israel in the face of Black Power attacks and in service to the beloved community of blacks and Jews working together for the rights of all was the venerable Bayard Rustin, and he did so with great vim and vigor.

BAYARD RUSTIN AND THE
PRO-ISRAELI COUNTERATTACK

It had seemed like a good idea at the time to Bayard Rustin. By mid-1970, the fifty-eight-year-old socialist, pacifist, labor advocate, and civil rights activist had participated in some of the most famous campaigns and events of the civil rights movement. He was also a passionate supporter of Israel, called by some

"Israel's man in Harlem." Placing a strongly pro-Israel advertisement in the *New York Times* and the *Washington Post* signed by dozens of prominent black Americans would go far in counteracting hostile Black Power attacks on Israel that emerged in 1967, he thought, and would in the process help frayed black-Jewish relations by showing Jews that pro-Arab blacks did not speak for most African Americans. Apparently, after drafting a statement and obtaining all the signatures, Rustin added a final section that called on the administration of President Richard Nixon to accede to Israel's request to purchase state-of-the-art American military aircraft.

The advertisement engendered a host of responses. American Jewish groups were thrilled with it. Others, however, expressed visceral hostility. Among the criticisms thrown at Rustin by some pacifist comrades of old was that he had betrayed his nonviolent heritage by calling for sales of aircraft to Israel. Black Power activists were livid for what they considered his "Uncle Tom" groveling to gain the approval of Jews. Additionally, at least two of the signatories, a member of Congress and an important civil rights figure, complained that the text was not the same as what they had approved prior to publication.

Overall, Rustin weathered the criticism and was pleased with what the advertisement had accomplished. But later in life, he confided that adding the sentence about the sale of jets to Israel had been a mistake.[18] How had it come to this? Why was Rustin so committed to the Jewish state that he had placed the advertisement in the first place, not to mention amending the text at the last minute in a way that angered some notable friends and allies and seemed so at odds with his own pacifist background?

If other traditional civil rights leaders and groups were not always certain about how to address the Arab-Israeli conflict, or tried to avoid speaking out on the topic, the attitude of Bayard Rustin stood in marked contrast: he charged right into the fray with a spirited, public, and long-lasting defense of Israel in the face of black attacks. For this and other reasons Rustin was despised by Black Power activists. Rustin was certainly no stranger to criticism and controversy by the time he took up Israel's cause in the late 1960s. A homosexual black man who was a pacifist, labor activist, socialist, and civil rights activist, he had done much over his varied and active career to upset friend and foe alike as he fought for peace and equal rights. "He had," recalled his friend and fellow pacifist David McReynolds, "paid his dues."[19]

Rustin's early career as an activist was steeped in the tradition of nonviolent resistance. He was imprisoned by the American government during the Second World War for refusing to serve in the military and traveled to India in 1948 to study the discipline of nonviolence with some of the followers of Mohandas K. Gandhi. Rustin also worked for the pacifist group the War Resisters League in the late 1950s. Moreover, he was a leader of the early civil rights struggle. He helped to form CORE in 1942 and, later, worked with Martin Luther King Jr. to establish the Southern Christian Leadership Conference. Rustin was close to labor activist A. Philip Randolph and organized the famous August 1963 March on Washington, at which both Randolph and King spoke. It is difficult to overstate Rustin's importance on the world of nonviolent direct action, both in the wider pacifist sense and the more specific case of nonviolence during the civil rights era.

But Rustin began moving away from direct-action activism and toward the conventional political realm in about 1964, focusing particularly on building coalitions and working through the Democratic Party and the AFL-CIO to address blacks' socioeconomic problems—something he called moving "from protest to politics." Beginning in 1965, Rustin based his work out of the A. Philip Randolph Institute, which he founded with the institute's namesake that same year along with financial support from the AFL-CIO. It was the beginning of a rightward turn that ended up baffling many of his former associates.

Among Rustin's many passions was an interest in Jewish issues and Israel. Years later, David McReynolds recalled that Rustin's deep feeling about Jews came from the fact that he identified with them as an oppressed people.[20] Beyond that, Rustin had long associated with Jewish liberals in his political work, civil rights activism, and labor efforts and had built particularly strong ties with Jews and Jewish groups over the years. He also had visited Israel. Not only did Rustin disagree strongly with Black Power, however; he could not stand its attacks on Israel and Zionism, and he feared these would rupture the liberal black-Jewish coalition he was committed to expanding.

Rustin therefore had little sympathy with SNCC and its increasingly radical orientation that emerged in 1966. Gene Guerrero, chair of the Southern Student Organizing Committee, recalled attending a "disturbing" fund-raising meeting in New York around that time at which Rustin railed against SNCC. Guerrero met with Rustin and two people close to him—the venerable Norman Thomas, leader of the Socialist Party of America, and Tom Kahn, a member of the League for Industrial Democracy. Thomas and Kahn said nothing, Guerrero recalled, but Rustin pounded the table in anger when talking about SNCC, saying it had become a dangerous organization.[21] Not surprisingly, then, Rustin blasted SNCC during the newsletter controversy. In a statement released to the press on August 15, 1967, he stated he was "appalled and distressed by the anti-Semitic article."[22]

After several years of Black Power attacks on Israel, Rustin was deeply concerned by 1970. Exacerbating his angst was the fact that the black-Jewish relations that already were frayed by the mid-1960s had worsened after 1967. In the midst of their relief and joy at Israel's perceived salvation, Jews were mortified to see blacks attack Israel as the aggressor in the war and hold up the Arabs as victims of Israeli imperialism. For many American Jews, black support for the Palestinians and concomitant denunciations of Israel first leveled by SNCC and the National Conference for New Politics in the summer of 1967 were disturbing because they evoked deep-set fears about their own security as a minority community in America. Moreover, the massive black uprisings in Los Angeles in August of 1965, both Detroit and Newark in July 1967, and dozens of cities in April of 1968 had seen many Jewish-owned businesses looted and burned. These events precipitated a wave of fear among those Jews who continued to live and work in black areas of other American cities. Adding further fuel to the fire were tensions in 1968 in the largely black Ocean Hill–Brownsville school district in Brooklyn, New York. Conflicts there between a new locally controlled black school board and the United Federation of Teachers led to strike actions by mostly white teachers, a large percentage of whom were Jewish. The strikes in the fall of 1968 spread and involved teachers throughout the New York City public school system.

Bayard Rustin therefore had reason to worry by 1970 about Jews abandoning ongoing political work with blacks. His vision of black identity and his future place in America were threatened, and he decided to take forceful, if controversial, action to prove to Jews that not all blacks echoed Black Power attacks on Israel. The erstwhile pacifist decided on a public relations campaign to urge the United States to supply Israel with advanced weapons. Rustin's full-throated, public offensive on behalf of the Jewish state was aimed as much at showing American and Israeli Jews that some blacks were on their side, and therefore part of the liberal mainstream, as it was trying to influence American politicians to back the Jewish state fully.

Something else motivated Rustin to publish his newspaper advertisement on behalf of Israel in mid-1970. The first half of 1970 saw the Republican administration of President Richard Nixon exert great efforts to create a framework for Arab-Israeli peace in the form of the Rogers Plan, named after Secretary of State George Rogers. Rogers spent several months in 1969 trying to broker an end to the Egyptian-Israeli fighting along the Suez Canal known as the "War of Attrition." The Israelis were strenuously opposed to some of Rogers's ideas, which to them meant making important concessions to Egypt without securing any binding concessions in return. American Jewish groups leapt to Israel's defense. Two dozen such organizations met in Washington on January 25, 1970, under the auspices of the Conference of Presidents of Major American Jewish Organizations to express their concern with the plan. The president of the Zionist Organization of America, Jacques Torczyner, denounced Nixon's policy as "appeasement" of the Arabs.[23]

As part of Rogers's efforts, the Nixon administration later announced in March of 1970 that it was holding up Israel's request for additional American-made military aircraft. In part this was to discourage the Soviet Union from providing even more weapons to Egypt than it already had in the years following the disastrous Egyptian defeat in 1967. Yet Jewish groups found the news about delaying the shipment of planes to Israel highly disconcerting. When Soviet pilots actually began flying aircraft painted in Egyptian colors in combat patrols a few weeks later, both the Israelis and their American Jewish advocates again jumped into action to lobby for delivery of the aircraft.

With this background in mind, we can begin to understand why Rustin suddenly decided to swerve from his labor and civil rights work in mid-1970 to assist the diplomatic efforts of both Israelis and American Jews by harnessing his pedigree, and that of "respectable" American blacks, to the offensive against the Rogers initiative and the withholding of aircraft for Israel. His solution was to place a full-page advertisement in the *New York Times* and the *Washington Post* calling for the administration to support Israel, a statement that would be signed by a number of prominent black Americans. Rustin hoped it would not only help the Israelis and their American Jewish supporters but also go far in repairing black-Jewish relations that had been damaged by Black Power advocates' attacks on Israel.

These various themes were stated clearly in the letter that the A. Philip Randolph Institute sent to prominent American blacks on June 12, 1970, soliciting their agreement to lend their names to the advertisement. The letter, mailed under Randolph's signature, told recipients that the United States must take a role in creating Middle East peace but only in such a way that was "consistent with the democratic values upon which we have based our own struggle in America"; in other words, American efforts to bring about Middle East peace must be solidly pro-Israeli. Randolph's letter stated that he was encouraging potential supporters of the advertisement to speak out in defense of Israel's right to exist as the most democratic country in the Middle East. The letter also noted that Israel had helped black African nations, certainly more than the Arabs had.

Beyond encouraging diplomatic support for Israel in advance of when Rogers was set to issue his final plan later in the fall of 1970, the Randolph letter also stated clearly Rustin's other main objective: to repair black-Jewish relations by showing that some blacks were not supportive of Black Power stances on Israel. Randolph wrote: "Such an advertisement is also important from the point of view of the relationship of the black and Jewish communities in America. In the past few years there have been some tensions between these two communities which have negatively affected the attitudes of a minority of blacks toward Israel. . . . It is in the interests of both groups [blacks and Jews] that the ties that bind them be nourished, not severed." This concern was kept quiet; a press release issued two days before the advertisement appeared mentioned nothing about this last point.[24]

Rustin solicited funds for the expensive advertisement from sympathetic Jewish supporters, and the broadside eventually appeared in the June 28, 1970, issues of the *New York Times* and the *Washington Post*. It was titled "An Appeal by Black Americans for United States Support to Israel" and advocated full support to Israel. While not directly mentioning the Rogers initiative, it made clear that the signers were solidly behind Israel and were calling on the United States to act in such a way that would be "unequivocally guaranteeing Israel's security." The statement then revealed the signers' faith in Israel as the Middle East's only example of a democracy and thus eminently worthy of American support.

The advertisement also stated that the signers were concerned about the Palestinian refugees but with important political caveats. It did not use the term *Palestinian*; it implied that the signers knew what the "real interests" of the refugees were, and it claimed that the "real" interests of the Arab world were not political but socioeconomic.[25]

The advertisement then veered into an attack on Black Power critiques of Israel:

Some Americans, including a small minority of blacks, have expressed the feeling that the Middle East crisis is fundamentally a racial conflict between nonwhite Arabs and white Israelis. We think that this point of view is not only uninformed but dangerously misleading. It ignores the fact that approximately half the Jewish Israeli population consists of immigrants from Asia and Africa [i.e., Mizrahi/Sephardic Jews]. And it also implies that there *is an inherent solidarity* of nonwhite people. . . . We should add in this regard that Israel, with its impressive program of foreign technical aid, has contributed far more than any of its Arab enemies to the development of black African nations.[26]

It then drove home that black support for Israel was consistent with the black freedom struggle: "We, therefore, support Israel's right to exist for the same reasons that we have struggled for freedom and equality in America."[27]

The final sentence of the advertisement that Rustin added at the last minute contained a political bombshell. It pointedly stated: "For the present this means providing Israel with the full number of jet aircraft it has requested." This statement represented a serious break with Rustin's pacifist background and would prove to be the most controversial portion of the advertisement, coming as it did in the midst of the Nixon administration's dithering about when to deliver the planes. The advertisement also included a section that readers could cut out, sign, and return to the A. Philip Randolph Institute indicating that they had sent President Nixon a letter urging him to send the aircraft to Israel and "bring the Israelis and the Arabs to the conference table." It also solicited a financial contribution.

Rustin managed to secure sixty-four signatures for the advertisement, including his and Randolph's. The signers ran the gamut of black American life, from politicians to athletes, from clergymen to labor leaders, and from civil rights leaders to publishers and academics. Political figures included United States Representatives Shirley Chisholm, William L. Clay, John Conyers Jr., Charles C. Diggs, Augustus F. Hawkins, and Louis Stokes. Famed former baseball player Jackie Robinson signed. So did state and local politicians such as Georgia M. Davis, Richard Hatcher, Leroy R. Johnson, Eleanor Holmes Norton, Basil A. Paterson, and Carl Stokes. Civil rights figures such as Ernest

Green, Vernon E. Jordan, John Lewis, Roy Wilkins, and Whitney Young lent their support. Business and publishing leaders joined academics in lending their names, as did clergymen such as Thomas Kilgore Jr., Martin Luther King Sr., Wyatt Tee Walker, and William J. Walls. Rustin later claimed that what motivated these people to sign was their solidarity with the "*progressive ideals and values* which a nation like Israel represents."[28] The black mainstream was fighting back vigorously against Black Power and its pro-Palestinian internationalism. The battle for black identity had been joined.

REACTIONS TO RUSTIN'S ADVERTISEMENT

The Jewish reaction to Rustin's advertisement was immensely positive, bordering on giddy. This was not a surprise given that Jewish organizations and donors had paid for some of its cost. The venerable left-wing Yiddish newspaper *Morgen Freiheit* opined in its July 1, 1970, issue that Rustin's advertisement "must be strongly greeted" as a good antidote to "extremists" who want to depict the Arab-Israeli conflict as part of a black struggle in America and an African struggle against imperialism.[29] I. L. "Si" Kenen, vice chairman of the American Israel Public Affairs Committee (AIPAC) and Israel's main public relations man in the United States, waxed effusive in a letter to Rustin in which he described the advertisement as a "remarkable achievement" and assured him that "we are deeply grateful to you."[30]

Eager to champion his efforts on behalf of Israel and black-Jewish amity, Rustin wrote to Israeli prime minister Golda Meir shortly after the statement appeared telling her that more than eight hundred people had filled out the mail-in coupon to President Nixon that accompanied the ad (calling on him to provide the aircraft to Israel). Rustin also was sure to mention the other reason why he had carried out this initiative. "I hope," he wrote, "that the ad will also have an effect on a serious domestic question: namely, the relations between the Jewish and Negro communities of America. . . . I hope that the ad will help to heal the divisions between the two groups so that their important alliance for social justice can be maintained."[31]

In contrast to Jewish responses to Rustin's advertisement, black reactions varied. One of the midwestern congressional representatives who signed the statement later admitted that he had signed it for political purposes: "fifteen percent of my constituency is Jewish." Another politician who did not sign applied that same reasoning in reverse, saying, "twenty-five per cent of the people I represent are Klansmen. Would that be an excuse to support their priorities?"[32] In the black press thirteen newspapers carried the full ad. Three of them—the *Chicago Defender*, the *Pittsburgh Courier*, and the *Louisville Defender*—praised it. Two others—the *Afro-American* and the *San Francisco Sun Reporter*—were critical of Rustin's efforts. The latter paper opined, "In the event the ads were subsidized by non-Blacks, then these 60 individuals described as 'Black Leaders' have become tools in the world-wide propaganda campaign of the hawks in the Golda Meir regime in Israel."[33]

The advertisement elicited a torrent of outrage and complaints from ordinary blacks sympathetic to Black Power. For them, Rustin had become the epitome of an Uncle Tom, a docile "negro" willing to do anything to please white people and secure their friendship and financial aid, as opposed to being a proud and independent "black" man. Rustin in their eyes was nothing more than a Zionist toady trying to harness the black freedom struggle for Israel's needs instead of standing up for issues near and dear to blacks in America. Phiefer L. Browne of New York wrote as much to Rustin: "You are the type of Negroes who are considered sell-outs and 'Uncle Toms,' " Browne accused Rustin and his cosignatories, "because you are more concerned with the security of a people thousands of miles away than with the oppression of blacks here and in Africa."[34]

John Grimes and Evelyn Nixon were two others who wrote to Rustin in a similar vein: "We find it impossible to recommend support of Israel because such support *would* create further oppression of Blacks," referring to peoples of color overseas. They also laid into Rustin: "It is the epitome of Uncle Tomism in all its negative connotations to support your Great White Father in his further oppression of Blacks. . . . America has presumed to set up a white watchdog in this Black stronghold to insure that oil will be regulated to American industries. Israel's geopolitical position separates Asia and Africa and insures imperialist supervision of natural resources on both continents." The two then offered some unsolicited advice to Rustin about "Uncle Tomism": "It is time that we no longer serve as tools for white politicians. We must begin to have opinions that are in our interests and to say what we feel and not what our oppressors want to hear."[35]

Beyond sending angry letters, some Black Power advocates enacted resolutions and made statements denouncing Rustin. At an August 1970 conference at Howard University in Washington, Jomo Logan of the New York–based African Americans for Friendship and Retainment of Our Image, Culture and Arts (A.F.R.I.C.A.) offered a resolution entitled "A Resolution by African americans [*sic*] Condemning the Appeal by So-called Black Leaders Calling for United States Support to Israel," which ripped into Rustin and his fellow signatories for betraying their race: "It is pathetic that in this day and time these so-called *elite* Blacks are unsympathetic to the implications of their endorsement of Israel and to the negative meaning it has for all people of African descent." It, too, accused Rustin of "uncle tomming to appease Jewish interests [and] must be considered an act of ABSOLUTE TREASON against the BLACK RACE." The conference adopted Logan's resolution unanimously.[36]

Another denunciation of Rustin came from the Republic of New Afrika (RNA). The RNA emerged from a March 1968 conference called by the Malcolm X Society in Detroit that proposed creating an independent black country called the Republic of New Afrika in the present-day states of Louisiana, Mississippi, Alabama, Georgia, and South Carolina. Shortly after Rustin's advertisement appeared, Ray Nero, minister of information for the RNA's consulate in New York, published "An Appeal to Reason: A Message to the Negroes Who Support Israel." It called Rustin and his cosigners "naive" for believing that by supporting Israel, the United States was supporting democracy and justice in the Middle East. Nero wrote that "their statement signed by 'non-violent' Negroes, 'pacifist' Negroes, and 'good Christian' Negroes . . . only endorses more criminal acts against the Arab population."

Nero also castigated them for urging nonviolence at home at the same time they were urging America to send military hardware to Israel. "More jets to an already militarily superior people does not seem in line with a policy of nonviolence," Nero's statement said, adding: "They say that more jets will '. . . guarantee Israel's right to exist as a nation.' Do they think more of the right to exist on stolen land than they do of their own right to exist here? What is to guarantee our right to exist here when faced with . . . mace, riot tanks and shot guns?" Finally, Nero blasted Israel for its treatment of fellow "colored people": "Israel continue[s] to annex Arab land, expel its inhabitants, deny political rights to those born and raised there, and force the growth of refugee camps.

It was Israel that forced a move for survival and dignity. It is only justice the Palestinians want, but they will not bury their dignity to get it."[37]

James Lawson and his Harlem Council for Economic Development also denounced Rustin and the statement he engineered and published. Lawson established the United African Nationalist Union in 1948 and long was involved in labor and black nationalist causes. He chided Rustin by writing that the estimated $10,000 it took to publish the statement in the *New York Times* and the *Washington Post* could have been spent on a revolving loan fund for black businesses, ten $1,000 scholarships for black students, or as a down payment on a cooperative. Besides, he said, "no Black man is rich enough to afford a quarter [of a dollar] for the Zionists! The Zionists are already rich and influential." Lawson also offered a color analysis of the Arab-Israeli conflict: "Furthermore, how can those who pretend to be of African extraction advocate war machines to a predominantly white nation (Israel) to destroy their own kind? Many Arabs are Black *and* African! It is ironical, and tragic, that a group of 'Negroes' would take this course against their own kind."[38] Black Power advocates clearly were fighting back.

Much as Black Power groups had done, traditional civil rights organizations publicly took sides in the Arab-Israeli conflict in the 1960s and 1970s in ways that reflected their own respective ideological positions on questions of black identity and political action in America. Organizations like the NAACP and the National Urban League, and individuals like Bayard Rustin, were reformers, not revolutionaries, and not surprisingly they denounced the Palestinians and stood squarely behind Israel as a sign of their fealty to a multiethnic vision of measured civil rights gains. Rustin's efforts on behalf of Israel provoked a viscerally hostile response on the part of blacks who viewed the Jewish state as the enemy of a fellow country of color, Palestine. Interestingly, the dean of the civil rights movement, Martin Luther King Jr., was much more conflicted and nuanced about what he said about the Arab-Israeli conflict in public. His hesitance reflected his own efforts at projecting a certain image and a certain vision of black political activity.

CHAPTER 4

BALANCED AND GUARDED

*Martin Luther King Jr.
on the Arab-Israeli Tightrope*

IT WAS AFTER MIDNIGHT on a summer night in 1967, and a dejected Martin Luther King Jr. was on the telephone speaking frankly about his depressed feelings. On the evening of July 24 King had begun a lengthy telephone conference call with several of his trusted associates. One topic dominated the discussion. At the end of the conversation, which lasted into the early hours of July 25, one of King's advisers, Harry Wachtel, tried to encourage the dejected civil rights leader: "Martin do not despair, you are on the right track." King responded gloomily: "There were dark days before, but this is the darkest."[1] What did he mean? He had lived through many difficult times. What were King and his associates talking about that made him so depressed that he called those days "the darkest" in his life?

The subject was the Arab-Israeli conflict, particularly how the war that had broken out in the Middle East the previous month might affect the public pilgrimage to the region that King had been planning for more than a year. He told his aides that if he went ahead with the pilgrimage after Israel's lightning victory and occupation of the Christian holy sites in Jerusalem and the West Bank in the first week of June 1967, "I'd run into the situation where I'm damned if I say this and I'm damned if I say that no matter what I'd say, and

I've already faced enough criticism including pro-Arab. . . . I just think that if I go, the Arab world, and of course Africa and Asia for that matter, would interpret this as endorsing everything that Israel has done, and I do have questions of doubt. . . . I don't think I could come out unscathed."[2] Too much was at stake: his vision of how to continue the fight for civil rights, how to respond to the challenges to that vision posed by rival Black Power militants, his need to speak out against war and uphold the principle of nonviolence, and his need to maintain good ties with Jewish supporters. The Arab-Israeli conflict was a headache King did not need.

Martin Luther King Jr. was one of the most significant figures in the United States during the 1960s. He cofounded the Southern Christian Leadership Conference (SCLC) in 1957, and his advocacy of peaceful change and nonviolent resistance, combined with his eloquent oratory and piercing sense of moral authenticity, catapulted him quickly to national and international recognition. The latter was pointedly indicated by the bestowal of the Nobel Peace Prize on him in October of 1964. Yet King did not simply champion the struggle of American blacks; he also spoke out against war, poverty, and injustice more generally. In particular, he watched events in Africa, Asia, and Latin America as anticolonial struggles broke out left and right in the 1950s and 1960s. He called for a boycott of the racist regime in South Africa, and in December of 1957 he gave a speech in which he acknowledged the interconnectedness of global struggles for independence with that being waged by blacks in America: "The determination of Negro Americans to win freedom from all forms of oppression springs from the same deep longing that motivates oppressed peoples all over the world. The rumblings of discontent in Asia and Africa are expressions of a quest for freedom and human dignity by people who have long been the victims of colonialism and imperialism."[3] Ten years later, in April of 1967, amid much controversy, he denounced the Vietnam War. By that fateful year, King had become a strong voice on the side of peace and justice throughout the world and an outspoken critic of American foreign policy.

Like other black leaders, King came face-to-face both with the intricacies of the Arab-Israeli conflict and the need to respond to the 1967 war carefully. Contrary to what generally is written about King, he was not a knee-jerk supporter of Israel to the detriment of the Palestinians and other Arabs. To be sure, King worked closely with Jews and Jewish organizations. He addressed Jewish groups early in his career, speaking, for example, at the annual convention of the American Jewish Congress in Miami Beach, Florida, in May of 1958. Prominent Jews such as American Jewish Congress president Joachim Prinz and theologian Rabbi Abraham Heschel supported King's civil rights efforts. Heschel even awarded King the Synagogue Council of America's Judaism and World Peace Award in December of 1965. Jews also were disproportionately well represented among those who contributed financially to the SCLC. All of this afforded him the opportunity to learn about Israel and the depth of American Jews' feelings about it.

As a Protestant Christian clergyman, King was also intimately familiar with the Bible and its stories about how God gave the ancient Hebrews the Promised Land in ancient Canaan. It was a standard feature of black Protestant Christianity to relate black suffering to that of the ancient Hebrews. Thus, the modern Zionist saga of the Jews returning to the Promised Land was well known to King; in fact, the night before he was murdered, King eerily compared himself to Moses—whom God did not allow to enter the Promised Land along with the Hebrews according to the biblical account—when he said to a gathering of black admirers in Memphis, Tennessee, "I may not get there with you, but I want you to know tonight, that we as a people will get to the Promised Land."[4]

KING IN PALESTINE

In fact, King's interest in the biblical Holy Land led him to make a short trip to East Jerusalem and the West Bank in March of 1959. His sojourn to the region came at the end of a trip he and his wife, Coretta, made to India in February of 1959 to study the life and teachings of the famous Indian freedom fighter and advocate of nonviolent resistance, Mohandas K. Gandhi. Coming four months before Malcolm X's trip to the city, it marked the first time that a major figure in the black freedom struggle actually visited the Palestinians' homeland. The trip allowed King to come face-to-face with Palestinians and hear their story, something that led him to understand the Palestinians' plight in ways that hitherto has escaped the attention of historians.

On their return trip to the United States from India, the Kings briefly visited the Middle East. After flying to Beirut, Lebanon, on March 10, 1959, and spending the night, the Kings flew the next day to Qalandiya Airport just north of

East Jerusalem, in the Jordanian-controlled West Bank. Shortly after 3:00 p.m., Dr. Vicken Kalbian received a telephone call from Lucy Khuri of the Jordanian government tourist office at the airport. She told the young Armenian doctor that none other than Martin Luther King Jr. and his wife had just arrived on the daily Middle East Airlines flight from Beirut and needed to see a doctor. Taken aback, Kalbian asked, "Are you sure it's him?" "Yes," Khuri replied. Kalbian then took his medical satchel and traveled the short distance to where the Kings were staying at the YMCA hostel in East Jerusalem right near the cease-fire line with Israeli West Jerusalem. When Kalbian made his house call, he found himself face-to-face with America's most famous civil rights leader.[5]

Dr. Kalbian was the son of a very prominent physician, Vahan Kalbian, who was born in Diyarbakir (now in Turkey) and who received his M.D. in 1914 from The American University of Beirut. Despite being an Armenian, the elder Kalbian was drafted into the Ottoman military and appointed by the military governor of Syria, Jemal Pasha, to administer all hospitals in Jerusalem during the latter years of the First World War. With the British army's entrance into Jerusalem in late 1917, Kalbian defected from the Ottoman army, stayed in Jerusalem, and served Palestine's new rulers for many years as the private physician to all the British high commissioners who served from 1920 to 1948. His son, Vicken, was born in the city, grew up speaking Arabic as well as Armenian, and was well-integrated into Arab life in the city.

The Arab-Israeli conflict changed all that. In early 1948 the Kalbian family fled its spacious home in West Jerusalem's Talbiyya District following orders to evacuate that were broadcast over loudspeakers by the Hagana, the main Zionist militia in Palestine. Like virtually all other Palestinian refugees, the Kalbians—even though they were not ethnic Arabs—were barred by the Israelis from returning, lost their home, and took up permanent residence in the eastern part of Jerusalem, which was controlled by Jordan as a result of the 1948 war. Vicken thereafter followed in his father's footsteps and became a doctor, obtaining his MD from The American University in Beirut in 1949. He soon joined his father working at Augusta Victoria Hospital in East Jerusalem.[6]

When he entered the Kings' room at the hostel that day in March of 1959, Kalbian found the couple in their beds. His first thought was that the famous African American looked exactly like the image of him that Kalbian had seen on the cover of *Time* magazine two years earlier.[7] In the course of examining

King, the latter showed him the scar he had from the emergency surgery he underwent the year before after he was stabbed by a would-be assassin in New York. After he was finished examining King, Kalbian called in a prescription to a local pharmacy. Before he could leave, however, King then told him, "Sit down; we'd like to talk." King confessed to the doctor that he never had heard the Arab point of view about the Arab-Israeli conflict and wanted to hear about it. Kalbian told him about the situation; thus, the noted American civil rights leader heard about the plight of the Palestinians directly from someone whose own boyhood home was one of thousands left behind by the fleeing refugees eleven years earlier.[8]

Kalbian also told King that he really should meet and talk to some Palestinian officials while in Jerusalem and that he would arrange it. After he left, Kalbian informed the owner of the YMCA, Labib Nasir, about the famous guest staying in his hostel. "Why didn't someone tell me he was here?" replied the startled Nasir. Kalbian and Nasir decided to invite some prominent Palestinians to a dinner for King that was held later at the National Restaurant. Attendees included Ruhi al-Khatib, the mayor of East Jerusalem; Musa Nasir, an academic; Anton Atallah, a judge; Raja al-Isa, a journalist; and Anwar Nusseibeh, a politician and statesman. Kalbian himself could not make the dinner, but King apparently enjoyed it, for he later thanked him for arranging it.[9]

The Kings were well enough to tour the sites and shrines in East Jerusalem the day after their arrival. On their third day the couple traveled to the holy sites in Bethlehem and Hebron, home, respectively, to the Church of the Nativity, where church tradition says Jesus was born, and the Ibrahimi Mosque, which reputedly contains the tombs of the biblical patriarch Abraham and some of his family. The following day, the Kings traveled to Nablus, the biblical Shechem, which contains the Tomb of Joseph and is close to Mount Gerizim, home of the Samaritan community. They attended a Samaritan religious ceremony there and later rented a car and drove to the ancient city of Jericho, near the Jordan River, before returning to the United States after a stop in Cairo.[10]

Visiting the Middle East and meeting with Kalbian and Palestinian dignitaries in East Jerusalem appears to have made an impact on King. Just over two weeks after landing at the East Jerusalem airport, he was back home in Atlanta delivering his Easter sermon at the Dexter Avenue Baptist Church on March 29, 1959. On that particular Easter morning, King's recent sojourn to Jerusalem and the West Bank was clearly still on his mind, as he titled his sermon "A Walk Through the Holy Land." He may have been including the Middle East when he spoke these words about the Third World and the struggles of its people, words that also were relevant to the black Americans sitting in the pews before him: "I think we know today there is a struggle, a desperate struggle, going on in this world. Two-thirds of the people of the world are colored people. They have been dominated politically, exploited economically, trampled over, and humiliated. There is a struggle on the part of these people to gain freedom and human dignity." That the Palestinians and the Arab-Israeli conflict were still in his thoughts was also illustrated by the fact that the next day, King wrote a letter in which me mentioned that while in Jerusalem, he had talked to "many people" about the conflict. Given that he had stayed in the Arab-side of the divided city, these "many people" could only have been Palestinians.[11]

THE MIDDLE EAST PILGRIMAGE IDEA

The plight of the Palestinians and the Arab-Israeli conflict remained on King's mind as the 1950s turned into the 1960s. In October of 1964, for example, he received a letter from an American living in Israel who brought to his attention Israel's discriminatory policies toward its Palestinian minority. Richard Krech was an American Jew who had been involved in the civil rights movement in the United States but by that point was living on the left-wing kibbutz of Sasa, in Israel's northern Galilee region—a kibbutz built on the ruins of a destroyed Palestinian village, Sa'sa. He wrote King a plaintive letter describing the situation faced by Israel's Palestinian citizens, including the fact that they lived under a martial law regime and were required to carry travel passes to move around just like blacks were required to do in apartheid South Africa. Krech urged King to use his "great moral influence" to dissuade Israel from continuing these policies.[12]

The Middle East continued to garner King's attention, factor into his career, and perhaps increase his ambivalence about taking sides in the Arab-Israeli conflict. Various Jewish quarters clamored for him to visit Israel. The Israelis no doubt believed that successfully wooing such a man of high moral standing to visit their country would be a major public relations coup. The Israeli government invited him in the summer of 1962, but Ze'ev Dover, Israeli consul in Atlanta, advised the Israeli embassy in Washington that the time was not right. He explained that Israeli officials were trying to cultivate relations with southerners, and King was too controversial among southern whites.[13]

The next year, King was invited by Ben-Zion Ilan of the Israeli Histadrut labor federation in Israel. King accepted the offer and was scheduled to visit Israel along with his close SCLC associate Ralph Abernathy in July of 1963 for an eight-day visit. In the end, however, King cancelled the trip at the last minute.[14] In the spring of 1965 the American Jewish Committee proposed a trip to Israel, where King would be a guest of the Israeli government. He accepted this invitation in May of 1965 but never acted on it. The following year, Israeli ambassador to the United States Avraham Harmon wrote King, reminding him that the invitation was still open.[15]

King did not accept these invitations, but about that same time, he began developing plans to travel to the Middle East on his own. He started planning a huge pilgrimage of American Christians who would travel both to Israel and the West Bank in late 1967. King must have been affected deeply enough by his own pilgrimage to the Holy Land that he wanted to return in the company of others, although on his own terms, not as an honored guest of Israeli and Jewish groups. He and his SCLC colleagues also were going to use the pilgrimage as a fund-raiser for the SCLC.

King's pilgrimage idea was ambitious. Its origins apparently lay in a letter he received from Sandy F. Ray, president of the Empire State Baptist Convention and an official in the SCLC. King then wrote to a black-owned tour company set up by Ray and two other clergymen, Concreta Tours, on June 24, 1966, with a proposal for the trip. The tour company envisioned a pilgrimage of at least thirty-five hundred people, at $775.00 per person, who would travel to the Middle East on one of three different itineraries. The highlight of the pilgrimage would be a sermon that King would deliver for all three groups on the Mount of Olives in East Jerusalem on November 11, 1967, followed by another sermon at the Sea of Galilee (Lake Tiberias) in northern Israel on November 16. The trip would also take pilgrims to Paris, Rome, and Athens.[16]

In November of 1966 King dispatched a trusted confidant to the Middle East to assess the possibilities of undertaking such a trip. Andrew Young had become the SCLC's executive director in 1964 at the tender age of thirty-two. Young did not travel using SCLC funds, however; earlier that June, he had been invited to participate in a twelve-day "study mission" in Israel by Irving M. Engel, the American Jewish Committee's (AJC) honorary president. Engel explained that the AJC was inviting twelve black leaders from the United States to participate in one of three groups that would undertake a twelve-day study mission in Israel. Young ended up accepting the invitation and planned to go with the second group, which traveled to the Middle East from November 17 to November 28, 1966. The trip took Young and his wife, Jean, to a number of locales in Israel, including Rehovoth, Tel Aviv-Jaffa, Caesaria, Haifa, Acre, Nazareth, Tiberias, Jerusalem, and Beersheba, as well as some Druze Arab villages and Kibbutz Lavi. While there, Young swam in the Jordan River and even met the legendary Israeli politician David Ben-Gurion.[17] In addition to the study tour's itinerary, Young spent some time looking into some preliminary details of King's proposed pilgrimage.

Young also crossed from Israeli-controlled West Jerusalem into East Jerusalem and met with Dr. Vicken Kalbian. Young had heard about Kalbian from King and wanted to discuss with him some of the medical details about that part of the pilgrimage that would take place in East Jerusalem and the West Bank. Kalbian was quite impressed with Young. He described the young SCLC official as "a most impressive guy: polished and cultured," and he found Young's wife, Jean, "beautiful" and "statuesque." Young explained to the doctor that King wanted to bring as many as two thousand pilgrims with him on the pilgrimage. Because many of them would be elderly, Young said that the organizers would need to prepare for possible medical emergencies, including providing ambulances to drive people with medical conditions down into the Jordan Valley for that part of the pilgrimage.[18] Young and his wife also attended a reception hosted by Hanna Nazzal, the Palestinian owner of Terra Santa Tours.

Young wrote to Kalbian after his return to the United States, thanking him for the conversation, which had included talk about the Arab-Israeli conflict. "Your view of the Palestine situation was most helpful," he wrote. At the same time, Young confided to his colleagues that he was not sure whether the 1948 Palestinian refugees really still wanted to go back home or if that was just being stated for propaganda purposes.[19]

Starting in November of 1966, King began wondering whether he should cancel the pilgrimage because of the increasingly worrisome political situation in the Middle East. On November 13, 1966, several thousand Israeli forces crossed into the West Bank and raided the Palestinian village of Sammu' in response to the killing of three Israeli border patrolmen by a mine two days earlier (for which Israeli blamed al-Fateh guerrillas entering from the West Bank). The Israeli forces destroyed dozens of homes in the village and engaged in fighting with Jordanian troops before withdrawing. Israel's actions drew widespread international condemnation and planted seeds of doubt in King's mind about the advisability of the pilgrimage idea. In a November 23, 1966, conversation that King had in Atlanta with his close aide Stanley Levison, he mentioned that he was reconsidering traveling to the Middle East.[20] Young returned from the region the next day and later spoke with King about the situation, the trip, and the political delicacies King might face in stepping into the Arab-Israeli conflict now that violence in the region was resuming.

The FBI was tapping Levison's telephone and monitored a conversation he had with Young on December 1, 1966. Young told Levison that while he was in the Middle East the previous month, he had told both Israeli and Jordanian officials—who were anxious for the high-profile American to visit—that King's primary purpose in traveling there would not be political but that he could not guarantee that King would remain silent on the issue. Young reported that they did not seem concerned with that and that, overall, he did not foresee any problems with the pilgrimage unless the region exploded into an actual war. Levison and Young also discussed other potential problems, including how ordinary blacks would interpret the pilgrimage idea and the money and attention that would be focused on it.[21]

News of King's hesitancy began to spread. Hearing of his concern, the American ambassador to Jordan, Findley Burns Jr., wrote to him in January of 1967 urging him not to cancel the trip. He admonished King: "Cancellation at this time, giving as the reason conditions in the Middle East, could lead to misunderstandings which, in my opinion, would be disadvantageous to all concerned."[22]

The June war six months later, combined with Israel's resultant occupation of East Jerusalem and the West Bank, obviously posed even more serious challenges for King's plan to lead a peaceful pilgrimage into an area at least part of which was now under Israeli military rule. Within three weeks of the war's conclusion, Emily Fortson of the company handling the pilgrimage details, Concreta Tours, traveled to Israel and the West Bank to assess the situation and determine how the war had affected planning for the event. The local tour organizers and others were upbeat about the prospects (no doubt desperate for tourism in the war-torn region), but King remained hesitant.[23]

Another reason for King's reluctance to proceed with the pilgrimage was that the Middle East put him in a difficult position politically. King was a Nobel Peace Prize laureate who had come out against the Vietnam War publicly in April of 1967 and needed to maintain his reputation as a peacemaker. Would the pilgrimage be interpreted as a backhanded endorsement of Israel's preemptive attack on the Arabs in the June war and subsequent military occupation of Arab territory? Furthering his dilemma was the fact that King also had long enjoyed good relations with American Jews and Jewish organizations, and he wanted to retain their support. He knew that Jews had been deeply concerned about Israel's fate as the crisis grew in May of 1967 and had been virtually unanimous in hailing Israel's subsequent victory as a momentous deliverance from what they had feared was the country's imminent destruction.

In fact, to shore up his credentials with Jewish allies, King had lent his signature to a pro-Israeli advertisement placed in the *New York Times* on June 4, the day before hostilities broke out. The group responsible for the advertisement was a new one called Americans for Democracy in the Middle East, headed by journalist and editor at *Forbes* magazine Charles E. Silberman.[24] The advertisement was titled "The Moral Responsibility in the Middle East" and stated that "men of good faith must recognize their moral responsibility to maintain freedom of passage at the Straits of Tiran."[25] King did not actually read the text of the advertisement, but two days after it appeared, the savvy civil rights leader conceded to Levison that his signature probably would help his standing in the Jewish community. Levison, who was Jewish, disagreed, telling King that only 10 percent of SCLC's donations came from Jews.[26]

At the same time, King worried about appearing too supportive of Israel. He obviously knew about the Palestinian perspective on the conflict from his 1959 trip to the West Bank and East Jerusalem. King was also aware of the growing Black Power movement and the degree to which its militancy had eaten into his civil rights constituency, especially among young people. Sensitive to the intersection of racial politics and the Arab-Israeli conflict, he therefore was not eager to compromise his standing among black radicals further. King admitted to Levison on June 6, 1967, that he had not seen the advertisement's text before agreeing to support it and, after actually reading it in the newspaper, thought that it was unbalanced and tilted too much toward Israel. He believed it made him and the other signatories seem like hawks on the Middle East and doves on Vietnam. King's ambivalence also came out in a June 8, 1967, conference telephone call he had with his aides when he confessed to being aware that SNCC had criticized him and the advertisement. His sensitivity about being attacked by SNCC may have been a factor in his refusal to condemn SNCC when the newsletter controversy erupted later that August.[27]

King was clearly conflicted about the Middle East and concerned about his image as an internationally known peacemaker. During that same June 8, 1967, conference call, King sought out advice from Young, Levison, and Harry Wachtel about what to say regarding the Middle East. He believed that if pressed to speak out, he could just emphasize his overall philosophy that war does not solve social and political problems. The fact that the apostle of nonviolence had come out strongly against the American war in Vietnam in his famous "A Time to Break Silence" speech at the Riverside Church in New York in April of 1967 was another reason why it was becoming increasingly difficult for King to be associated with Israel's preemptive strike and subsequent military occupation of Arab territory, territory that included the holiest shrines in Christianity. King was also worried about Israel becoming "smug and unyielding" after its massive victory.[28]

With the short war over and King still worried about both the pilgrimage and what to say publicly about Israel, he decided on a course of action that he hoped would satisfy all sides whenever he was asked about his thoughts on the recent hostilities. It was developed in conversations with his aides. As far back as December of 1966, Young had mentioned to Levison that while he was in the Middle East, he held a conversation with a man from the Middle East Council of Churches who mentioned that Arab-Israeli peace would only come when the Arab world became more developed.[29] Six months later Young repeated this idea during the June 8, 1967, conference call, noting that this idea of peace through development also was expressed in the February 1965 "Pacem in Terris" conference in New York, which had discussed Pope John XXIII's 1963 "Pacem in terris" encyclical.[30] Wachtel then wrote a draft telegram to President Lyndon Johnson and Soviet premier Alexei Kosygyn ten days later on June 18—presumably it was written on behalf of King—in which he used this approach to explain how to solve the Arab-Israeli conflict peacefully: "For Israel peace requires firm and unequivocal insurance of their territorial integrity so that their people may continue with security to build their nation without diverting their resources towards armament and war. For the Arab world peace requires the elimination of poverty, illiteracy and disease which has prevented these Third World nations from developing stable, viable lives for their many millions of people."[31]

King seems to have been pleased, for his public comments thereafter reflected what his aides had suggested. King decided to emphasize his solid support for Israel's right to exist, if not for Israeli actions during the war or thereafter. Whatever he may have thought about the intricacies of the Arab-Israeli conflict, King clearly believed that Israel had a right to exist as a state, and he had no qualms about affirming this point. But he also he understood enough about the Palestinians from firsthand experience to know that unless their plight somehow was addressed, the conflict would continue.

King therefore chose to balance his public assertion of Israel's right to exist with an indirect acknowledgment of the Arab point of view—but in economic, not political, terms. He chose to speak out about how poverty and the lack of economic development in the Arab world kept the pot of violence and war boiling, and he eschewed any overt discussion of the *political* bases of Arab grievances, such as Palestinian dispossession, the fate of the 1948 refugees, compensation for their property losses, and so forth. This was about as close to expressing overt sympathy for Arab perspectives as King was willing to go in public while still maintaining his identity and his vision of political allies and action.

This two-track approach was made clear a week after the war ended, when on June 18, 1967, journalists from the ABC television program *Issues and Answers* interviewed King and asked him about the recent fighting. King stated that prewar Arab talk of driving Israel into the sea was "terribly immoral" and that the Jewish state offered a good example of what people can do together to transform "almost a desert land into an oasis." Peace required security for Israel. Yet King also acknowledged that so long as people are poor, as many Arabs were, they are going to make "intemperate remarks. They are going to keep the war psychosis alive"—which was a tacit comparison with the socioeconomic bases of American black anger and violence. Peace therefore required a type of "Marshall Plan for the Middle East" to spur economic development for all.

When pressed to comment about whether Israel should return the Arab territories it occupied during the war, King was forced to get off message and go beyond palatable platitudes to answer that specific political question. Still, he chose his words carefully and used qualifying language: "I think for the ultimate peace and security of the situation it will probably be necessary for Israel to give up this conquered territory because to hold on to it will only exacerbate the tensions and deepen the bitterness of the Arabs."[32] These were prescient words indeed.

King was also worried that the recent war would derail the peace movement that was trying to organize additional large, national protests against the Vietnam War. Even before war broke out, his aides believed that the peace movement was "suffering badly" because Jews, who were highly represented within antiwar ranks, had all become hawks when it came to events in the Middle East. Levison complained on June 6, 1967, that the war had become a "real monkey wrench" in the peace movement and that King's hopes for a major peace march in August were now pointless. King agreed, but he remained anxious to keep public attention focused on Vietnam, even though war in the Middle East had "confused it a great deal."[33]

In the end the 1967 war and the political concerns surrounding a trip to the Middle East led King to cancel his planned pilgrimage. By mid-June of 1967 Levison claimed that only about two hundred people had made reservations for the trip instead of the several thousand that King had hoped for.[34] King called his close aides on July 24 to determine what to do. King feared that his presence in Jerusalem in particular would be problematic inasmuch as "they [the Israelis] have annexed Jerusalem, and any way you say it they don't plan to give it up."[35]

After a lengthy discussion, King finally opined that his instincts had usually proven to be sound and that his instincts in this instance told him that "I don't think I could come out unscathed" from the trip. His image as a peacemaker would be tarnished, and his mind seemed to be made up.

King wrote to the head of Concreta Tours on September 6, 1967, expressing his desire to cancel. The SCLC leader cited a flare-up of Egyptian-Israeli shelling across the new front lines along the Suez Canal as a reason. King also stated that it would "compromise" his beliefs in nonviolence and democracy to take a trip to Greece and risk appearing to support the Greek Colonels— the leaders of the military coup that had overthrown the Greek government in

April of 1967—given that the pilgrimage's itinerary included Athens. He followed that up with a letter to El Al Israel Airlines, the Israeli national carrier, officially cancelling the pilgrimage. His letter cited four reasons for doing so. First, he claimed that he could not conduct a trip that was "free from political over tones [*sic*]"—a direct reference to his desire to avoid embroiling himself in the political questions raised by the war and the Israeli occupation of the West Bank. Second, while he agreed that it was safe for Americans to travel to Israel and the West Bank, ordinary American citizens who read about the ongoing violence along the new Arab-Israeli cease-fire lines might feel that the situation was too dangerous. Third, he did not want to do something that might connote support for the Greek junta. Finally, King claimed that the Newark, Detroit, and other inner-city black rebellions that summer were placing great demands on his time and energy.[36] King's 1959 trip remained the only time he ever visited the Middle East.

KING ON THE TIGHTROPE

Public perceptions about King's stance toward the Arab-Israeli conflict continued to trouble him thereafter. Just six days after writing to El Al Israel Airlines, King felt compelled to write another letter dealing with Israel. In mid-August the SNCC newsletter controversy erupted. King had been traveling and when pressed by the media for comment deftly demurred by stating that he had not read that particular issue of the *SNCC Newsletter*. Two weeks later, the National Conference for New Politics in Chicago adopted the statement condemning Israel and Zionism for starting the June war. This time it was harder for King to sidestep the issue, given that he had opened the conference with the keynote speech. Several major American Jewish organizations—among them the American Jewish Committee, the American Jewish Congress, the National Jewish Community Relations Advisory Council, the Union of American Hebrew Congregations, the Union of Orthodox Jewish Congregations of America, the United Synagogues of America, and the Anti-Defamation League of B'nai B'rith—sent King a telegram shortly after the conference ended asking that he publicly distance himself from the gathering because of the statement on Israel. The telegram argued that because King had opened the conference with a speech, he might be perceived as endorsing its subsequent resolutions.

King felt forced to act. He had in fact been suspicious of the direction the conference seemed to be taking even before it began, and the storm of controversy that emerged no doubt confirmed his concerns. His aides had been told in advance that issues relating to Israel were hindering the work of conference planning. Levison had held a phone conversation on August 24, 1967, shortly before the conference began, with Richard A. Russell, a Jewish businessman, activist, and part owner of *Ramparts* magazine. Russell was close to King and occupied a seat on the executive board of the National Conference for New Politics. He indicated that he was resigning from the committee because he had tried and failed to have fellow board member Stokely Carmichael removed. Russell could no longer work with Carmichael given his "pro-Arab, pro-Nasser point of view," and inasmuch as he had encouraged King to become involved with the conference, he told Levison to let King know of his action.[37]

Second, King must have believed that he could not ignore a communication directed to him by such high-profile Jewish allies. Much therefore rode on how he responded, and King chose his words carefully when he responded to the telegram. As far back as June 6, Levison had advised King that if he must make a statement on the Middle East that he include something to the effect that Israel's existence and territorial integrity were "incontestable."[38] King adopted this suggestion almost verbatim. "*Israel's right to exist as a state in security,*" King diplomatically wrote to the Jewish organizations on September 28, 1967, "*is incontestable*"—a statement that Levison seems to have written and that, while not repudiating the conference or its condemnation of Israel, nonetheless served to assure the Jewish groups about his support of Israel's right to exist. The American Jewish Committee seemed pleased and thereafter issued a press release that quoted from King's letter.[39]

King and SCLC leaders continued to deal with the Arab-Israeli conflict and its domestic ramifications for blacks and Jews. They believed that beyond the question of Israel, they had to say something about the delicate question of whether SNCC and the National Conference for New Politics went beyond being anti-Israeli and were in fact being anti-Semitic in their statements, as Jewish groups and even certain black leaders were claiming. The SCLC issued a statement titled "Anti-Semitism, Israel, and SCLC: A Statement on Press Distortions" soon after King wrote back to the Jewish organizations about his position on the New Politics conference, Israel, and anti-Semitism.

The statement essentially repeated for public consumption what King had written in his response to the Jewish organizations. It upheld Israel's right to exist but took care to follow King's two-pronged approach, balancing support for Israel with recognition that the roots of the problem lay in the region's economic underdevelopment. It noted, inter alia: "SCLC and Dr. King have repeatedly stated that the Middle East peace embodies the related problems of security and development. *Israel's right to exist as a state in security is incontestable. At the same time, the great powers have the obligation to recognize that the Arab world is in a state of imposed poverty and backwardness that must threaten peace and harmony.* Until a concerted and democratic program of assistance is effected, tensions cannot be relieved. Neither Israel nor its neighbors can live in peace without an underlying basis of social and economic development." It also was careful to note that ultimate peace required action and vision on both sides: "The solution will have to be found in statesmanship by Israel and progressive Arab forces who in concert with the great powers recognize that fair and peaceful solutions are the concern of all humanity and must be found. . . . Neither military measures nor a stubborn effort to reverse history can provide a permanent solution for peoples who need and deserve both development and security." Rather than simply blaming each side, especially the Arabs, for intransigence or fanaticism, the statement instead offered a left wing–sounding economic analysis by noting that "at the heart of the problem are oil interests." Finally, the SCLC statement condemned anti-Semitism firmly and clearly: "*SCLC will continue tirelessly to condemn racism whether its form is white supremacy or anti-semitism.*"[40] King was being measured, cautious, and nuanced.

King continued to be cognizant of the conflict and the fine line he was forced to walk in his approach to it. He had a vision of working carefully within the system to uphold. Some of his advisers pushed him to come out more forcefully for Israel, despite the apparent contradictions inherent in an advocate of nonviolence championing a country that was now subjecting the West Bank, Gaza, Golan, and Sinai to a military occupation. SCLC board member Wyatt Tee Walker wrote him in late August of 1967 to ask him to sign another pro-Israeli statement. "Israel deserves a chance to survive," Walker wrote. "I remain a pacifist; but the information I have seems to justify Israel's response to the Arab threat—fight or die!"[41] Despite such advice, King knew that the Palestinian question was only going to grow in intensity unless it was resolved; merely having Israel use its military power to subdue the Arabs was no solution, as he noted in "Anti-Semitism, Israel, and SCLC: A Statement on Press Distortions." Years later his aide Jesse Jackson recalled King mentioning that the Palestinian question was going to grow into a major problem. "I remember Martin telling me before he died," Jackson noted, "that was gonna be the next big new tension in the world, about the Palestinians."[42]

As 1967 turned into 1968, King remained obliged to dance among the raindrops of racial and ethnic politics and to keep in mind how they intersected with the Arab-Israeli conflict. Publicly, he stuck with his two-pronged strategy about how to respond to questions concerning Israel and the Middle East. King continued to speak out in support of Israel's right to exist, if not its policies, and took pains in this regard to set himself apart from Black Power advocates' position on the Middle East. This helped him burnish his insider credentials. All the while, however, he balanced this with his call for improving Arab standards of living in hopes that this would lessen Arab rejection of Israel, which helped his image as an outsider prophet of peace and justice.

King exemplified this approach when he spoke at the Rabbinical Assembly's convention at Kiamesha Lake, New York, on March 25, 1968, telling his Jewish audience that the 1967 war engendered "various responses" in the United States, stressing that "the response of some of the so-called young militants again does not represent the position of the vast majority of Negroes." He took a swipe at black nationalists and their vision of racial solidarity with the Third World by stating that such people were "color-consumed" and "see a kind of mystique in being colored" that prompts them to condemn anything that is not. King then assured the conference that he considered Israel to be "one of the great outposts of democracy in the world," an "oasis of brotherhood and democracy."

True to form, King did not ignore the Arab world in his address, taking pains once again to state that while peace for Israel meant physical security, peace for the Arab world meant "economic security." Dismissing the Arabs' hostility to Israel as a "quest to find scapegoats" to blame for their economic insecurity—and thus continuing to ignore public discussion of what he clearly knew by that point were the political bases for Arab grievances—King argued that alleviating Arab economic insecurity could lead to peace: "Peace for Israel means security. . . . On the other hand, we must see what peace for the Arabs means in a real sense of security on another level. Peace for the Arabs means the kind of economic security that they so desperately need. These nations, as you know, are part of that third world of hunger, of disease, of illiteracy. I think that as long as these conditions exist there will be tensions, there will be the endless quest to find scapegoats."[43]

Ten days later King was dead, killed by an assassin's bullet in Memphis, Tennessee. As is the case with Malcolm X, we can only speculate about how King's stance toward the Arab-Israeli conflict might have evolved had he lived. He knew the realities faced by all sides in the conflict, yet he took his role as peacemaker seriously enough not to champion either side's behavior in a consistent manner. King also knew that the issue was not going away and that as a peacemaker he no doubt would continue to have to face it. Like other mainstream civil rights leaders and Black Power activists, King's vision of black identity and place within America undergirded his stance on the Arab-Israeli conflict.

What is clear after King's death, however, is the way that certain partisans of the conflict strove to paint him and his legacy as being supportive of their side of the issue. Such a powerful moral voice belonging to a man who epitomized much of what Americans considered good about the 1960s was considered a prize catch, and activists of various stripes long have tried to claim him as an advocate for the justice of their cause. In the years since his death, pro-Israeli commentators in particular have claimed that King lined up solidly behind the Jewish state. Suspicion about the veracity of some of his alleged expressions of support for Israel and Zionism emerged when a book appeared in 1999 that contained a letter supposedly written by King in 1967 claiming that anti-Zionism was really just a form of anti-Semitism. But "Letter to an Anti-Zionist Friend" turned out to be a hoax. A number of persons have tried to track down where the counterfeit letter first appeared, or who created it, to no avail.[44] Regardless of what really happened, it shows the degree to which being able to lay claim to King's prestige and legacy continues to be seen as valuable political currency vis-à-vis the Arab-Israeli conflict in the twenty-first century.

Despite whatever proponents of Israel or the Palestinians claim that King thought or would have thought about the Arab-Israeli conflict, King clearly understood the pain and suffering of both Israeli Jews and Palestinian Arabs alike from his travels and contacts, and he tried to remain balanced and guarded in his public pronouncements about the conflict. In this way his approach to the Middle East was markedly different both from Black Power militants like those in SNCC and from fellow civil rights leaders like Roy Wilkins and Bayard Rustin. Beyond his own ambivalence about being a pacifist taking sides in an armed conflict, King's caution also emanated from his fear of alienating Jewish supporters, on the one hand, and further antagonizing Black Power detractors, on the other. His views on racial identity and his mission as an advocate of wider nonviolent socioeconomic change in the United States found him straddling the divide between Jewish solidarity and Black Power concepts of revolutionary Third World identity. He surely spoke positively about Israel as a country and its right to exist, but these attitudes did not extend to condoning Israeli conduct.

Black Power pro-Palestinian criticisms of Israel quickly began to spread starting in 1967. King and other mainstream black leaders soon found themselves contending with the intellectual and cultural power of militant black attitudes about global issues such as the Arab-Israeli conflict, notably voices emerging from the Black Arts Movement.

THE POWER OF WORDS
The Black Arts Movement
and a New Narrative

FOR HARLEM-BASED WRITER Askia Muhammad Touré there was a clear link between the situation faced by blacks in America and that facing Third World peoples. This included the Palestinians. Born Roland Snellings, Touré worked at the SNCC office in Atlanta and joined the Revolutionary Action Movement in early 1964 before becoming a poet. In 1970 he wrote a poem entitled "A Song in Blood and Tears" that specifically compared the black struggle in Harlem with the guerrilla war being waged by the Palestinians against Israel:

Black Brown Red Yellow Brothers starving
in the streets of Calcutta, dying on
the reservations, nodding in the Harlems,
napalmed in Vietnam, or marching with
the people's armies down the streets
of PEKING/GUINEA/TANZANIA/
PALESTINE GUERILLA
armies marching . . .[1]

Touré's sense of identity as a black man was wrapped up tightly with that of other peoples of color, as symbolized by his conflation of black, Asian, African,

American Indian, and Palestinian peoples and their respective armed struggles. His poem clearly showed that Black Power support for the Palestinians extended beyond politics and was surfacing in cultural expressions of black identity by the early 1970s.

The high profile Black Power internationalism advocated by Malcolm X and SNCC helped spread black consciousness about international events, and the Arab-Israeli conflict in particular, throughout the rest of the 1960s and into the 1970s. One particularly important example is how support for the Arab struggle against Israel emerged among black writers. An essential dimension of Black Power was its commitment to forge a new, revolutionary political image for blacks that was reinforced on a cultural level by black men and women of the arts and letters. This culture was designed to be an essential dimension of overall black empowerment and an important vehicle for expressions of both black identity and sense of place within America. The Black Panther Party's artist-in-residence, Emory Douglas, once noted the power of a new revolutionary, internationalist black culture: "This new born culture is not particular to the oppressed Black masses but transcends communities and racial lines because all oppressed people can relate to revolutionary change which is the starting point for developing a revolutionary culture."[2]

The fact that an awareness of Palestine was spreading among blacks and appearing in forms of black cultural expression underscored its importance for African American identity. From the poetry of the Black Arts Movement to articles in publications like *Negro Digest/Black World* and to manifestos in underground newspapers, black cultural expression reinforced the shared sense of struggle between black Americans and the Palestinian people. Support for the Palestinians therefore contributed to formulation of an anti-imperialist, revolutionary cultural identity by which blacks could define themselves and subvert the dominant white American cultural hegemony.[3] No dimension of this process better exemplified this than the Black Arts Movement.

THE BLACK ARTS MOVEMENT

The Black Arts Movement has been described as the cultural wing of the political Black Power movement. It refers to a host of persons and cultural fora that witnessed the collective expression of black pride and cultural production at the same time that others paraded Black Power on the American political stage.[4] The Black Arts Movement proposed creating a vigorous black artistic and cultural community as part of the political attempt to create vibrant, independent black communities and organizations. The roots and development of the Black Arts Movement were varied, but certainly one of its towering figures was Harold Cruse. A major intellectual force and critic of integration, Cruse created a stir when he published *The Crisis of the Negro Intellectual* in 1967. As part of his discussion of black intellectuals, he famously wrote about the tensions between blacks and Jews during a decade when this was becoming a hot-button issue, particularly for Jews who had been sympathetic with the black freedom struggle but were feeling uneasy about blacks by the mid-1960s.

Cruse directed his attention overseas and criticized Israel and Zionism. He understood the Zionist movement that successfully created the Jewish state of Israel out of a predominantly Arab part of the Middle East as a clear example of European imperialism. In *The Crisis of the Negro Intellectual* he wrote, "The European experience also shows that European imperialism was not exclusively a Christian affair: Witness the international machinations that brought about the State of Israel." Cruse also derided the United Nations for its role in causing the Arab-Israeli conflict, describing its partition of Palestine in 1947 as having done "violence" to its own charter.[5]

Cruse saw black political activism in America both as revolutionary and as linked with the wider anticolonial struggles going on around the world. He noted in 1968 that "the revolutionary initiative has passed to the colonial world, and in the United States is passing to the Negro."[6] Addressing black-Jewish relations in the United States and the "crisis" of black intellectuals, Cruse had written in 1967 about transnationalism when he noted that affairs in the Middle East could not help but affect Jews' relationships with American blacks as the latter became more and more concerned with anticolonial movements in Africa. American Jews' attachment to Israel after 1948, he claimed, had "special significance" to such relations: "*Black Nationalism, Zionism, African affairs, and Negro Civil Rights organizations are intimately interlocked on the political, cultural, economic and international fronts, whether Negro intellectuals care to acknowledge it or not.*"[7]

Amiri Baraka was another great figure associated with the founding of the Black Arts Movement in the 1960s, and he concurred with Cruse's sentiments.

Born as Everett LeRoi Jones, he first became a poet and writer associated with the Beat movement in New York City before changing direction radically after the assassination of Malcolm X in February of 1965. Along with Cruse, Jones went on to establish the Black Arts Repertory Theater/School in Harlem later that same year. Constantly reinventing himself, Jones changed his name to Ameer Barakat a few years later after studying Islam with Heshaam Jaaber, a black American who claimed Sudanese roots. Barakat then changed his new Arabic name shortly thereafter to its Kiswahili (Swahili) variant, Amiri Baraka, under the influence of the Los Angeles–based black cultural nationalist figure Maulana Karenga.[8]

In 1968 Baraka coedited and published one of the early seminal works of the Black Arts Movement, an anthology of literature titled *Black Fire*, which featured a poem by Charles Anderson that mentioned Israel and the Arabs. It was titled "Finger Pop'in," and one stanza of Anderson's poem dealt with how Israel raised money to bomb Egypt:

And in Israel a monster was put on stage, in a blood campaign to sell bonds in order
    to buy more bombs to drop on Cairo.
And the rats skipped across the floor.
Finger pop![9]

Baraka continued to champion the Palestinians from his base of operations in Newark, New Jersey—the city that exploded in violence during the black rebellion in July of 1967. His increasingly virulent criticisms of Israel were given voice by the Congress of Afrikan People, which emerged from the Pan-African Congress that Baraka had helped organize in Atlanta from September 3 to September 7, 1970. As a writer, it was not surprising that Baraka used the congress's newspaper, *Unity and Struggle*, to launch strident attacks on Israel and Zionism. In one issue the paper denounced Zionism as "a form of colonialism," noting that "Israel was created by, for and because of imperialism." In a 1975 issue *Unity and Struggle* commented on the "Zionism is racism" issue being raised at the United Nations by asserting that Zionism was indeed racism, as well as reactionary nationalism, and that racism long had been one of the main weapons used by imperialism against peoples of the Third World: "progressive forces in the world will hold up a mirror to zionism [*sic*]," the paper declared, "so the world can see the ugly face of racism." Another article in that same issue proclaimed, "Zionism is a form of colonialism, which has erected the settler colony of 'Israel.' The land that is supposedly called 'Israel' is Palestine."[10]

Cruse and Baraka were not alone. Another indication of the pro-Palestinian sentiments in the Black Arts Movement was the fact that Baraka coedited *Black Fire* with Lawrence P. Neal, who also was strongly anti-Zionist. Neal also was involved in the formation of the Black Arts Theater Repertory Theater/School and helped form a group in Harlem called the Black Panthers based on what SNCC had done in Lowndes County, Alabama.[11] The same year that *Black Fire* came out, Neal published a piece in which he bemoaned the fact that black nationalists could not compete with the pro-Israeli propaganda issued by the mainstream black leaders in America during the 1967 war. There was, he claimed, "no adequate means of presenting the Arab side of the conflict." What black support there was for Israel came not from "Biblical mysticism" but rather from "good propaganda for over forty years." Neal called for educating the black community about the fact that "Zionist interests are decidedly pro-Western and . . . these interests are neo-colonialist in nature and design."[12]

Other poets associated with the Black Arts Movement expressed similarly strong support for the Palestinian struggle. One of these poets was Don Lee (he adopted the Kiswahili name Haki R. Madhubuti in the 1970s). Lee helped found the Third World Press in Chicago in December of 1967 and two years later traveled to Africa, where he attended the Pan-African Cultural Festival in Algeria, at which a representative from al-Fateh spoke. His feelings about the Arab-Israeli conflict were evident in his 1970 poem "A Poem for a Poet," which was dedicated to the famous Palestinian poet Mahmud Darwish, a refugee from the 1948 war who, as the Palestinians' modern poet laureate, was noteworthy for his aching poetry of exile from Palestine. Lee's poem links the Palestinian exile with that faced by American blacks, who had been exiled from Africa by the evil of slavery. Part of the poem noted, "Our enemies eat the same bread."[13]

Lee blasted pro-Israeli blacks in another 1970 poem titled "See Sammy Run in the Wrong Direction," which was a scathing attack on a group of black editors and publishers from the National Newspaper Publishers Association (NNPA) who visited Israel—what Lee called "occupied Palestine"—in November of 1969. Lee accused the journalists of being untrue to themselves as black people by trying to imitate Jews. Like many Black Power activists, Lee used *negro* as a term of denigration, referring to blacks who tried to please whites by acting in ways deemed submissive and respectable in white eyes. The title and several parts of the poem refer to Sammy Davis Jr., a famous black American performer who converted to Judaism several years after losing an eye in an automobile accident. Lee introduced his poem as follows:

(for the ten *negro* editors representing n.n.p.a.
who visited occupied *Palestine* [known as Israel]
on a fact finding trip, but upon their return—
reported few facts, in any.)[14]

In addition to the likes of Cruse, Baraka, and Neal, another noteworthy pro-Palestinian voice in the Black Arts Movement was the influential writer and editor Hoyt W. Fuller. Fuller lived abroad for several years in the late 1950s as a refugee from American racism, and after returning in 1960, he began editing the *Negro Digest*. The periodical changed its name in 1970 to *Black World* to keep pace with the changing times and was a leading intellectual organ of the Black Arts Movement. One of Fuller's earliest comments on the Arab-Israeli conflict came in 1969, when he covered the Pan-African Cultural Festival in Algeria and noted the mingling of American blacks with Palestinians from the al-Fateh guerrilla movement: "They [al-Fateh members] are indeed heroic figures. . . . They apparently are particularly interested in making contact with the American blacks, and *vice versa*."[15]

Fuller continued to express black concerns about the Middle East throughout the early and mid-1970s. In July of 1973 he wrote and published the short article "Possible Israeli Attack in Africa?" in which he referred to comments made by Senator J. William Fulbright (D-AR) about the possibility of an Israeli attack on Libya.[16] Much like Stokely Carmichael had done earlier, Fuller linked blacks' concerns about the African motherland with those Arab states, like Libya, that were part of that continent.

Fuller's strident comments elicited concern from some who worried about the direction *Negro Digest/Black World* was taking. Fuller was, as one writer noted presciently in late 1974, questioning Zionist statements "even at the risk of his job."[17] In February of 1975 Fuller wrote that American blacks were not going to fight the Arabs for oil, echoing the boxer Muhammad Ali's famous refusal to fight against the Vietnamese people, who had done nothing to harm him as a black man in America. "There are thousands of Black men in and out of uniform," Fuller wrote, "who stand ready to refuse to fight the Arabs on the very same grounds: The Arabs have done nothing to Black People."[18] Later that year, Fuller published a hard-hitting article by Ronald Walters that not only accused Israel of "military imperialism" but also noted the degree to which American Jews had veered away from supporting struggles for justice by giving their support to Israel. "Since the Israelis have no intention of returning to the *status quo ante*," Walters wrote, "they are guilty of military imperialism, with the material support of the United States." Israel was now part of a "Western power structure" that put the Jewish state in a "defense role *vis-à-vis* those interests and the oppressed."[19]

Several months later, in February of 1976, John H. Johnson, the famous black publishing magnate, decided to stop publishing *Negro Digest/Black World*, thereby depriving Fuller of his pulpit. Johnson was no Black Power zealot. Several years earlier, in June of 1970, he had lent his signature to Bayard Rustin's strongly pro-Israeli advertisement in the *New York Times* titled "An Appeal by Black Americans for United States Support to Israel." Yet some have claimed that the real reason Johnson shut down *Negro Digest/Black World* was because Fuller's very public anti-Zionist and pro-Palestinian statements had led to Jewish threats to stop buying advertising space in *Jet* and *Ebony*, two of Johnson's widely read and more mainstream magazines targeting black audiences.[20] The intrablack war over what to say about the Arab-Israeli conflict continued unabated.

BLACK ESSAYISTS AND JOURNALISTS

In a fiery article published a month after the three-week-long October 1973 Arab-Israeli war, noted writer Shirley Graham Du Bois forcefully articulated Black Power's view of a global color line whereby peoples of color were struggling against white imperialism. The conflict between Arabs and Israelis was just one front in this wider contest: "[In the Middle East] it is 'colored folk' battling with the 'white folk' of Israel! . . . Surrounded as they are by an ocean of suntanned peoples, Israel has repeatedly, defiantly and arrogantly asserted its superior 'whiteness.' . . . Nobody was allowed to forget that the State of Israel belonged to the dominant, 'enlightened' *white* world." Du Bois also hailed the pan-African support extended to Egypt during the 1973 war, deriding the

Israelis and other "white folks" who were surprised that all of Africa stood up and stood by their fellow African state:

Israel had no idea that when Egypt's Anwar el Sadat lifted his hand signaling, *now is the time* and dark-skinned troops crossed to the occupied east bank of the Suez Canal throwing themselves against the "invincible" invaders, with their mighty US armaments, dug deep in African soil—no white folks dreamed that all Africa would get the message and line up! . . . I do not believe he [al-Sadat] was putting his entire trust in "superpowers." He knew thtt [*sic*] the world's majority peoples were behind him— that dark-skinned majority ingenuously referred to as the Third World. He trusts *them* to enforce the just peace to which he aspires.[21]

The early 1970s witnessed more and more African American essayists and journalists adopt pro-Palestinian stances as part of the new black aesthetic and culture set in motion by the Black Arts Movement. One was the very significant woman of letters, Shirley Graham Du Bois. She studied music at the Sorbonne in Paris in 1929 before obtaining her BA and MA at Oberlin College in 1934 and 1935, respectively, and went on to become a nationally known playwright and author. She married the venerable W. E. B. Du Bois, the intellectual and cofounder of the NAACP, in 1951. She followed her husband to Ghana in 1961, the same year she helped found the influential black intellectual and cultural journal *Freedomways*.

As a widow, Graham Du Bois fled Ghana for Cairo in 1966 after a coup d'état toppled the government of Kwame Nkrumah, taking up residence in the Duqqi district of the Egyptian capital where the PLO maintained an office. While living in Cairo, Graham Du Bois followed Arab-Israeli affairs closely in the 1960s and 1970s, even publishing a biography of Egyptian president Gamal Abdel Nasser in 1972. The October 1973 Arab-Israeli war affected her deeply given Egypt's prominent role in the fighting. Graham Du Bois's sentiments of a racial fault line in the Middle East echoed those of her late husband, who more than fifty years earlier had prophesied that the main issue that would define the twentieth century was what he called the color-line.[22]

James Baldwin was a major American writer of the mid-twentieth century, and he, too, voiced criticisms of Israel. Baldwin visited the Jewish state in September of 1961 as part of a trip he intended to make to Africa. He traveled throughout the country and crossed over the cease-fire lines into Jordanian-controlled

East Jerusalem to visit the Christian shrines there. Despite appreciating see-
ing the holy places he had read about as a religiously oriented youth, Baldwin
came away from his journey with a clear view of what he considered the wider
Western imperialist purposes that Israel served. In a 1970 interview he mused:

When I was in Israel I thought I liked Israel. I liked the people. But to me it was obvious why the Western world created the state of Israel, which is not really a Jewish state.
The West needed a handle in the Middle East. And they created the state as a European pawn. It is tragic that the Jews should allow themselves to be used in this fashion,
because no one cares what happens to the Jews. No one cares what is happening to the
Arabs. But they do care about the oil. That part of the world is a crucial matter if you
intend to rule the world.

Baldwin hastened to tell his interviewer that he was "not anti-Semitic at all,
but I am anti-Zionist." He noted: "I don't believe they [Zionists] had the right,
after 3,000 years, to reclaim the land with Western bombs and guns on biblical injunction. When I was in Israel it was as though I was in the middle of
The Fire Next Time."[23]

Outside of the Black Arts Movement and the black intelligentsia, various
editors, journalists, and black newspapers in the late 1960s and 1970s were noteworthy for their hostility to Zionism and Israel. The Nation of Islam's *Muhammad Speaks* long had sided with the Arabs. In the run-up to the June 1967 war,
the paper carried an article that asserted an internationalist Black Power analysis
of the rising tensions in the Middle East: "a more profound appraisal indicates
that it [the crisis] is essentially a conflict between the newly emerging nations
of the East and the old West, led by White America."[24] The same sentiments
were expressed in a full-page title in the June 23, 1967, issue: "Arabs: By Proxy
the White West Is Sowing New Colonialism in Our Midst."[25]

Underground black political newspapers were another source of pro-Arab,
anti-Israeli sentiment in the 1960s and 1970s. Detroit's *Inner City Voice* exem-
plifies one publication that vocally supported the Palestinian cause. Established
in September of 1967 in the wake of the Detroit disturbances, it was edited
by John Watson, a young activist involved in a number of black working-class
issues in the city. Watson had a long history of activism, having worked with
SNCC's Detroit chapter until he and his colleagues were expelled for extolling
a more militant course for northern blacks than SNCC was willing to support

at the time. Watson studied Marxist thought and later was involved with the Negro Action Committee. In early 1963 he helped found UHURU (Kiswahili: freedom), a civil rights and black nationalist student group. UHURU members expressed a great interest in the Middle East that was fueled by the fact that several of them met some Middle Eastern revolutionaries during a 1964 trip to Cuba.[26] By the late 1960s, Watson was involved with the Dodge Revolutionary Union Movement. He later helped form the League of Revolutionary Black Workers (LRBW) in June of 1969 and served on its governing committee. Later, in 1971, the LRBW created a broader grouping in Detroit called the International Black Workers Congress.

Watson was also a journalist whose strong pro-Palestinian viewpoint was expressed in the underground publications with which he was associated. He edited the *Black Vanguard* in 1965 before starting the *Inner City Voice*, which became a major voice for the black community in Detroit. In November of 1969 the paper ran an article by student and journalist Nick Medvecky titled "Revolution Until Victory—Palestine al-Fatah." The piece reported on a trip Medvecky had made to Lebanon, Syria, Jordan, and Israel in August of that year.[27] Starting in the fall of 1968, Watson also edited the *South End*, the newspaper of Wayne State University in Detroit. When that newspaper ran a front-page story (also written by Medvecky) about al-Fateh, the response of Detroit's Jewish community was immediate and vociferously negative. Years later, Medvecky recalled, "We [Watson and I] had no idea that we were then grabbing hold of the third rail in American politics. We were quite literally astonished at the response."[28]

Just over a year later, in February of 1971, Watson traveled to Kuwait to attend the Second International Symposium on Palestine. He visited Jordan as part of the trip and interviewed writer and spokesman for the Popular Front for the Liberation of Palestine, Ghassan Kanafani, for the radical paper *The Guardian*. In a letter to *The Guardian* Watson wrote, "The major point is that the Palestinian Revolution is facing enemies on several fronts, struggling internally, and needs the wholehearted support, *materially* and verbally from all progressive forces at this time."[29]

Other black underground or political party papers supported the Palestinians, as well, in the early 1970s. Among them was the *African World*, published by the Youth Organization for Black Unity (YOBU) in Greensboro, North

Carolina, which ran an article in October of 1973 titled "How the Palestinian People Were Driven from Their Lands." An issue the following year asserted that YOBU would "never compromise in its struggle against Zionism."[30] Another newspaper was *Jihad News*, established in the wake of the September 1972 arrest of former RAM activist Max Stanford Jr. (Muhammad Ahmad). The issue that came out as the 1973 Arab-Israeli war was under way carried an article on the history of conflict that described Israel: "In short, Israel is a settler-state built on a foundation of oppression and discrimination of Arab peoples. In that regard it is similar to the South African or Rhodesian settler-states."[31] That same issue carried an editorial noting the whiteness of Israel: "The huge attacks by Israel on Egypt shows [*sic*] the emphasis the United States and the Israelis place on the military conquest of Africa by white troops." Toward the end the editorial noted, "A victory for the African and Arab people is a victory for us."[32]

Black essayists, journalists, and underground newspapers were not alone in articulating revolutionary international solidarity with the Palestinians in the early 1970s. The Drum and Spear Bookstore was opened in Washington, DC, in June of 1969 by former SNCC activists Charles Cobb Jr., Courtland Cox, and several others. Cobb had played an important role in running SNCC's famous Freedom Schools in Mississippi during the summer of 1964. Cox had been one of the founders of SNCC and was also deeply involved in SNCC's activities in Mississippi. He helped organize the 1963 March on Washington. Both men later attended the Pan-African Cultural Festival in Algeria in July of 1969 and had talked with Palestinians while there.

The short-lived bookstore they established became a major source of information and literature for the black community in Washington and was an important place for showcasing black poetry in particular. The year after Drum and Spear Bookstore opened, it established the Drum and Spear Press, which quickly decided to publish a series titled Poets of Liberation. The first book in this series was *Enemy of the Sun: Poetry of Palestinian Resistance* and contained poems from noted Palestinian poets such as Samih al-Qasim and Tawfiq Zayyad.[33]

Why did Drum and Spear Press decide to focus on Palestinian poetry in the first work to come out in its Poets of Liberation series? Years later Cobb and Cox credited Drum and Spear's managing editor, Anne Forrester, with coming up with the idea. Cobb also pointed out, "'Poets of Liberation': it seemed to us that the Palestinian struggle symbolized that. They wanted land, they wanted a nation."[34] Cox agreed:

This [pro-Palestinian stance] was not a big deal. We saw that the Palestinian struggle was part of our struggle against what was characterized as an imperialist nature of the United States and other countries. We also saw that Israel was engaged in very aggressive colonial activities. . . . My sense is that the book was one of several things that we were doing, relationships and conversations, around our support for the Palestinians and other people who we felt were oppressed. It was just a manifestation of that.[35]

Cox also noted that the two men's experience traveling in the Arab world in the late 1960s had further sensitized them to the issue of the Arab-Israeli conflict and its relevance to the black freedom struggle in America:

Charlie and I had been traveling in Africa. We were in Morocco when the Six Day War broke out. My sense was that there, [it] was not just an academic discussion of what was going on in the Middle East. We were in Morocco. We were getting the perspective of what was going on, on the ground from there, as opposed to what was going on in the United States. We understood that we had to make alliances with various people in the world. We were moving to becoming pan-Africanists. If we were going to deal with the situation in the United States, we were going to have to include Africa in the discussions. And we had to make allies of other people who were being oppressed in the world.[36]

Enemy of the Sun: Poetry of Palestinian Resistance ended up being the only book ever published by Drum and Spear Press that did not directly deal with black issues, demonstrating the importance that the Question of Palestine had for black cultural activists and poets by the 1970s. Black poet Samuel W. Allen noted the similarity between Palestinian and black American poetry in the book's preface: "It is striking that the powerful title piece of this volume, 'Enemy of the Sun' by Sameeh Al-Qassem seems to correspond to an earlier period in the Black American poetic experience."[37]

The Black Arts Movement, journals, underground newspapers, and other fora in which black men and women of letters wrote in the 1960s and early 1970s were sites in which the dominant discourse of American support for Israel was contested by black writers seeking to express a new black cultural identity. Like political Black Power advocates, they were embracing a culture of anti-imperialist resistance and African American solidarity with peoples of color struggling for independence and cultural-national authenticity overseas. Nor were they alone; other black voices began expressing their support for the Palestinians in the 1960s and 1970s in realms as varied as the world of sports and the world of national black political conventions. Here, too, the new discourse of pan–Third World support for the Palestinians began emerging as an integral part of the construction of a revolutionary black identity.

BLACK POLITICAL CONFERENCES

At the third National Conference on Black Power, held in Philadelphia from August 31 to September 2, 1968, Omar Abu Ahmed, a CORE activist from the Bronx in New York submitted a minority report describing Zionism as a threat to African Americans. Ahmed had been a Freedom Rider in 1963 and a member of Malcolm X's Organization of Afro-American Unity. His report stated: "The Black Power Conference recognizes that the Zionist Movement is a threat to the internal and external security of the Black people in America and in Africa. It is further recognized that the Zionist ideology is a force of colonialism, racism, and western imperialism, therefore, a threat to world peace." Ahmed included recommendations urging a condemnation of groups like the American Jewish Congress and American Jewish Committee for their "racist and violent attacks on the members of the Black American people," as well as a condemnation of Israel for attacking African states like Egypt, the Sudan, and Morocco. It also stated that Israel had attacked "occupied Palestine while expelling its people." Ahmed's recommendations concluded: "It is recommended that the Third International Conference on Black Power demand the withdrawal of Zionist forces from occupied lands in Africa and Asia. Finally, it is recommended that the Conference support the Palestinian people in their just struggle to liberate their land from Zionist colonialism. Finally, let it be known that the Third International Conference will oppose Zionism with all its strength and resources towards defeat of this racist, imperialist movement."[38] Strong words indeed.

Expressions of black support for the Palestinians began emerging from the various Black Power conferences that convened in the late 1960s and early 1970s. One of the most significant (and notorious) examples was at the National Black Political Convention (NBPC) in Gary, Indiana, from March 10 to March 12, 1972. The convention drew not only advocates of radical Black Power but more conventional civil rights organizers and black elected officials as well. The gathering was held in an industrial suburb of Chicago that was home to Richard Hatcher, one of the first elected black mayors of a major American city. Three men organized the convention: Hatcher, Representative Charles C. Diggs (D-MI), and Amiri Baraka. More than eight thousand blacks attended as delegates and spectators. The convention strove to adopt a common black political agenda to guide black political activity in the United States.

During the proceedings, a delegate from Washington, DC, Douglas Moore, offered a resolution denouncing Israel. Moore's mainstream pedigree was different from most black activists who had spoken up against Israel in the past. He was a Methodist minister who was active with the SCLC, NAACP, and SNCC and was famous as the "godfather" of the sit-in tactic. Moore was sensitized to anticolonial movements after serving as a missionary in Africa in the early 1960s. He later moved to Washington, DC, and became involved with the Black United Front in the capital city.

Despite his establishment background, Moore had a radical streak and shared Black Power advocates' inclinations about Israel and the Palestinians. He had criticized Israel's ties with South Africa at the first African Liberation Day in Washington several months earlier, and at Gary he introduced a resolution that reiterated this same criticism, plus several more. Moore's resolution included the following:

Whereas, the establishment of the Jewish State of Israel constituted a clear violation of the Palistinians' [sic] traditional rights to live in their own home land,

Whereas, Israeli agents are working hand-in-hand with other imperialistic interests in Africa, for example, South Africa,

Be it therefore resolved that the United States Government should end immediately its economic and military support to the Israeli regime . . . ; that the Arab peoples' land holdings be returned to Palestinians; and that negotiations be ended in the freedom of the representatives of Palistinians [sic] to establish a second state based on the historical right of the Palistinian [sic] people for self-government in their own land.[39]

The resolution was adopted, but controversy about the language on Israel immediately broke out and continued for another two months after the NBPC adjourned. As the National Conference for New Politics similarly had done in

1967, the NBPC eventually softened the language of the Israel subresolution for eventual inclusion in the final "National Black Political Agenda" (NBPA). The convention's continuations committee developed alternative language for the subsection on Israel that was presented at a May 19, 1972, press conference in Washington, during which the three NBPC cochairs announced the NBPA. The subsection on Israel had been changed significantly to read as follows:

Be it resolved that the convention go on record as being in agreement with the OAU [Organization of African Unity] positions that call for:

1. The Israeli government to be condemned for her expansionist policy and forceful occupation of the sovereign territory of another state.

2. Measures be taken to alleviate the suffering and improve the position of the Palestinian people in Israel.

3. The NBPC should also resolve to support the struggle of Palestine for self-determination.

4. The NBPC concurs also with the UN Position that Israel rescind and desist from all practice affecting the demographic structure or physical character of occupied Arab territories and the rights of their inhabitants.[40]

Even then, the controversy continued. Various mainstream black political figures took pains to distance themselves from the Israel subsection, including NBPC cochairs Diggs and Hatcher (Baraka did not). They issued a statement on the day of the press conference that read, in part, "We feel obligated to point out that in our judgment the resolution regarding Israel . . . [is] not representative of the sentiments of the vast majority of black Americans." Washington's congressional delegate, Walter E. Fauntroy (D-DC), also attended the press conference and concurred. Joining in the rejection was the entire Congressional Black Political Caucus.[41] Representative Louis Stokes, chair of the caucus, had issued a press release at the end of the convention that read: "As the black elected officials to the U.S. Congress, we affirm our position that we fully respect the right of the Jewish people to have their own state in their historical national homeland. We vigorously oppose the efforts of any group that would seek to weaken or undermine Israel's right to existence. . . . We pledge our continued support to the concept that Israel has the right to exist in peace as a nation."[42] Stokes's press release was politically motivated overkill. No portion of the resolution had denied Israel's right to exist or called for its dismantling. Quite the opposite: the original resolution had called for the right of Palestinians to create a *second* state in the area for themselves, leaving Israeli Jews to continue living in their own state.

The fact that the Arab-Israeli conflict continually emerged at African American political conferences illustrates how pervasive pro-Palestinian sentiments were becoming among left-leaning blacks and how much more conservative blacks were fighting back. At a time when the Vietnam War was the biggest foreign policy issue facing the country, the fact that black Americans continued to denounce Israel and support the Palestinians at one national conference after another reveals the depth not just of pro-Palestinian feeling among blacks but also the degree to which they viewed themselves as part and parcel of the same anti-imperialist forces in the Middle East opposed both by Israel and their own government. In the lens of the great racial divide predicted by W. E. B. Du Bois, they were people of color, and Palestine was a kindred country of color.

THE COMMITTEE OF BLACK AMERICANS FOR TRUTH ABOUT THE MIDDLE EAST

On November 1, 1970, a hard-hitting statement denouncing Israel, hailing the Palestinians, and opposing US military aid to Israel appeared in a full-page advertisement in the *New York Times*. The text was unequivocal: "We, the Black American signatories of this advertisement, are in complete solidarity with our Palestinian brothers and sisters, who, like us, are struggling for self-determination and an end to racist oppression. . . . We stand with the Palestinian people in their efforts to preserve their revolution, and oppose its attempted destruction by American Imperialism aided by Zionists and Arab reactionaries." It stated, furthermore, the signatories' absolute opposition to Zionism, which was linked to imperialism and colonial settler states like South Africa, as well as their support for the Palestinian resistance movement:

We are anti-Zionist and against the Zionist State of Israel, the outpost of American Imperialism in the Middle East. Zionism is a reactionary racist ideology that justifies the expulsion of the Palestinian people from their homes and lands, and attempts to enlist the Jewish masses of Israel and elsewhere in the service of imperialism to hold back the Middle East revolution. . . .

WE STATE that the Palestinian Revolution is the vanguard of the Arab Revolution and is part of the anti-colonial revolution which is going on in places such as Vietnam, Mozambique, Angola, Brazil, Laos, South Africa and Zimbabwe. Because of its alliance with imperialism, Zionism opposes that anti-colonial revolution and especially revolutionary change in the Middle East.

WE STATE that Israel, Rhodesia, and South Africa are three privileged white settler-states that came into existence by displacing indigenous peoples from their lands.

The advertisement appeared as a direct rebuttal to the advertisement that pro-Israeli acolyte Bayard Rustin had placed in the same newspaper six months earlier, and it was the work of a small group of activists called the Committee of Black Americans for Truth About the Middle East, which had been formed by Paul B. Boutelle of New York.[43] Boutelle had joined Malcolm X's Organization of Afro-American Unity, and in fact he was at Harlem's Audubon Ballroom to meet someone the day Malcolm was murdered there. In 1964 Boutelle ran for election to the New York State Senate on the Freedom Now Party ballot. The following year, Boutelle joined the Socialist Workers Party (SWP) and became active in the early movement against the war in Vietnam, founding Afro-Americans Against the War in Vietnam in December of 1965. He also served as secretary of the Black United Action Front and was the SWP's vice presidential candidate in the 1968 national elections.

In addition to all his other political activities, Boutelle was well aware of the Arab-Israeli conflict and had developed clear pro-Palestinian sympathies by the time of the 1967 war. "Israel was totally an extension of US imperialism," he recalled years later.[44] On July 15, 1967, he organized a small rally in Harlem to "tell the other side" of the war that featured black speakers like SNCC's H. Rap Brown and the SWP's 1964 presidential candidate, Clifton DeBerry.

Three years later, Boutelle was outraged by Rustin's advertisement and decided to respond. He and six others formed a group called the Committee of Black Americans for Truth About the Middle East (COBATAME). Boutelle served as COBATAME's chair; cochairs included Patricia Robinson, a writer from New Rochelle, New York; Lydia A. Williams, Adult Adviser for Youth Unlimited in Brooklyn, New York, and a member of the executive board of the American Committee on Africa (ACOA); and Gwendolyn Patton Woods, former national coordinator of the National Association of Black Students in

Washington, DC. Attorney Robert F. Van Lierop of New York City, who was another member of ACOA's executive board, served as COBATAME's secretary treasurer.

The activists quickly circulated a text among blacks who opposed US aid to Israel and managed to raise the $4,000 needed for the advertisement, which appeared in the *New York Times* on November 1, 1970. Entitled "An Appeal by Black Americans Against United States Support of the Zionist Government of Israel," it was specifically worded to mimic, in the negative, Rustin's advertisement, which had been titled "An Appeal by Black Americans for United States Support to Israel." COBATAME's advertisement decried Israel's affirmation of American policy in Vietnam: "WE STATE that Israel continues to support United States policies of aggression in Southeast Asia, policies that are responsible for the death and wounding of thousands of black youths." It championed groups like al-Fateh and the Popular Democratic Front for the Liberation of Palestine, and it ended by stating: "WE DEMAND THAT ALL MILITARY AID OR ASSISTANCE OF ANY KIND TO ISRAEL MUST STOP. IMPERIALISM AND ZIONISM MUST AND WILL GET OUT OF THE MIDDLE EAST. WE CALL FOR AFRO-AMERICAN SOLIDARITY WITH THE PALESTINIAN PEOPLE'S STRUGGLE FOR NATIONAL LIBERATION AND TO REGAIN ALL OF THEIR STOLEN LAND."[45] Like Rustin's advertisement had done, Boutelle's statement included a coupon that could be cut out and returned to COBATAME.

Boutelle managed to secure fifty-six signatures for inclusion, including his own. Some of those who signed were activists, such as Ella L. Collins, head of the Organization of Afro-American Unity and Malcolm X's half-sister; the advocate of armed black self-defense Robert F. Williams; Clifton DeBerry, SWP presidential candidate in 1964; Grace and James Boggs, intellectuals from Detroit (although Grace was not black; she was of Chinese ancestry); former SNCC chairman Philip Hutchings; and Albert B. Cleague, noted clergyman and activist from Detroit. Poets and writers added their names, including Askia Muhammad Touré and his wife, Halima; A. B. Spellman; and Earl Ofari, as did musicians Keito (L. McKeithan) and Mahade Mohammed Ahmed. Legendary Harlem bookstore owners Lewis H. Michaux and Una G. Mulzac signed, as did journalists John Watson and Charles Simmons. Three people associated with the ACOA, staff member Charles Hightower and board members Robert F. Van

Lierop and Lydia A. Williams, also signed. Finally, other signatories included union members, lawyers, students, and activists in the women's movement like Frances M. Beal and Maxine Williams of the Third World Women's Alliance. More than three hundred people responded to the COBATAME advertisement. They were about evenly split between positive and negative responses. Of the negative responses, Boutelle reported that more than 90 percent of the letters "were of a very vulgar, racist, emotional, ignorant nature with five of them being physically filthy i.e. contents of the envelope."[46]

COBATAME did receive some requests for speaking engagements, and in late 1970 Boutelle prepared a fund-raising proposal for writing a pamphlet or book to be titled "Black Americans, Jews, and the Middle East Crisis." He estimated that it would require between $1,200 and $3,500 and hoped to complete it by January 1971.[47] Apparently, he was never able to publish it, and ultimately COBATAME ceased to function fairly shortly thereafter. Funds were short, and its members all had regular jobs that kept them from performing too much free labor for the group. COBATAME's newspaper advertisement was the group's only contribution to Black Power's counterattack on Bayard Rustin.

The expressions of support for the Palestinian struggle against Israel that exploded out of the pages of black journals and newspapers and at black political conferences stood as testament to the growing sense among black activists that the Arab-Israeli conflict was a major component of their identity and sense of political mission. If Malcolm X and SNCC had opened the door of internationalist black solidarity with Palestine as a country of color, black women and men of the arts and letters pushed it further open. This kind of internationalism became a key element in the construction of a new black cultural identity envisioned by African Americans like those in the Black Arts Movement. They were not alone; a new force within the Black Power movement was emerging that also sought to create a new, revolutionary identity for black Americans. But it aimed not at educated blacks but rather those on the street corners in the inner cities it called the "lumpen" (after the Marxist term *lumpenproletariat*): the Black Panther Party.

CHAPTER SIX

STRUGGLE
AND REVOLUTION

The Black Panthers and the Guerrilla Image

ON JULY 22, 1969, in the Algerian capital of Algiers, El-dridge Cleaver publicly proclaimed that Israel was an American "puppet and pawn" and that "al-Fateh will win"—a reference to the largest and most important Palestinian guerrilla organization.[1] An al-Fateh official stood by his side as Cleaver, minister of information for the Black Panther Party, spoke these words in support of the Palestinian national resistance movement. What was Cleaver doing in an Arab-majority country, and why was one of the most notable leaders of Black Power's most visible group in the late 1960s denouncing Israel and hailing al-Fateh?

Without doubt, one of the most memorable manifestations of militant Black Power in the 1960s and early 1970s was the Black Panther Party (BPP). Much maligned and misunderstood by hostile, frightened whites, the Panthers conjured up the fear that blacks were rising up, bearing arms, and fighting back—eschewing the nonviolent resistance preached by Martin Luther King Jr. What is much less remembered is that the Black Panther Party also provided some of the sharpest and most vivid denunciations of Israel, and support for the Palestinians, of any other group in the Black Power movement. As with Malcolm X and SNCC, the reason had to do with the group's theoretical understandings of foreign policy, of its own stance vis-à-vis the anticolonial struggles that were raging throughout the Third World, and its imaginings of itself and its revolutionary role in America.

The Black Panther Party was formed in Oakland, California, in late October of 1966 by Huey P. Newton and Bobby Seale. Newton attended Merritt College and took law courses at Oakland City College and San Francisco Law School. By the mid-1960s he was familiar with the writings of revolutionaries like Mao Zedong, Ernesto "Che" Guevara, and Frantz Fanon. Seale also attended Merritt College, where he first met Newton in 1962. Two years later, Seale became an organizer with the black revolutionary organization the Revolutionary Action Movement (RAM).

The Black Panthers initially focused on domestic issues like police harassment of blacks in Oakland and the BPP's legal rights to carry firearms in public. Yet as black nationalists influenced by Malcolm X, RAM, and Marxist teachings, the BPP also quickly developed its thinking about foreign policy and the manner in which it intersected with the situation facing American blacks. In this regard the Panthers shared the deepening internationalism of SNCC and the understanding of the connection between the black freedom struggle at home and anticolonialist revolution abroad. As Eldridge Cleaver expressed it in 1968: "The link between America's undercover support of colonialism abroad and the bondage of the Negro at home becomes increasingly clear. Those who are primarily concerned with improving the Negro's condition recognize, as do proponents of the liquidation of America's neo-colonial network, that their fight is one and the same. . . . It is at this point, at the juncture of foreign policy, that the Negro revolution becomes one with the world revolution."[2]

THE PANTHERS' STANCE ON PALESTINE

The international attention garnered by armed Palestinian guerrillas from groups like al-Fateh and the Popular Front for the Liberation of Palestine (PFLP) in the years after 1967 caught the attention of Black Power militants. Of the Third World struggles being waged in the late 1960s, the Panthers could more easily relate to Palestinians as Arabs and Muslims than to Asian freedom fighters such as those in the National Liberation Front (Viet Cong) in Vietnam. The contemporary popularity of Fanon's *The Wretched of the Earth*, with its many references to "Negroes and Arabs" and descriptions of the Algerian war of independence—along with the film *The Battle of Algiers* and the travel to Algeria and elsewhere in North Africa and the Middle East carried out by a number of black Americans—helped further the bonds of revolutionary and cultural solidarity between American blacks and Arab Muslims like those in Algeria and Palestine. Images of Palestinian fida'iyyin (Arabic: those who sacrifice themselves, i.e., guerrillas) carrying their AK-47 assault rifles fit in well with the gun-toting Black Panthers.

The Black Panthers also saw a similarity between their struggle against the structural underpinnings of white supremacy and capitalism in America and that of the Palestinians because both were fighting alone against overwhelming odds. In South Vietnam the Viet Cong struggle against the Americans had been joined by the North Vietnamese army, whereas the Palestinians did not benefit significantly from the military intervention of surrounding Arab states. Black militants in the United States pounced on the image of the brave Palestinians, waging alone what they called a people's war against tremendous odds. This appealed to the Panthers' own sense of fighting alone against more powerful forces. Moreover, their attempts to build a vibrant, revolutionary culture, including on an artistic level, for American blacks were strengthened by the language and visual imagery supplied by Palestinian groups, who were adept and active in their publicity/propaganda efforts.

It comes as no surprise, then, that the BPP quickly embraced the Palestinian cause in 1967. In fact, the first expression of this support came fewer than nine months after the party was formed. In July of 1967 the party's paper, the *Black Panther*, printed its first article on the Arab-Israeli conflict shortly after the war. The "article" was actually just a reprint of an English-language Chinese government denunciation of the preemptive Israeli strike in the June war and offered "firm support for the Arab people's fight against U.S.-Israeli aggression."[3] Despite this early support for the Arabs, it would not be until October 12, 1968, that the newspaper again ran an article on the Arab-Israeli conflict, one that championed al-Fateh. The following month, the November 16 issue stated that Palestinian refugee camps run by the United Nations Relief and Works Agency (UNRWA) for Palestine refugees in the Near East were "concentration camps," and it boldly asserted that "Israel IS because Palestine's right to be was canceled."[4]

The following year the BPP dramatically increased its public and private statements and activities regarding the Palestinians and the Arab-Israeli conflict. In January of 1969 the *Black Panther* carried al-Fateh's first general international communiqué to the world press. That same issue carried a Third World Press news story, datelined Damascus and based on an al-Fateh military communiqué, about al-Fateh guerrilla activities.[5] Three months later, BPP field marshal Donald "DC" Cox hailed al-Fateh at a rally in San Francisco.[6] From then on, a torrent of stories about the Arab-Israeli conflict came out regularly in the party's newspaper. In fact, of the forty-three issues of the *Black Panther* that ran from June 1, 1969, until March 28, 1970, the party ran thirty-three articles or other items in support of the Arabs or attacking Israel.[7]

One reason for this sudden and dramatic increase in the BPP's interest in Palestine and the Arab-Israeli conflict in 1969 was that the BPP had begun finding out more about the conflict by that point, including through contacts with the PLO's office in New York. Richard Earl Moore, who later changed his name to Dhoruba bin Wahad, was one of those who served as a Black Panthers liaison to the office.[8] Yet the main reason for the BPP's growing support for the Palestinians starting in 1969 was no doubt the presence of Eldridge Cleaver in Algeria in June of that year and his close contacts with Palestinian political and guerrilla figures located there.

ELDRIDGE CLEAVER IN ALGERIA

Cleaver was the Panther's high-profile minister of information who in 1968 published the best-selling book *Soul on Ice*. He went underground in late 1968 to avoid prosecution for his involvement in a gun battle with police and eventually made his way to Cuba in December of 1968. After seven months there, the Cuban government arranged for him to fly surreptitiously to Algeria on a Cuban passport. Quite soon, however, Cuban officials in the country approached Cleaver and said that the Algerians had discovered he was in the country and were none too happy about the situation. Handing him a ticket to Amman, Jordan, the Cubans then said that they would help him get to an al-Fateh military camp in Jordan, where he could publicly surface and announce his exile.[9] In the end Cleaver and his entourage remained under cover in Algeria.

Cleaver surfaced publicly the following month when he officially opened the Afro-American Information Center in Algiers on July 22, 1969. No doubt, one reason for choosing that time to surface was because the Pan-African Cultural Festival had opened in Algiers the day before, drawing people from all over Africa and the world for the festivities, which lasted until August 1, 1969. Accompanying Cleaver were several other Panthers, including Emory Douglas, David Hilliard, and Cleaver's wife, Kathleen Neal Cleaver. The office was festooned with posters of Huey Newton, as well as artwork done by Douglas, the party's artist-in-residence. The Afro-American Information Center was located near the office of al-Fateh. On that day, in fact, an al-Fateh official stood by Cleaver's side at the new information center when he proclaimed that Israel was an American "puppet and pawn" and that "al-Fateh will win." The al-Fateh figure probably was Mahdi Saidam, who headed the al-Fateh information office in Algiers; Cleaver also gave a speech at Saidam's nearby office.[10]

The Palestinians were anxious to woo the small Black Panther delegation and the other American blacks attending the festival to their cause. One factor working in the Palestinians' favor was the fact that they spoke English. Alongside the distinctive Algerian Arabic dialect, most Algerian officials and other revolutionary groups the Panthers had encountered in Algeria spoke French. The Palestinians' ability to communicate with Cleaver and his entourage in their own language drew the two groups closer together than most. Kathleen Neal Cleaver also recalled that the al-Fateh cadre "had a knowledge of the United States and its devastating politics vis-à-vis their struggle," which also helped the Panthers see the interconnectedness between their struggle and that of the Palestinians.[11]

Al-Fateh made a statement at the festival even though it was not an African organization, a statement that the group also printed as an English-language pamphlet titled *To Our African Brothers*. The statement linked the Palestinians with Africa by asserting that even though the Palestinians and their struggle were not part of "Africa the continent," they *were* part of "Africa the cause." There was a *geographic* map of the world and there was a *political* map, al-Fateh asserted, the latter of which showed the divide between racism, colonialism, and repression vs. revolution, rebellion, and freedom. Such viewpoints no doubt made an impression on Cleaver.[12]

Cleaver also garnered the attention of higher-ranking Palestinian officials. Yasir Arafat, head of both al-Fateh and the PLO, reportedly asked to meet him.[13] Arafat got his chance later that year. From December 25 to December 28, 1969, Algiers was host to another international gathering called the Congress of Palestine Support Committees, which brought together Palestinian supporters from around the world. On December 26 a PLO official with the nom de guerre Abu Hassan spoke at the meeting, after which Arafat and a representative of the African National Congress did as well. Next up was Cleaver. Among other things, the Panther leader said, "The Party did not arrive at this position [on the Palestinians] after having read [about it]" but rather because of its own experience in America. "Black people in Babylon [America] were being blocked by forces we did not understand. We found there were certain people within the United States who wanted to define our struggle for us." This was a not-so-subtle swipe at those in the progressive movement in America who were opposed to the BPP joining the chorus of Black Power support of the Palestinians and criticism of Israel. Cleaver probably was referring specifically to Jews, although he made sure to note that blacks were not anti-Semitic but rather were "anti-imperialism and slavery because these are the things we have suffered from."[14] The next day, December 27, Arafat publicly embraced Cleaver in a news story broadcast around the world.

The Algerians did not quite know what to do with Cleaver and his comrades at first, and he was forced to cool his heels for a year, doing little besides granting interviews. A year later they decided to recognize Cleaver and the other Panthers officially and grant them formal status as a liberation organization on par with about a dozen other such groups they hosted. On September 13, 1970, Cleaver and his entourage officially opened the office of the Black Panthers' international section in Algiers, in the two-story Villa Boumaraf, which formerly had been occupied by the National Liberation Front of South Vietnam (the Viet Cong). Kathleen Cleaver put her competence in French to good use running day-to-day affairs for the office in a country where Arabic and French were the two main languages. Kathleen Cleaver was an impressive young woman. She studied at Oberlin College and Barnard College at Columbia University before dropping out in 1966 to work on the staff of SNCC in New York and Atlanta. She joined the BPP in 1967, the year she married Eldridge Cleaver, and rose to become the party's communications secretary and the first woman on the BPP central committee.

The new office was almost immediately busy with issues relating to the Palestinians. Three days after it opened, Jordan's King Hussein ordered his army to attack PLO guerrillas in his country in what came to be a bloody two-week conflict that Palestinians called "Black September." The statement that the BPP international section issued in the midst of the fighting on September 18, 1970, once again stated that the Palestinian struggle and the BPP's struggle were one and the same. It read in part: "The struggle of the Palestinian people for their freedom and liberation from US imperialism and its lackeys is also our struggle. We recognize that if the Palestinian people cannot get their freedom and liberation, neither can we."[15] It represented a sincere belief that the BPP and the Palestinians were fighting together in the same trench, for the Panthers' conceptualization of themselves as armed freedom fighters of color seemed to demand no less.

With Kathleen Cleaver's organizational help, the BPP international section continued to forge links with PLO cadres and supporters in Algeria and elsewhere in the Arab world. One notable example occurred in early 1971, when the BPP sent a representative to the Second International Symposium on Palestine, which was held from February 13 to February 17 in Kuwait. The al-Fateh office paid for the airline tickets. Kathleen Cleaver spent some time researching the Palestinian question and discussing it with Elaine Klein, an American who was advising the Algerian government, and then drafted a statement reflecting the BPP's position on Israel and the Palestinians. The speech was delivered at the conference by BPP field marshal Donald "DC" Cox, who had fled into exile and arrived at the BPP international section in Algeria in March of 1970.[16] It read: "The Palestinian liberation struggle stands in the vanguard of the struggle against the Zionist menace that plagues the people of the entire Arab world in general, and has usurped the national rights and freedom of the Palestinian people in particular. . . . The Black Panther Party unconditionally and firmly supports the just struggle of the Palestinian people and their war of national salvation against the lackey state of Israel and its imperialist backers."[17]

"ZIONISM (KOSHER NATIONALISM) + IMPERIALISM = FASCISM"

Back in "Babylon," as Eldridge Cleaver called the United States, Panther activists continued to raise the Palestinian cause in speeches and publications. The BPP leadership began escalating its public comments about the Arab-Israeli conflict and, like Cleaver was doing, defending the Panthers' stance against criticism among liberal allies. Just about the time that Cleaver first arrived in Algeria in mid-1969, BPP chair Bobby Seale published an article entitled "Our Enemy's Friends Are Also Our Enemies" in the *Black Panther*. He gave voice to the Panthers' anger at those on the Left who begrudged them their embrace of the PLO: "We want to make it clear to all the S.D.S.'s [Students for a Democratic Society members] and P.Lers [Progressive Labor Party members], the pigs and the fascists, that we have a mind of our own, and yes we support Al-Fath [*sic*] in the struggle. And that we make our decisions and we support who we want to support, and that we're here to make revolution."[18]

Connie Matthews, who was the BPP's international coordinator by 1970, also attacked whites—in this case, Jews—who turned against the Panthers after the party publicly came down on the side of the Palestinians. Matthews, born Connie Smith in Jamaica, was one of the few top Panther leaders who was not American. She published an article in the *Black Panther* that railed at flagging Jewish support for the BPP: "The White Left in the U.S.A. is comprised of a large percentage of the Jewish population. Before the Black Panther Party took its stand on the Palestinian people's struggle there were problems but the support of the White Left for the Black Panther Party was concrete. However, since our stand the White Left started floundering and became undecided. This leaves us to believe that a large portion of these people are Zionists and are therefore racists."[19] The Panthers took pains to stress the commonality of the struggle they waged alongside the Palestinians. The Palestinians felt the same way. The *Black Panther* quoted PLO chairman Yasir Arafat in December of 1969: "The Palestinian Liberation Movement considers itself a part of the people's struggle against international imperialism. We are fighting the same enemy. The mask may differ, but the face remains the same."[20]

BPP minister of education Raymond "Masai" Hewitt stated much the same thing earlier in August 1969 when he said, "We recognize that our oppression takes different forms—Zionism in Palestine and fascism here in America—but the cause is the same: it's U.S. imperialism."[21] Hewitt and the PLO may have shared more than just ideology; they may have been in direct contact. Hewitt later spoke at a March 11, 1970, Mobilization for Palestine teach-in in Montreal organized by the Québecois Palestine Solidarity Committee and various Arab student groups. According to the diary kept by Robert L. Bay, a top Panther lieutenant who accompanied Hewitt on the trip, Hewitt was in Montreal because the BPP central committee wanted him to "speak with PLO representatives."[22]

Kathleen Neal Cleaver agreed with Matthews, Hewitt, and other Panthers that this commonality of enemies drew the Panthers together with the Palestinians. She noted that this connection drew her and other Panthers in Algeria close to the PLO's representatives there: "The lack of any language barrier between the Black Panthers and the representatives of the liberation movements from South Africa and Zimbabwe made associations between them, in personal terms, the closest, but in political terms the Panthers found their strongest support among those directly harmed by the United States' policies: the Palestinians, the Vietnamese, and the North Koreans."[23]

In 1970 the Black Panthers went on an all-out public relations offensive against Israel and in defense of the Palestinians. When an interviewer asked him what had been the greatest inspiration for the BPP, Huey Newton replied, "I think that not only Fidel [Castro] and Che [Guevara], Ho Chi Minh and Mao [Zedong] and Kim Il Sung, but also all the guerrilla bands that have been operating in Mozambique and Angola, and the Palestinian guerrillas who are fighting for a socialist world."[24] During this period, when party cofounders Newton and Seale were in jail or on trial, BPP chief of staff David Hilliard essentially assumed leadership of the party in the United States. As a high-profile Panther, he, too, began speaking out on the Arab-Israeli conflict. The February 17, 1970, issue of the *Black Panther* quoted him: "We want to make it very clear that we support all those who are actively engaged in the struggle against U.S. Imperialism and Zionism, which means to us racial supremacy."

The *Black Panther* became a major source of BPP commentary on the Middle East in 1970. In January it published an article titled "Zionism (Kosher Nationalism) + Imperialism = Fascism." It was rife with revolutionary rhetoric: "Victory to the people's struggle of Palestine! Victory to Al-Fat'h! Victory to Al-Assifa [Fateh's military wing]!" It claimed that the Zionists were replicating what the Nazis had done, and it repeated the belief that Israel was a mere tool of Western imperialism. "The Zionist fascist state of Israel," the article proclaimed, "is a puppet and lackey of the imperialists and must be smashed."[25]

As it had done for SNCC, artwork became an important medium for explaining ideology to Black Panther members. To a much greater extent, however, the BPP made its revolutionary art one of the cornerstones not only for spreading its ideas to a constituency unaccustomed to reading heavy theoretical writings but also for creating a new black revolutionary culture. The Panthers made extensive use of the art of the BPP's minister of culture, Emory Douglas, who had studied art at San Francisco City College prior to joining the BPP in early 1967. Soon he was put in charge of the *Black Panther*, but he is most remembered for his cartoons and other vivid political artwork.

Believing, like Huey Newton did, that the black community in the inner cities did not possess a culture of reading, Douglas worked hard to make his graphics tell a visual story to match what the articles in the paper were saying. His evocative images became classics of revolutionary art in 1960s–1970s America. Douglas described this new revolutionary culture in this way: "Just as the liberation struggle brings about new politics, it also brings about a new culture, a revolutionary culture. . . . Also out of the struggle for liberation comes a new literature and art. Based on the people's struggle, this revolutionary art takes on new form. The revolutionary artist begins to arm his talent with steel, as well as learning the art of self-defense, becoming one with the people by going into their midst, not standing aloof, and going into the very thick of practical struggle."[26]

The *Black Panther* ran two of Douglas's evocative cartoons about the Arab-Israeli conflict in March of 1970. Their purpose was to translate Panther ideology about Israel and the Palestinians into a simple graphic form that linked Israel with the ever-present "pig" so often denounced by the Panthers in the 1960s and 1970s. *Pig* was often used as a negative epithet referring to a police officer, although it also had a broader connotation of those in control, those in authority. As early as an article titled "Palestine Guerrillas vs Israeli Pigs," which ran in a January 1969 issue of the *Black Panther*, the BPP sometimes referred to the Israelis as pigs.

Douglas used the image of the pig in the cartoons he drew for the March 21, 1970, issue. An article titled "Al Fath [*sic*] Does Not Intend to Push the Jews into the Sea" was accompanied by cartoons featuring America and Israel as pigs. The first cartoon depicted the United States as a large-breasted female pig sitting atop an American flag, nursing two piglets, one labeled West Germany and the other Israel. Other piglets, bearing the names of American allies like France and Japan but also Rhodesia and South Africa, clamored to suck as well. The other illustration featured two drooling pigs standing nose-to-nose. One was labeled "U.S. Imperialism" and wore a Statue of Liberty–type crown; it held an American flag under one arm while the other arm raised a torch like the Statue of Liberty. Its nose read "Nixon." The second pig wore an eye patch and carried an Israeli flag tucked under one arm that clutched an automatic rifle while the other hand raised a scepter bearing the Star of David. Its nose read "Moshe Dayan."[27]

Douglas's cartoons symbolized one of the important functions that the Palestinian cause served for the BPP and the wider Black Power movement in the late 1960s. It afforded them the chance to deepen their own attempts to create a revolutionary black culture of resistance at home by linking it to the Palestinians' culture of resistance, which was becoming increasingly popular throughout the global Left, particularly in terms of visual culture. Palestinian groups like al-Fateh and the Popular Front for the Liberation of Palestine already were adept at producing posters and other publicity/propaganda vehicles that were replete with images of steely, armed guerrillas—both men and women—to enhance their written narrative. Indeed, Palestinian poster production was among the largest in the world in the 1960s and found audiences in many countries.[28] Like the BPP, the Palestinians were reaching out both at home and abroad to audiences that often responded better to images than to the written word.

The BPP used Palestinian-themed art and sloganeering not only to generate support for the Palestinians but, equally important, to bolster the domestic revolutionary image they were creating for themselves as armed revolutionaries.[29] As Stokely Carmichael and Charles V. Hamilton noted in 1967, self-definition through culture and other means was an essential part of Black Power: "Black people must redefine themselves, and only *they* can do that. Throughout this country, vast segments of the black communities are beginning to recognize the need to assert their own definitions, to reclaim their history, their culture."[30] Black Power's stance alongside the Palestinians was therefore more than just another chapter in its storied history in the 1960s; it was part and parcel of the very revolutionary identity it sought to create.

Of the various Palestinian guerrilla/political groups, al-Fateh received the lion's share of the Black Panther Party's attention. The *Black Panther* carried a number of articles about al-Fateh, as well as al-Fateh communiqués, photos, and statements of its leader, Yasir Arafat. The reason no doubt was because Cleaver became close with al-Fateh officials in Algeria and because al-Fateh, the best funded of the Palestinian groups, had a good public relations apparatus both in the Middle East and in the United States. It published numerous statements and periodicals in English that were available in the United States. This was an interesting alliance given that al-Fateh was basically a conservative nationalist movement that eschewed the kind of socioeconomic revolutionary talk emanating from the BPP.

HUEY NEWTON'S EVENTUAL ABOUT-FACE

Attacks on the Panthers' stance on the Middle East eventually prompted Huey Newton to speak out publicly about their embrace of the Palestinian cause and attacks against Israel. Shortly after his release from two years in jail, he held a press conference on August 26, 1970, at which he spoke at length about the BPP's stance on the Arab-Israeli conflict and on anti-Semitism. While solidly supportive of the Palestinians, Newton's statement nonetheless revealed his own shifting view of the conflict. Instead of simply attacking Israel in the strident revolutionary prose familiar to readers of the *Black Panther*, Newton spoke of Arab-Jewish coexistence and was careful to distinguish between the Israeli government and the Jewish citizens of Israel. Newton was beginning to change his overall vision of what the BPP needed to be doing in America, and this extended to his views on the Middle East. It is instructive to quote from his statement at length.

Newton spoke of Jewish-Arab "harmony," and pointed out the difference between criticizing Jews and criticizing the Israeli government, even noting that some Israelis were against Zionism:

We have respect for all people, and we have respect for the right of any people to exist. So we want the Palestinian people and the Jewish people to live in harmony together. We support the Palestinians' just struggle for liberation one hundred percent. . . . As far as the Israeli people are concerned we are not against the Jewish people. We are against that government that will persecute the Palestinian people. . . . Our view is that the people led by the Palestinian people should be led into a struggle, a revolutionary struggle in order to transform the Middle East into truly a people's republic.[31]

He also broke with the previous BPP consensus by conceding that while the Zionist case for a separate, ethnoreligious state exclusively for Jews might not be acceptable "politically" or "strategically," he perhaps could accept it "morally":

Israel was created by Western imperialism and maintained by Western fire power. The Jewish people have a right to exist as long as they solely exist to down the reactionary expansionist Israeli Government. Our situation is similar in so many ways; we say, that morally perhaps, the Jewish people can make a case for separatism and a Zionist state based upon their religion for self-defense. We say, morally, perhaps we could accept this, but politically and strategically we know that it is incorrect.[32]

Gone was the talk of smashing the "Zionist fascist state of Israel."

A few months later, the Black Panther Party began to change significantly, which pushed Newton further down the road of rethinking the BPP's stance on the Middle East. First, the party began disintegrating owing to factionalism and misinformation calculated to inflame this factionalism that was fed to party activists by the secret COINTELPRO program run by the FBI.[33] The most high-profile split within the party occurred in early 1971 between Cleaver, still in Algeria with the BPP international section, and Newton in the United States. One of these contentious issues pertained to whether the BPP should continue to work for revolution and armed confrontation with the powers of the state or move toward becoming a more aboveground, community service–oriented group. Cleaver still favored the former, Newton the latter. Each man ended up expelling the other from the BPP shortly thereafter, but the Newton faction ended up retaining control over the bulk of the party's operations and publications in Oakland, including the *Black Panther*. The Cleaver faction, based in New York while Cleaver himself remained in Algeria, debuted a new publication titled *Right On!* in April of 1971.

Thirty-one-year-old Newton ally Elaine Brown became BPP chair three years later in 1974 after Newton fled into exile in Cuba. She recalled that after the Cleaver-Newton split rent the party, Newton and the main party apparatus adopted a "new stance." The party stopped being what she called a "revolutionary cult" working for systemic revolutionary change through armed struggle and decided to work instead on what the party called "survival programs" to serve black communities. The Black Panthers even ran candidates in local elections: in 1972 Bobby Seale ran for mayor of Oakland, California, and Brown ran for city council.[34]

The Newton faction's changing strategies also corresponded to a different theoretical and practical approach to the Arab-Israeli conflict. The fact that the Palestinian armed resistance movement had been severely mauled by the Jordanian army in September of 1970 and again in July of 1971, and was less and less on the radar screens of the Black Power movement by 1974, also contributed to this new approach. BPP activist Austin Allen was witness to some of Newton's changing thoughts about the matter.

Allen became active with the party at the time of the Newton-Cleaver split and eventually grew close to Newton and his faction. According to Allen, Newton's attitudes toward the Arab-Israeli conflict began changing because he believed that the Arab world, which had plenty of power, was not really serious about defeating Israel on behalf of the Palestinians. Newton therefore thought that the only possibility was a two-state solution: Israel and a Palestinian State. Newton said, in Allen's words, "There had to be two states, and the Arabs ain't coming clean." As Allen noted in an interview, Newton argued that "the Palestinians served the other purpose within the structure of the Arab world. . . . You're saying you want to get something you're not going to get because you don't want to get it in the first place. So let's really talk reality and it's going to have to be two separate nations which was quite different. Most people expected us as an organization to say it's got to be the Palestinian state period."[35]

Newton's evolving attitude toward Israel and the Palestinians was already evident at his August 26, 1970, press conference. It became, in fact, one of several issues that contributed to the nasty split between Newton and Cleaver that broke out in the winter of 1971. In a famous February 26, 1971, overseas telephone call between the two men that Cleaver taped, the latter questioned Newton about his new thinking about the coexistence of a Palestinian state along with Israel.[36]

In the wake of both the BPP split and the October 1973 Arab-Israeli war, Newton's new thinking led him to issue a dramatically different, formal BPP policy statement on the Arab-Israeli conflict in May of 1974. David Horowitz, a radical journalist who worked with the Panthers in the early to mid-1970s, claims that it was he who actually wrote this new policy statement.[37] After reading a piece in the *Black Panther* that ran after the 1973 Arab-Israeli war and lambasted Israel as a "racist" state, Horowitz questioned Newton about the BPP's position. After hearing him out, Horowitz said Newton asked him to draft a new policy statement for the Panthers.[38] Newton then showed a draft of a new BPP policy to David Du Bois, the new editor of the *Black Panther*. The son of the author and activist Shirley Graham Du Bois and the stepson of the famous activist W. E. B. Du Bois, David Graham Du Bois was familiar with the Arab-Israeli conflict from his experience living in Egypt in the 1960s, working as an announcer for Egyptian radio, and writing for the English-language newspaper the *Egyptian Gazette*.[39]

Du Bois was very enthusiastic about the new policy document Newton showed to him. "This is, in my opinion, a brilliant position paper on the Middle East Conflict," he wrote to Newton on May 2, 1974. "It's [*sic*] basic humanism devastates arguments against its proposals from both sides. The only forces it exposes for attack are U.S. imperialism, Zionism and Arab reaction." He also made a few suggestions.[40] It is unclear whether the draft that Du Bois read was the one that Horowitz had been asked to write, or was a document drawn up by Newton, or was something else altogether. In any event the final wording was Newton's decision, given his position as "chief theoretician" of the party.

The BPP's new position paper on the Middle East was published in the May 25, 1974, issue of the *Black Panther* and marked a major shift away from a stridently pro-Palestinian stance toward one that emphasized justice and human rights for all peoples in the Middle East. An accompanying editorial noted the purpose of the new policy: "It is to contribute to ending the suffering and dying in the Middle East that the Black Panther Party has drawn up and distributed its Position Paper on the Middle East Conflict. The Black Panther Party's overriding concern is securing the human rights of all the people in the Middle East, Jew and Arab alike; and first, the right to life."[41] No longer was the BPP's mission to support the Palestinians as fellow revolutionaries of color fighting American-backed imperialism in the form of the State of Israel. The new BPP policy was titled "The Issue Is Not Territory, but Human Rights" and stated: "We can no longer accept an unprincipled posture, in the interest of misguided subjective notions. We can no longer allow our posture to be characterized as simply 'pro-Arab,' for we support the right of all human beings to freedom and human dignity."[42] The approach emphasized human rights and human understanding for all parties in the conflict. Its vision for the Middle East was bold:

We believe that the real issues are internal to each territory: the fact of the existence of the State of Israel will prove no real hardship to the Arab peoples, if the Jews and their 400,000 Arab comrades living in Israel will throw off their mutual yoke of oppression, and build a people's government serving the human interests of all. In like fashion, the peoples of the Arab nations need only turn their attention and energies away from the so-called Holy War over what is now called Israel to their own oil-rich countries, and throw off the yoke of their oppressive regimes, claiming for themselves, the wealth beneath their own national soils.

Even though the new Panther policy statement recognized that "the issue is not territory," it conceded that national statehood was a necessary "transitional stage of development" for Jews and Palestinians in the Middle East. The policy therefore upheld the legitimacy of Israel and called for creation of a truncated Palestinian political state—something that the PLO itself had not yet officially accepted. The statement claimed that ultimate justice and security would come for the Jews and Arabs of the Middle East when a global revolution overthrew capitalism and imperialism and when both peoples recognized the humanity and claims of the other side.

However broadminded and balanced this sentiment may have appeared, the document actually seemed to favor the Israelis over the Palestinians in terms of humanistic concessions. It was careful to ask Israelis merely to recognize the Palestinians' claim to "independent national institutions"—the words *independent state* were not mentioned in this passage—while asking Palestinians and the Arab states to recognize Israel both as a state and as the expression of global Jewish sovereignty. Stemming from this, the new policy called on Arabs and Jews worldwide to change their thinking. It urged Jews to show compassion for Arab and Palestinian suffering, and called upon progressive Jews in the United States in particular to give up their "uncritical support to the Israeli government in power" and apply toward Israel the same standards and expectations that they apply toward other countries.

What impact did this dramatic volte-face have on Panthers and their supporters? Elaine Brown recalled that Newton's new policy toward Israel and the Palestinians "sent everything into a state of confusion" and "befuddled his troops." It also was one of several factors that drove some Newton loyalists to begin to question the reformist direction in which Newton was taking the party. Brown claimed that Newton believed that the reason the BPP needed to change its policy was because what occurred in the 1948 Arab-Israeli war "was a *fait accompli*. The resultant State of Israel had to be reckoned with, therefore. Life, like revolution, he said, looked forward, not backward."[43]

Even more astonishing, Brown claimed that "Huey found a certain private delight in taking that position." According to her, several days before Newton announced the party's new position on the Middle East, he confided in her that his father, Walter, was half-Jewish. He claimed that Walter's own father was a Jew named Simon. Huey somehow connected his father's subsequent self-hatred and bitterness toward whites, as well as the bitterness that lay deep in the hearts of many American blacks, with the bitterness felt by Arabs and Jews in the Middle East. In neither case did Newton believe that focusing on the past was worthwhile. Rather, people needed to focus on the future. "There was, therefore," she wrote, "something poetically proper, healing, even, he thought, for the black son of the bastard son of a Jew to take that position."[44]

Newton visited the Middle East six years later, in 1980. According to his lawyer, Fred J. Hiestand, the PLO invited Newton to visit the Israeli-occupied West Bank. Newton agreed but insisted on visiting Israel and Lebanon as well. The PLO paid for Newton and six other people, including Hiestand and two instructors from the Intercommunal Youth Institute that the BPP had established in 1971.[45] Newton traveled to Beirut on April 21, 1980, where he visited several social service centers run by the PLO: a Palestine Red Crescent hospital, a SAMED (Palestine Martyrs Works Society) workshop, and a school. While in the city, he met Yasir Arafat. Newton also traveled to south Lebanon, where he visited Palestinian refugees at the al-Rashidiyya refugee camp and observed fragments, bearing American markings, of bombs dropped by Israeli jets. The Israeli government dashed Newton's plans to visit Israel, however, by refusing his entrance into the country.[46]

The *Black Panther* detailed Newton's visit and published a cover photo of him shaking hands with Arafat. An article stated, "Huey believes that the only viable solution will be the creation of a separate entity for the Palestinians." Voicing support for a "separate entity" was something significantly different from supporting a "separate state," something formally called for by the PLO in March of 1977.[47] That linguistic technicality indicated just how far the Black Panther Party had come since its days of total support for the Palestinians' guerrilla struggle against the Israeli "pigs" for the purpose of destroying the "fascist Zionist state of Israel."

The Panthers were the force within the Black Power movement that did the most in the final years of the 1960s and first years of the 1970s to place the Palestinian cause squarely on the political map in the United States through constant reiteration of their supportive position on the Palestinian struggle. The BPP picked up on the internationalism, Third World identity, and pro-Palestinian sentiments first expressed by Malcom X in the late 1950s and early 1960s and first articulated in a dramatic and public fashion by SNCC in 1967, and institutionalized them. Especially given Eldridge Cleaver's exile in Algeria and frequent contact with Palestinians from al-Fateh there, solidarity with the Palestinians and what they called their revolution became part of the Panthers' own activism during the period 1967–73. This included its theoretical understandings of American-backed imperialism, its self-proclaimed identity as a revolutionary organization, and its daily organizational efforts. Solidarity with the Palestinians also became more than just part of the BPP's ideology. It became part of the group's communications and publicity/propaganda efforts, as well as its attempts to create a visual revolutionary image and culture for the blacks it was mobilizing and organizing on the street corners of urban America.

As was the case for SNCC, the fact that the Panthers viewed the American government as the enemy both of their movement and of the Palestinians helped solidify their ties with the Palestinians perhaps more than any other revolutionaries outside of the Vietnamese. BPP member Mumia Abu-Jamal recalled decades later: "To the average Panther, even though he worked daily in the ghetto communities of North America, his thoughts were usually on something larger than himself. It meant being part of a worldwide movement against US imperialism, white supremacy, colonialism, and corrupting capitalism. We felt as if we were part of the peasant armies of Vietnam, the degraded Black miners of South Africa, the Fedayeen in Palestine."[48]

By the time the BPP adopted Newton's new, less-radical position on the Arab-Israeli conflict in 1974, both it and the wider revolutionary Black Power movement were in decline. Gone were the visions of guns and revolution. Newton by that time envisioned a party that would work within the system for incremental change. The new BPP stance toward the Arab-Israeli conflict clearly reflected this new understanding of the party's new vision of itself, black identity, and political activism and was reflected in its stance vis-à-vis the Arab-Israeli conflict. In a way this symbolized something deeper: black support for the Palestinians was outlasting the heyday of Black Power and becoming more mainstream.

CHAPTER 7

MIDDLE EAST SYMBIOSIS
Israelis, Arabs, and African Americans

ISRAELI PRIME MINISTER GOLDA MEIR was not amused. It was April 13, 1971, and she was having a meeting at her office in West Jerusalem with five young Jewish activists from a new protest group calling itself the Black Panthers Organization. The group was made up of Mizrahi/ Sephardic Jews, Jews whose origins were from the Middle East and North Africa and who tended to occupy the lower socioeconomic strata within Israeli society as compared to Ashkenazic Jews (Jews of Central and Eastern European background). Meir kept asking the men—Ya'akov Elbaz, Rami Marciano, Sa'adiya Marciano, David Levi, and Re'uven Abergil—how and why they chose the particular name "Black Panthers" for their group. They liked its shock value, Sa'adiya Marciano replied.

Clearly not satisfied, the prime minister followed up with, "Did you not hear of this name somewhere else?" Marciano admitted to her that they knew of the American Black Panthers. "We know they support Fateh and are against Jews," he said. Then why, the prime minster wanted to know, did they take this particular name? "Because it gives us shock value [Hebrew: *mahats*]," Marciano responded with the bravado of Huey Newton and Eldridge Cleaver. He thought that the name would help the organization make "noise" in Israel.

Abergil picked up where his comrade left off: "We may share 40 percent of the ideology of the Black Panthers in the United States, who were also disenfranchised and screwed-up. The fact is that they are violent—we are not." Meir noted acidly, "They are also anti-Semitic."[1] Black Power had arrived in Israel, and as in America, the ruling elite were not happy.

There was a significant cross-cultural mixing of ideas, information, and people around the world during what some have called the "Global 1960s." One of the fascinating aspects of black Americans' engagement with the faraway Arab-Israeli conflict is how those experiences impacted the people actually living in the midst of that conflict. African American stances on Israel and Palestine, in fact, played a symbiotic role; they not only mirrored and amplified their own attitudes toward race and identity but also affected Middle Easterners' views both of American blacks and themselves. The best example of this was the emergence of the Israeli Black Panthers, who coalesced as an Israeli version of the BPP in early 1971.

THE ISRAELI BLACK PANTHERS

The Zionist movement that succeeded in creating the Jewish state of Israel developed as a movement of Ashkenazic Jews in Europe, who created the outlines of a state, and later ruled that state, along European political and sociocultural lines. While Mizrahi/Sephardic Jews from Arab and Islamic countries had always been present in small numbers in pre-1948 Palestine, it was the waves of Jewish immigration from countries like Iraq, Yemen, Morocco, Egypt, and Libya during and after the establishment of Israel in 1948 that quickly changed the previously Ashkenazic-dominated demography of the new Jewish state. Coming from Middle Eastern and North African cultural backgrounds, these Jews often found it hard to adjust to a new secular, European-oriented Ashkenazic lifestyle and political system. A number of them came from poorer, less-educated, and more traditionally religious backgrounds than their Ashkenazic compatriots. The result was that when they were eventually integrated into Israeli life, they were disproportionately well represented in the lower socioeconomic strata and outside the political structure. For their part, many Ashkenazic Israelis looked down on the new Mizrahi/Sephardic immigrants as primitive and apt to cause the "Levantinization"—the Middle

Easternization—of the European nature of the country via their high birth rate and Arab-like cultural attributes.

The founders of the Black Panthers in Israel tapped into the discontent felt by the Mizrahi/Sephardic population and decided to use confrontational tactics, just as American blacks were doing, to confront a power structure that they believed excluded them. Most of the group's founders were Moroccan immigrants: Shalom "Charlie" Biton, Robert "Re'uven" Abergil, and Sa'adiya Marciano. Another, Kokhavi Shemesh, was born in Iraq. The fountainhead of the new movement was the Musrara District of West Jerusalem, also called the Morasha District in Hebrew. Just north of the Old City, it was formerly a middle-class Palestinian neighborhood that, after the 1948 war and the depopulation of its Arab inhabitants, abutted the cease-fire line with Jordanian-controlled East Jerusalem from 1948 until 1967. During this time, several hundred Mizrahi/Sephardic families (mostly Moroccan, with some Iraqis) were settled there in homes abandoned by Palestinian refugees.

The Israeli Black Panthers clearly were aware that they were borrowing a name—as well as an image, a vocabulary, and an attitude—from the American Black Panther Party. As early as January of 1971, they had used the name in press interviews when referring to their new movement: "We will be the Black Panthers of the State of Israel."[2] In fact, the young activists seemed to revel in the ominous connections that the name *Black Panthers* seemed to evoke among Ashkenazic Israelis. Kokhavi Shemesh had this to say about the name: "We hunted around for a name which would attract attention, which would help to get our problem into the headlines. Since a black group with the same name had arisen in the United States, and since Israel's propaganda had claimed that its members were the enemies of Israel and since most of Israel's foreign capital comes from the United States we chose the name 'Black Panthers' in order to give a jolt to Jews both here and abroad."[3] Shemesh also claimed that the idea first came to them after a statement made by a member of the Jerusalem municipality: "We have no connection with them [Black Panther Party in America]. But the name caused a stir, and that is what we wanted. It came about purely by chance, when Mrs. Miyuhas, a member of the Jerusalem Municipality, made a statement on youth organizations in Jerusalem in which she compared the youth to the Black Panthers in the United States. We jumped at the idea, and adopted the nickname applied to us by Mrs. Miyuhas."[4]

There are other stories about how they came by the name *Black Panthers*. Some have to do with cross-fertilization from the Israeli anti-Zionist group known as Matzpen. According to one story, a Matzpen activist named Shimshon once spent a night in jail in the Moscobiya police complex in West Jerusalem with Sa'adiya Marciano and Charlie Biton, before the Israeli Black Panthers had been formed. Supposedly, the man regaled his two fellow prisoners with tales of the Black Panthers in America, after which they decided to use that same name when they later formed their organization.[5] Another alleged Matzpen connection to the name *Black Panthers* stems from early 1971, when the Israeli police, through an informant, had begun monitoring the nucleus of activists that came to be called the Black Panthers. According to the informant, a Matzpen activist inspired a group of the soon-to-be Black Panthers with stories he told about the exploits of the Black Panther Party in the United States.[6]

For all the eventual publicity surrounding the Black Panthers in Israel taking the name and the crouched panther symbol from the American Black Panther Party, did they actually have any contact with Americans connected with the BPP? An oft-circulated story claims that black American activist Angela Davis met with the group while visiting Israel in 1971, after which they decided to use the name *Black Panthers*. Davis, however, did not visit Israel in 1971, so the story is not true. Later that year, in October of 1971, a delegation of Israeli Black Panthers, including Charlie Biton, did in fact meet with some of their American namesakes at a Marxist conference in Florence, Italy.

One American who definitely did have contact with the Panthers in Israel, and who was quite important in their development, was not African American but rather a Jewish veteran of civil rights struggles named Naomi Kies. Kies received a PhD from the Massachusetts Institute of Technology and, after first visiting Israel in 1965 to conduct research, immigrated permanently in 1967. Thereafter she taught sociology at The Hebrew University of Jerusalem. Kies became a close adviser to the Israeli Black Panthers starting in March of 1971—once they learned to trust her as an Ashkenazic Jew—as a result of her research on social conditions in Jerusalem. She was one of several people who worked with them as they cultivated the media and sought to broadcast their message, and she even allowed them to use her home as their base of operations when their headquarters burned down. Kies also helped arrange a tour of the United States that the Panthers announced in July of 1971, although the trip never materialized.[7]

The Black Panthers immediately raised the hackles of the Israeli political establishment, dominated as it was by Ashkenazic Jews like Prime Minister Meir. Meir's government refused their application for a permit for their demonstration and took several of them into preventative custody in an attempt to stop it from happening. On May 19, 1971, when discussing a violent demonstration that had been staged by the Black Panthers in Jerusalem a day earlier, a politician told Meir at a press conference that he had met some of the Panthers and that they were "nice guys." Meir famously retorted, "They are not nice guys" if they threw Molotov cocktails at the police.[8]

The Israeli press regularly reported on the New Left and Black Power movements, as well as the American Jewish reaction to both movements. In June of 1971 the newspaper *Yediot Aharonot* described the Black Panther Party in the United States as "an extreme organization, with an anti-Semitic character, that has strong ties with Arab terror organizations and preaches armed revolution in the U.S. to undermine the current regime which it deems rotten."[9] The fact that the Israeli Panthers took the name of a militant black American group widely known and reviled in Israel for its anti-Israeli stances only added to their dangerous mystique. So did their deliberate appropriation of Malcolm X's famous phrase "by any means necessary."[10]

The direct connection between the Black Panther Party and the Black Panthers in Israel offers an instructive example of the impact of the transnationalism of the "Global 1960s." By borrowing directly the name of their American namesakes, as well as the tactics and discourse both of the Black Power movement and the New Left in the United States, which they learned in part from American immigrants, the Israeli Panthers show the degree to which a symbiotic relationship existed between the new attitudes of American and Israeli young people when it came to matters both of ethnicity and of the Arab-Israeli conflict. American Jews long had been deeply connected with their Israeli counterparts. Yet here was a case where Israeli Jews in turn were identifying with American *blacks*, not American Jews.[11] They shared the same idiom of dispossession: "The Blacks are being screwed," "white power," "masters and slaves," "police state," "brothers," "equality of rights," and others.[12]

Beyond their rough-and-tumble style and rhetoric, and their drawing public attention to distinctive Mizrahi/Sephardic grievances in defiance of the conventional wisdom that Israeli Jews constituted one people, the Panthers also were perceived as radical because they proposed allying themselves with Palestinians in creating a revolutionary new society. In April of 1972 Shemesh and some other Panthers spoke at a gathering near Bet She'an, in northern Israel. They articulated the Panthers' vision of a new society built in cooperation with the Palestinians: "We intend to initiate in this country a social revolution, build a new society of which there is still no example anywhere in the world: leftist, but not like the USSR or China; something like the kibbutz, but not exactly. We shall establish a 100 percent egalitarian society. We must reach a situation in which we shall fight together with the 'fucking' Arabs against the establishment. We are the only one who can constitute a bridge of peace with the Arabs in context of a struggle against the establishment." Clearly the American Black Panthers were not the only ones who felt akin to the Palestinians' concerns; "black" Israelis did, too.[13]

The Panthers went a step further than their American counterparts in identifying with the Palestinians. Whereas Black Power advocates in America had supported the Palestinians as kindred people of color fighting against imperialism, the Panthers in Israel actually believed that Mizrahi/Sephardic Jews and Palestinians were culturally part of the same people. All that separated them was religion; other than that, the Panthers argued, they and Palestinians both shared a common Middle Eastern/North African cultural heritage. And as indigenous Middle Eastern peoples, both Jews from Arab and Islamic countries and Palestinians experienced the same discrimination from an Israeli establishment dominated by Ashkenazic Jews and Ashkenazic culture and values. Shemesh once wrote: "Ever since I came to consciousness people have tried to convince me that there is a big difference between me and the Arabs, that is, they have tried to instil [sic] into me that Jews are better than Arabs and that we, the Jews, are a chosen people. . . . Reality shows, at least to me, that there is no difference between the Arabs and me. The only difference is in the religious origins."[14] From their name to their tactics, the experience of the Israeli Black Panthers reveals a deep connection with and influence of the Black Panther Party in the United States and the wider Black Power movement's attempt to change ethnic relations in America. Like the Newton faction of the Black Panther Party, elements of the Israeli Black Panthers eventually moved in the direction of conventional politics in the 1970s, even running as candidates for election to the Knesset. Hearing about the militant stances of the American

Panthers and even being guided by Americans like Naomi Kies, the Israeli Black Panthers offer a tangible example of how the experience in the United States affected Israeli politics and society in a profound way during the Global 1960s.

ARAB SUPPORT FOR BLACK LIBERATION

On May 16, 1967, amid the tension in the Middle East that ultimately led to the June war, a pro-Arab rally was held in Sproul Plaza, the center of student political life on the campus of the University of California at Berkeley. A leaflet entitled "Zionism, Western Imperialism, and the Liberation of Palestine" was distributed that in all likelihood was the work of Arab students at Berkeley. Clearly trying to connect the Arab-Israeli conflict with the black freedom struggle, it stated that "the Zionist settler-state was founded on an exclusivist racial basis" and that this racial discrimination continued to be practiced on the Palestinian citizens who remained in Israel after 1948. Although Zionism constituted a type of apartheid, the broadsheet claimed, it did not generate the same degree of negative criticism in the West as did the white minority states in Rhodesia and South Africa. Furthermore, it noted, Israel acted as a tool for imperialism in the Middle East.[15] Two weeks later, and across the country, blacks and Arabs made common cause when activists from SNCC took part in a pro-Arab demonstration staged on May 31 in front of the White House by the Organization of Arab Students (OAS).[16]

Three months later the OAS came out strongly in support of SNCC after the infamous newsletter controversy. The OAS held its sixteenth annual convention at the Massachusetts Institute of Technology in Cambridge, Massachusetts, from August 28 to September 2, 1967, just a few short weeks after the newsletter brouhaha broke out. Among the resolutions adopted at the convention was one condemning the "character assassination" of SNCC for its criticism of Israel. It also included the "black people in the American ghettoes," along with the Palestinians as a kindred people in need of liberation. OAS vice president Ali M. Baghdadi was quoted as saying: "As a civil rights organization they [SNCC] are being true to their principles when they condemn those who regard territorial integrity and freedom from terrorism as rights to be enjoyed by Western nationals, but not by African or Asian nations."[17] Like Israelis of color, Arabs were being influenced by American Black

Power and were reciprocating black militants' feelings of commonality and solidarity with them.

Black Power figures began capitalizing on this by meeting with Arab students and delivering orations at OAS gatherings. In August of 1968 Stokely Carmichael gave a speech titled "The Black American and Palestinian Revolutions" at the OAS convention in Ann Arbor, Michigan. He told the assembled students that black Americans would stand with the Arabs, both those in the United States and those in the Middle East: "We will work more closely with the Arab students wherever we can. Our eyes are now open. . . . We want to make it clear that we see the Arab world, not only as brothers, but also as our comrades-in-arms. . . . They [the American government] cannot stop us from going to the United Arab Republic [Egypt]," Carmichael added. "They cannot stop us from going to Syria. As long as you invite us we will come."[18]

Palestinian information professionals in the United States also were keenly aware of the benefits of cultivating ties with the blacks. The Arab Information Office's Randa Khalidi al-Fattal was one of them. Looking back decades later, al-Fattal noted: "I started one of the very first efforts to get to know black Americans. When [they] finally politicized their cause they looked around for allies, and I was one of the Arabs in America who felt that they may very well fall under Israeli influence. . . . It was then our duty to draw their attention—of the Black Panthers and other groups—to the fact that we had a very legitimate cause."[19]

So much for Palestinians and other Arabs in the United States. What about Palestinians in the Middle East itself? The PLO occasionally tried to cultivate black support through the media, for example when its Palestine Research Center in Beirut produced a pamphlet in 1969 written by the American academic Richard Stevens that linked Zionism and South African apartheid. Stevens plainly stated the connection between American blacks and the Middle East: "And in the broader sense, the inter-relationship of Zionism, apartheid and Israel possess problems of fundamental morality which will be of greater concern to the Black American community not only as it ponders its relationship to the moral and political aspects of the Israeli-Palestinian Arab relations, but as it asserts its concern for the well-being of the disenfranchised Black minority of South Africa."[20]

PLO chair Yasir Arafat personally extended solidarity messages to black Americans on occasion. So did other Palestinian militants. In 1970 Welsh journalist Colin Edwards asked famed Palestinian airplane hijacker from the Popular Front for the Liberation of Palestine (PFLP), Leila Khaled, about the black freedom struggle in America. "If you were now talking to the black revolutionaries in America, the Black Panther Party," Welsh asked her, "what would you say to them?" Khaled responded: "I'm with those people because they are defending their rights as human beings and the worst thing you or anyone can face is when you are not treated like a human being. And I'm with them in their revolution against what is called a democratic government in the US. It's not at all a democratic government. So those people, I *hope* they can have their rights and they can't have their rights except by force. That is the motto of this century because force is the only way they can be heard."[21]

Black Power supporter Yuri Kochiyama summed up the reciprocal feelings of solidarity and mutual struggle between African Americans and Palestinians when she recalled one small example of how Americans of color left a symbolic impact on Palestinian guerrillas and activists in the 1960s. She was quite familiar with the Black Power movement, even though she herself was not black. Born to Japanese immigrants in California, Kochiyama and her family were interned in a prison camp during the Second World War, as were other Japanese Americans. She married and moved with her husband to Harlem in 1960, where Kochiyama became friends with Malcolm X—she held him in her arms as he died—and went on to be an activist in the black freedom movement and a number of other causes. Kochiyama once recalled that some of the Palestinian activists who came to the United States in the late 1960s related to her that Palestinian guerrillas sometimes used code names like Malcolm X, Stokely Carmichael, and Black Panther.[22] Black Power had indeed spread to the Middle East.

SOLIDARITY TRIPS

On March 4, 1974, one of the most famous American athletes in the world gave a press conference in Beirut, Lebanon, at which he said, "America is the headquarters of Zionism and imperialism."[23] The man later visited two Palestinian refugee camps in southern Lebanon, much as his friend and mentor Malcolm X had done ten years earlier when he was in Gaza. Palestinian fighters in the camps fired their guns in the air in welcome, and the visiting American told the crowds, "In my name, and in the name of all Muslims in America, I declare support for the Palestinian struggle to liberate their homeland and oust the Zionist invaders."[24] The man? The world-famous heavyweight boxer, Muhammad Ali. How is it that the man *Sports Illustrated* magazine declared the "Sportsman of the Century" in 1999 found time amid his busy schedule to visit Palestinian refugees and offer his support for their cause?

Muhammad Ali has been described as the most famous Muslim on Earth in the 1960s, a highly visible black American well known to the peoples of the Third World.[25] Yet his action in support of the Palestinians is largely forgotten today. The famously loud and opinionated young boxer became the Olympic heavyweight boxing champion in 1960 and the world heavyweight professional champion four years later. He hobnobbed with celebrities from the Beatles on down, but significantly, the young athlete also became close friends with Malcolm X. What garnered Cassius Clay significant, often negative, attention was the fact that the day after he earned the world heavyweight title in February of 1964, he announced his conversion into the Nation of Islam and his new name: Muhammad Ali. He traveled to Egypt several months later, in June of 1964, as part of a tour of Africa, met President Gamal Abdel Nasser, and prayed at the medieval Husayn Mosque in Cairo.

Ali's conversion and name change were treated with derision by a confused white public. He became even more controversial three years later when he refused to be inducted into the army in April of 1967. Ali stated that his religious beliefs prohibited him from doing so. After his conviction of draft evasion and his expulsion from the world of professional boxing, Ali was out of the ring until 1971. Soon thereafter, he made the Islamic pilgrimage (hajj) to Mecca in Saudi Arabia in January of 1972.

Two years later, Ali again traveled to the Middle East. After arriving in Lebanon on March 2, 1974, he met with Prime Minister Taqi al-Din al-Sulh and other notables, visited the al-Maqasid Hospital, and held a press conference. Yet he departed from such customary events on March 5 by taking some unusual steps. He began the day with an early morning exercise run in Beirut in the company of several US Marine Corps embassy guards. Ali then traveled to southern Lebanon, where he toured the al-Ayn al-Hilwa and Mi'a wa Mi'a refugee camps while escorted by uniformed Palestine Liberation Army soldiers sporting maroon berets. Fighters fired bursts of automatic weapons in celebratory

welcome, after which he spent more than an hour visiting the camps and signing autographs. While there, Ali hailed the Palestinians' "great fighting spirit."[26]

Lesser-known black Americans who sympathized with the Palestinian
cause visited the Middle East in the early 1970s, as well. One was the activist
Paul B. Boutelle.[27] Boutelle was contacted by Randa Khalidi al-Fattal of the
Arab Information Center in New York and asked if he would be interested in
traveling to the Arab Middle East as part of a delegation of black American
activists. Three years earlier she had escorted Stokely Carmichael during his
September 1967 trip to Syria. Boutelle and about ten other men and women
ended up traveling to Lebanon, Syria, and Jordan in August of 1970.[28] With
al-Fattal as a guide, the Americans visited Palestinians in their homes, refugee
camps, and guerrilla training camps.[29]

In Amman, Jordan, the group achieved a diplomatic coup of sorts by attending the meeting of the Palestine National Council, the PLO's highest decision-
making body, which took place August 27–29, 1970. While at the meeting the
group even met with Arafat; a picture of Boutelle and the others shaking hands
with a smiling Arafat, wearing his trademark kefiyya headdress and dark sun-
glasses, graced the cover of *al-Fateh*, the official newspaper of Arafat's al-Fateh
organization. That same issue of the paper ran a quotation from a member of
the group, who was described as a "representative of the movement for the liberation of blacks." The person expressed support for the Palestinians' struggle,
stating, "It is better to die as men than die as slaves. . . . Our revolution is exactly like the Palestinian revolution, and it is a drop of blood, a drop of sweat,
and a drop of ink that will accept nothing except the liberation of every one."[30]

A fascinating follow-up to the visit involving an African American friend
of Boutelle's occurred just a few days after the group returned to the United
States. On September 7, 1970, the PFLP hijacked two airliners and diverted
them and their passengers to Dawson Field, a deserted Second World War–era
airfield in the Jordanian desert that PFLP militants renamed Revolution Field.
Two days later, a PFLP sympathizer diverted a third airliner to the field, as well.
Barbara Mensch, a young Jewish American from Scarsdale, New York, who had
turned sixteen a mere thirty days before the hijacking, was among the hostages
being held by the PFLP at the airfield. She had been returning to the United
States from Israel, where she had spent the summer living on a kibbutz. Her
father was Martin Mensch, a lawyer working in the New York City law firm of

Fleischer, Dornbusch, Mensch, and Mandelstam. Worried about his daughter, Mensch approached one of his associates at the firm, a young black attorney named Robert Van Lierop, for help inasmuch as he knew that Van Lierop was sympathetic to the Palestinians.

Mensch asked Van Lierop if he could use his contacts to arrange for a message to be delivered to his captive daughter in Jordan. Knowing that Boutelle had just returned from meeting with Palestinians in Jordan, Van Lierop contacted his friend and asked for assistance. The young lawyer soon was on the telephone with none other than Bassam Abu Sharif, the PFLP's spokesperson on the ground at Dawson Field. After asking Abu Sharif to deliver a message from the girl's father, Abu Sharif reportedly told Van Lierop that the PFLP was offering to release her instead as a gesture of solidarity with the black American fugitive, Angela Davis, and other blacks in the United States, and to challenge the American government to drop all charges against Davis. Martin Mensch was thrilled and agreed to travel to Jordan to pick up his daughter.

Accompanied by Van Lierop, Mensch was soon on a plane flying to Jordan to arrange for his daughter's release or offer himself as a hostage in her place. The two Americans finally arrived in Amman via Beirut on September 15, 1970, and quickly met with Abu Sharif and others from the PFLP at the Intercontinental Hotel in Amman. By that time the PFLP had moved the hostages and blown up the three empty aircraft because, they told the crestfallen Mensch, the Jordanian army was preparing to move against the Palestinians, and the PFLP wanted to move them to safer locations. Indeed, the following day, King Hussein of Jordan ordered his army on the offensive and attacked PFLP and other Palestinian armed forces in the country—putting an end to talk of Barbara Mensch's quick release.

The fierce fighting, known as Black September, lasted several days, trapping Mensch and Van Lierop in the Jordanian capital. Eventually, both men managed to survive the ordeal and arrive back in the United States safely on September 22. The PFLP released Barbara Mensch and the other remaining hostages five days later, after which they were flown home via Cyprus. Mensch's young daughter returned from her lengthy stay in the Middle East with a new and different understanding of the Palestinians and the Arab-Israeli conflict. She told the press after her release that the PFLP hijackers had taken good care of them, even providing kosher food to one Jewish hostage. More remarkably, considering her ordeal, she also said, "I must say I'm more sympathetic now that I've seen how they [Palestinians] live in the refugee camps."[31]

The travels to Arab countries undertaken in the 1960s by political figures like Malcolm X, Stokely Carmichael, and Eldridge Cleaver were being replicated in the early 1970s by famous black athletes and more ordinary activists alike, who visited Palestinian refugee camps in Lebanon, attended PLO congresses in Jordan, and even met with PLO leaders. Such encounters reinforced the cross-cultural connections present in the Global 1960s and reinforced a visceral sense of solidarity and shared destiny between blacks and Palestinians that was essential to the formulation of a new black identity. The shared identity of blacks and Arabs championed by Frantz Fanon in *The Wretched of the Earth* was deepening.

THE MYTH OF THE PLO TRAINING BLACK MILITANTS

On May 14, 1970, the FBI wrote a report for President Richard M. Nixon claiming that members of the Black Panther Party might be traveling to the Middle East to receive training at the hands of al-Fateh guerrillas. By August of 1970 the *New York Times* was reporting on BPP members in Jordan. Both the FBI and the CIA began looking into the reports. Could the worst nightmares of Nixon's paranoid administration turn out to be a reality? Were domestic blacks receiving training or other material support from Palestinian groups? The meteoric rise in global prominence of the Palestinian guerrilla movement after the 1967 war did lead to some American blacks visiting the Middle East. But were they returning with more than just a firsthand perspective on the Palestinians and the Arab-Israeli conflict? Was their pro-Palestinianism extending into actual military training at the hands of Palestinian guerrillas?

The story began in the spring of 1969, when reports began circulating in Washington that al-Fateh agents in the United States were trying to recruit Americans. In response to an inquiry Assistant Attorney General J. Walter Yeagley informed Representative J. Herbert Burke (R-FL) on May 6, 1969, that the FBI would investigate such reports and that the Department of Justice would deport any foreign students involved in illegal activities of this sort.[32] More stories and reports surfaced in 1969 about al-Fateh recruiting Western radicals to attend a type of course in Jordan that summer. The August 18, 1969, issue of *Newsweek* carried a story that 140 students, mostly European but allegedly including four Americans, attended a five-week al-Fateh course in Amman, Jordan, the month before.[33]

The press was not the only group to believe the story: the FBI wrote in a classified June 1970 report that it believed that "representatives of black extremist and domestic subversive groups" would "probably be invited to camps in the Middle East for guerrilla and political training."[34] The CIA also believed that al-Fateh had been inviting groups of Americans and Europeans "to participate in training and indoctrination courses in the summers of 1968 through 1970."[35] The FBI also claimed that at least one American *was* recruited successfully to work with al-Fateh against Israeli interests about that time.[36]

The FBI continued to look into reports of recruitment. The bureau claimed that al-Fateh agents attended an Arab conference in Montreal that was attended by some American students in Students for a Democratic Society (SDS), and discussed the formation of some kind of "international brigade" of Americans and Europeans who would go and fight in Jordan in the summer of 1970.[37] This latter report may have referred to a March 11, 1970, teach-in in Montreal that was part of the Mobilization for Palestine organized by the Québecois Palestine Solidarity Committee and various Arab student groups. Some Americans, including high-ranking BPP official Raymond "Masai" Hewitt and other Panthers, attended the gathering.[38]

The arrival of Eldridge Cleaver in Algeria in mid-1969 helped set in motion the rumor of a particular connection between Palestinians and the BPP. Cleaver's close ties to al-Fateh personnel in Algeria, particularly an official who went by the nom de guerre Abu Basim, gave rise to stories about Black Panthers undergoing training by al-Fateh. On January 30, 1970, CBS news correspondent Richard C. Hottelet reported from Algiers that Abu Basim had told him that he had spent two months in the United States and Canada in 1969 and had studied the BPP. He claimed he wrote a report to his al-Fateh superiors urging that they support the Panthers, including with training. Hottelet also reported that Cleaver was going to travel to Jordan in mid-February of 1970 and spend two to three weeks as a guest of Yasir Arafat. The FBI picked up on the story, although the bureau cautioned that an al-Fateh spokesman in Amman denied the allegation. The *New York Times* then reported in August 1970 that "well-placed Palestinians" said that "some Panthers" already had been trained by al-Fateh in Jordan during the previous year.[39]

Despite the rumors and reports, the above-cited FBI report of June 1970 discounted the possibility that al-Fateh *actually* had trained BPP members at that point. The report had this to say about the subject: "There is no information which would indicate that the Fedayeen have given military training to black militants in the past. On the contrary, the United States Department of State during February, 1970, advised that the American Embassy, Beirut, has no information that BPP members have visited Fedayeen camps to receive military training. According to the State Department, American newspapers have made inquiries on this point in the Middle East and uncovered no evidence of BPP training by the fedayeen [*sic*]." The same FBI document stated that although no evidence existed showing that Black Panthers had been trained by al-Fateh, the bureau *had* found indications that Panthers and Palestinians had at least discussed the issue. The report stated that the New Haven, Connecticut, chapter of the BPP discussed the possibility of sending two members to the Middle East to be trained by al-Fateh. The two would then return to the United States to set up training camps.[40] A former CIA official who worked in the MH/CHAOS Program and who was responsible for monitoring the BPP claimed years later that the al-Fateh did agree to train BPP members in 1970.[41]

That same June 1970 FBI report also stated that two male employees of the Arab Information Center, along with the wife of a Syrian diplomat—no doubt a reference to Randa Khalidi al-Fattal—posted to the United Nations in New York asked a BPP member on April 30, 1970, if he was interested in attending a "revolutionary school" in Egypt starting in late June of that year.[42] It was this report that the FBI passed on to President Nixon two weeks later in its May 14, 1970, report. That report went further, stating that the training would last two weeks and that the BPP member would then return to the United States and establish similar schools at home.[43]

That same FBI report added to the confusion by discounting some other suspicions about the Black Panthers. First, it noted that the FBI had not found any indication that the Panthers were involved with violent actions inside the United States on behalf of Palestinians: "While there is no question that black extremists in this country politically support the Arab position in the Middle East, there has been no evidence that they have carried out any violence to underscore their support for the Arabs." Second, the FBI possessed no "information which would indicate that the BPP is being financed by Middle Eastern sources." The document did, however, hold out the possibility that Palestinian guerrillas might someday invite Americans to train in the Middle East as activism against the war in Vietnam receded and as more "establishment" figures supported Israel. As noted above, it stated that "representatives of black extremist and domestic subversive groups will continue contacts with and support of Fedayeen and members of both groups will probably be invited to camps in the Middle East for guerrilla and political training."[44]

Reports surfaced again in August of 1970, two months after that FBI report was written, indicating that the Panthers might indeed be in the Middle East—in Jordan. The *New York Times* ran a story on August 27, based in part on an article that appeared in the Palestinian guerrilla newspaper *al-Fateh*, reporting that several Black Panthers arrived in Jordan on August 22 to attend a meeting of the Palestine National Council, the legislative body of the PLO. The group of Americans allegedly included a woman and came to Jordan overland from Syria. The *Times* story quoted one of the "Panthers" who arrived in Jordan: "There is a large similarity between the status of the Palestinian people and the status of blacks. The Palestinian people represent the vanguard of the peoples in the Middle East area in the conflict with imperialism and racism." The *Times* based its story on another Arab source as well: Baghdad Radio. Iraqi radio apparently reported something similar: that early in the week of August 23, some Panthers arrived in Jordan who were committed to waging a "people's war of liberation" in the United States, much like the Palestinians were doing in the Middle East.[45]

Based on what it had heard several months earlier about Panthers attending a "revolutionary school" in the Middle East, the FBI believed these new press reports. An FBI document written four years later mentions what appears to be the same story as reported by the *Times*: six "American black extremists" traveled to the Middle East with a representative of al-Fateh in August 1970 to receive firearms and explosives training. The group supposedly met Arafat and was urged to conduct propaganda upon returning to the United States.[46] Some people even said that Stokely Carmichael was among them.

So what really did happen in the summer of 1970? Did a delegation of Black Panthers travel to the Middle East for training? No. The facts are that several black Americans did arrive in Jordan in August of 1970. They did attend the Palestine National Council Meeting from August 27 to August 29, and they did meet with Arafat. They were not, however, a delegation of visiting Black Panthers but rather Paul Boutelle and the group of black Americans that was being shown around the region by the Arab Information Center's Randa Khalidi al-Fattal. The details of this trip match almost identically with the shadowy reports of "Black Panthers" in Amman at the same time. Adding to the confusion was the fact that the Jordanian press mistakenly reported that the Americans were a delegation from the Black Panthers. This mischaracterization appeared in the Jordanian daily newspaper *al-Difa'* on August 27, 1970, which reported that the head of this alleged BPP delegation spoke at the Palestine National Council meeting and said that they preferred to "fight to the death as men rather than die as slaves."

The Palestinian newspaper *al-Fateh*, which had been the basis of the *New York Times'* erroneous report, had, in fact, reported correctly what actually transpired: a delegation from the "movement for the liberation of blacks" in the United States—Boutelle and his colleagues—attended the Palestine National Council meeting that met in Amman, Jordan, August 27–29, 1970. The words about dying like men rather than slaves also appeared in the August 29 edition of *al-Fateh* and also included a photo of the delegation shaking hands with Arafat. In fact, *al-Fateh* made it abundantly clear that these American visitors were *not* Black Panthers when its August 30 issue carried the text of a telegram sent to the meeting by the actual Black Panther Party specifically stating that the BPP regretted that it was not able to send delegates to attend the meeting in person.[47]

Al-Fattal, who had arranged Boutelle's trip, commented years later on the American government's suspicions about her real intentions and how those suspicions followed her for a long time thereafter. In a 2013 interview she noted: "The Americans chose not to see it as an innocent invitation. They saw it as an effort by me to train them in warfare. . . . They made me persona non grata in America for quite some time, though I was the wife of a diplomat. . . . Eventually he became an ambassador and there was a big issue about that. But I'm very proud of it, because I really felt that I could at least draw their attention to our cause."[48]

The exaggerated "Panthers in Jordan" reports were false. The FBI, the *New York Times*, and others mistook Boutelle and his colleagues for Black Panthers. Regardless of the real circumstances, the confusion at the time was genuine, and by the end of 1970 the FBI had decided that it now had proof of some kind of Palestinian-BPP connection. The venerable director of the FBI, J. Edgar Hoover, issued a statement several months later on November 11, 1970, in which he indicated that the Black Panther Party was being supported by terrorist organizations. The FBI continued to monitor alleged Panther-Palestinian ties thereafter. In February of 1972 the bureau claimed that the faction of the BPP loyal to Eldridge Cleaver was trying to obtain weapons and ammunition for two or three al-Fateh operatives in the United States who were planning to attack an American airport somewhere in the eastern part of the country.[49]

The FBI's great rival, the CIA, correctly dismissed the possibility that Palestinian fighters were training Black Panthers. A massive May 1973 CIA report written by the agency's director of security, Howard J. Osborn—a report that famously became known as the CIA's "Family Jewels"—revealed that the agency had examined the FBI's evidence in 1970 and concluded that no such training ever took place. On December 10, 1970, the CIA's deputy director of intelligence read press reports of Hoover's earlier November 11 statement about terrorist support for the Black Panthers. In the words of the May 1973 CIA document, which was part of the famous "Family Jewels": "He said that we have examined the FBI's related files and our own data and find no indication of any relationship between the fedayeen [sic] and the Black Panthers. He provided the Director with a memorandum on this topic."[50]

The discourse of global black revolution against the powers-that-be found receptive audiences among those most directly affected by the Arab-Israeli conflict: Israeli Jews and Palestinian Arabs. Moreover, African Americans were in direct contact with Israelis and Palestinians both in the Middle East and at home. Black Power's connection to the conflict in the Middle East thus played itself out in more than just domestic African American politics, highlighting the fact that Black Power internationalism was deeply embedded in the Global 1960s and that transnational links stretched far and wide during that turbulent period.

CHAPTER 8

RED, WHITE, AND BLACK

Communists, Guerrillas,
and the Black Mainstream

ON JULY 28, 1970, the director of the Washington office
of the American Committee on Africa (ACOA), Charles Hightower, wrote
an angry letter to some of those who had signed Bayard Rustin's pro-Israeli
advertisement in the *New York Times* expressing his "profound opposition
and outrage" at what they had done.[1] Hightower's action triggered a strong
backlash from Rustin and led to a small avalanche of intra-ACOA meetings
and letters lasting several months. Hightower's bitter opposition to Rustin
and his establishment cohorts represented a challenge to the very sense of inside-the-system legitimacy that ACOA represented and brought up the same
issue of white paternalism that SNCC had confronted several years earlier.
Hightower found that he was not alone among his ACOA colleagues in his
outrage—a feeling that led to some profound soul searching within ACOA
about who really controlled the organization and what its purpose was. Who,
then, was Charles Hightower, and why did his letters of pro-Palestinian pique
set off such a chain reaction? And why was it that the question of Israel and
the Palestinians set off the brouhaha within a mainstream organization focused on Africa?

CONTROVERSY WITHIN THE
AMERICAN COMMITTEE ON AFRICA

The ACOA hired thirty-six-year-old Charles Hightower in 1970 to head its Washington, DC, office. The committee had been formed in 1953 to support anticolonial struggles in Africa. ACOA emerged from an earlier ad hoc group, Americans for South African Resistance, which had been formed by two ministers in New York to support the African National Congress call for a "Campaign of Defiance Against Unjust Laws" in South Africa. From its headquarters in New York, ACOA tried to reach out to a broad coalition of labor, religious, and civil rights groups, as well as politicians and other constituencies, to draw attention to the black anticolonial and antiracist struggles emerging on the African continent. In 1967 ACOA established a branch office in Washington to monitor Congress and bring attention to African struggles in the seat of American power.

On July 28, 1970, one month to the day after Rustin's advertisement appeared, Hightower wrote his angry letter to some of the blacks who had signed it. He wrote the letter on ACOA stationery and signed it as the Washington director of ACOA. The letter expressed Hightower's "profound opposition and outrage" at each signatory for having signed a statement "of support for Israeli aggression against the Arab peoples of the Middle East," as well as for the fact that "you have incorrectly attempted to justify your action by relating Israel to the world-wide movement for social justice." Given that ACOA was created out of support for blacks suffering from official racism in South Africa, Hightower went on to write about Israel's relationship with the apartheid regime and the degree to which both oppressed people of color: "Apparently, you are ignorant of the fact that Israel is supported by South Africa, that each of these states keep about 5,000 political prisoners in detention, that in the Arab territories occupied by Israel [in 1967], there is not even the pretense of democracy, and that closer political and economic ties are currently being extended between South Africa and Israel."

He continued by pointing to the racism he saw within Israeli society, the discrimination experienced by what he called "dark-skinned" Mizrahi/Sephardic Jews who immigrated to Israel from Arab and other Islamic countries in North Africa, the Middle East, and Southwest Asia. By contrast, Hightower pointed out that the "Arab Revolution" was seeking to improve the lot of all peoples in the region. Finally, he excoriated the signatories in a personal attack: "Your support for Israel and request to the United States Government to supply that aggressive country with American-made jet aircraft for use against the Arab population is a criminal and reactionary position of policy which calls into question your fitness to serve as a representative of Afro-America." As if to show temperance after writing those words, Hightower signed the letters, "Yours in continuing struggle, Charles Hightower." For good measure Hightower also issued a press release with his comments and sent copies of his letter, along with a statement he had signed against American support to Israel, to the staff at various embassies in Washington, including those of Zambia, Tanzania, and the Soviet Union.[2]

Some of those to whom Hightower sent letters responded angrily. Both Rustin and Representative Charles Diggs (D-MI) complained about Hightower to ACOA's office in New York. The NAACP's Roy Wilkins, who happened to sit on the National Advisory Board of the A. Philip Randolph Institute that Rustin headed, complained as well. One of the main reasons that Rustin was upset was because ACOA was not a radical Black Power group but one more in line with his approach. It was a liberal, within-the-system organization that reached out to many of the same constituencies that the A. Philip Randolph Institute did. What is more, some of the same people worked with both groups. None other than Randolph himself was one of two cochairs of the ACOA, and some of the signers of Rustin's advertisement sat on the ACOA national committee.

Rustin was also an old colleague-in-struggle with ACOA's executive director, George M. Houser. Well-known in civil rights circles, Houser had helped found CORE in 1942 and ACOA in 1953, and he had served as ACOA's executive director since 1955. Rustin held nothing against Houser as a result of Hightower's actions: Houser had been on leave from his ACOA post since May of 1970 and thus was not involved with the controversy. Still, Rustin believed that Hightower had drawn a line in the sand to which Houser needed to respond.

The ACOA decided to act. Its steering committee met to deal with the issue a few days after Hightower sent his letter. Committee members discussed how ACOA's ability to work with people in Congress like Representative Diggs depended on Hightower's contacts with them, which now clearly were called into question by the angry letter he had sent them. Someone from the committee apparently told *Jet* magazine that the steering committee's members had voted three to two to ask Hightower to send the follow-up letter—a close vote indicating that Hightower had support within the committee. The magazine

also reported that an angry Representative Stokes had said he would not conduct any business with ACOA as long as Hightower remained director of the
Washington office.[3]

The committee delegated ACOA president Peter Weiss to contact Hightower and ask him to send a second letter to all who received his first one,
clarifying to them that he had been expressing his own opinion and not that
of the ACOA.[4] Weiss himself was no stranger to issues relating to Israel. He
was born in Vienna to a Jewish family and fled with his family in 1938 after
the Anschluss united Nazi Germany with Austria, the land of Adolf Hitler's
birth. In 1950 he became a member of Americans for Progressive Israel and later
became a member of the governing council of the American Jewish Congress.

Weiss wrote to Hightower on August 7, 1970. He was somewhat sympathetic
toward Hightower's attitudes, if not what he wrote and how he had written
it. "I think it hardly needs saying that the only matter at issue was the use of
the Committee's letterhead and of your ACOA title, and not the substance
of the letter," Weiss wrote. He also added that he himself was "quite annoyed
by the 'Black Americans' ad. I thought it was inaccurate, stupid and not helpful either to the cause of Israel or to that of peace in the Middle East." Weiss
made clear that he did not agree with everything Hightower wrote, especially
about the "Arab revolution": "I have serious doubts whether El Fatah, being
supported largely by feudal oil money, is really committed to the cause of the
'Arab revolution.'"[5]

Weiss then dived into the real issue. He was requesting that Hightower
write back to everyone who received his July 28, 1970, letter and make it clear
to them that he was speaking for himself, not ACOA. He also pointed out to
Hightower that some on the steering committee had worried that Hightower's
"rather strong language" might impair his future ability to work with congressional officials on matters relating to Africa.[6]

On August 10, 1970, Hightower wrote back to Stokes and the others to
whom he originally had written, as Weiss had suggested. He simply wrote
tersely that while he hoped that his first letter had been clear in expressing his
own feelings, not those of ACOA, subsequent communications to ACOA's
New York office made it necessary for him to "clarify" the matter. Hightower's
second letter certainly was not good enough for Rustin, who complained in an
August 28, 1970, "Dear Friend" letter he sent to all the persons who had signed

his advertisement. The letter bemoaned the fact that ACOA did not "apologize" to each of them, although it acknowledged that Hightower himself had subsequently made it clear to them that his letter did not represent ACOA's views.[7]

That may have ended the matter for Rustin, but the incident provoked continued conversation and controversy within ACOA. One of the basic premises of the Black Power movement was that blacks should manage their own affairs, run their own organizations, and pursue their own objectives—free from white control and influence, however liberal or well-intentioned. Because of such control, Black Power advocates argued that groups professing to work on behalf of black issues sometimes were not really in touch with what African Americans themselves really wanted and needed. ACOA, in fact, epitomized such a well-meaning liberal group, whose president, executive director, and many of its executive board and national committee members were white. And in this case ACOA's black staff wanted the group to take a stand against Israel.

On September 14, 1970, ACOA staff member Prexy Nesbitt decided he had had enough. Like Hightower, Nesbitt was a smart, black, relatively new staff person from Chicago who had begun working for ACOA as its Chicago field representative in January of 1970. Nesbitt sent a memorandum to the staff and executive board of ACOA in the wake of the Hightower incident threatening to quit unless certain "central issues" within ACOA were resolved. He lashed out against ACOA for its failure of nerve, not only for not supporting Hightower vigorously in the recent controversy with Rustin but also for not pushing for radical action on African issues that were near and dear to the black community.

In his lengthy memorandum Nesbitt made sure to state that his charges did not constitute a "character assassination" of individuals within ACOA. If anything, they could "be labeled as a character assassination upon the political role and impact of the organization known as the ACOA." Nesbitt began his statement with a firm condemnation of what the steering committee did to Hightower, a question about what the implications of that act meant for relations between the committee and the paid ACOA staff, and a round denunciation of ACOA for not taking a stand against Israel in light of clear evidence that it enjoyed a cozy relationship with apartheid in South Africa:

As a staff member, I deplore and reject the recent act by the Steering Committee asking Charles Hightower to issue a letter stating that his views on Israel were not those of ACOA. (Such an act raises serious questions about the political rights of an ACOA

employee and about the relationship between the Board and the Staff.) I wholly support Charles' condemnation of those Black Americans who requested U.S.A. support
for Israel, and moreover, I hasten to condemn ACOA for the fact that Charles' views
are not the views of ACOA. One must ask at a time when the role of Israeli support
for the fascists in South Africa is so clearly established, how can the ACOA (an organization pruporting [*sic*] to support the struggle of African peoples in Southern Africa)
fail to condemn Israel for its imperialist role in Southern Africa as a whole.

After raising other complaints about how ACOA operated, including charging that overall strategy is determined by the executive director independent of
any consultations with the staff, Nesbitt drove his main point home: ACOA
had failed its "mandate" and had not moved "into the mainstream of history."
He contended that ACOA had criticized Hightower for doing what it should
have done itself. "We have failed the struggling comrades from South Africa
who are most immediately the victims of the Israeli–South African Axis," he
charged. ACOA was a group that only "feigns" to support liberation movements
in southern Africa, and that was not consistent with the kind of revolutionary
change to which he was committed.[8]

Houser responded to Nesbitt's allegations in a September 25, 1970, "comment." But with the gauntlet thrown down, ACOA's executive board decided
to hold a special meeting to discuss the entire Hightower issue and its ramifications for ACOA. Because he could not attend that meeting, one member of
the board weighed in on the issues raised by Nesbitt in a memorandum to the
staff and his fellow board members. No doubt to Nesbitt's pleasure, Lincoln
University professor Richard P. Stevens not only wrote in defense of the issues
Nesbitt had raised but wrote in support of Hightower as well.[9] Stevens wrote
that he agreed with Nesbitt that demanding that Hightower write the second
letter to signers of Rustin's advertisement was "unwarranted." He doubted that
any fair-minded person reading Hightower's first letter could have come away
feeling that he had spoken on behalf of ACOA and not merely himself. What
ACOA should have done was to defend Hightower's right to speak, and use
his title with ACOA as an identifier, rather than ask him to write the follow-
up letter.[10]

Stevens's letter then turned to Nesbitt's criticisms. He agreed that Nesbitt
had raised an important issue about the consistency with which ACOA approached African issues and how that affected the group's relations with the

black community. Speaking as a white professor teaching at a historically black university, Stevens wrote that there was a growing divide in the black community between establishment "leaders" and younger blacks who we are more attuned to Third World liberation issues. One manifestation of this, he remarked, was a keen sense among younger blacks to take their commitment to black liberation seriously enough to call attention to any forces or individuals standing in its way. He then drove the point home: "This might indeed involve singling out for attack states, person[s], movements which liberal white opinion would not oppose"—like Israel.[11]

Stevens also expressed his personal incredulity that Rustin and his fellow signers had spoken out as blacks in support not of black Africa but of Israel. Britain had just announced resumption of arms shipments to South Africa, and these black "leaders" (the quotations were his) could not see fit to speak out on that subject but rather on arms for Israel? He also sharply noted that if the Zionist Organization of America had spoken out against British arms for South Africa, "then Black Americans might have adequate reason to support Zionism; if not, should the concern of Blacks move in support of Israel? Young militants are asking these questions." In conclusion, Stevens said that ACOA must be sensitive to "new questions and approaches" that reflect "new moods."[12]

With the memoranda of Nesbitt and Stevens in hand, Houser wrote a memorandum to the board in advance of the October 6, 1970, meeting. A longtime white civil rights activist who had helped establish CORE in 1942, Houser's mainstream vision of ACOA was clear. Noting that "we are essentially non-establishment, interracial, and reformist in our impact," Houser concluded that "our emphasis should be essentially [what] it has been but even further focused because of financial restraints." Regarding the Arab-Israeli conflict, therefore, he wrote, "I would hope that we would stay out of it to the extent possible." Passing resolutions on issues tangential to ACOA's central mission would have "relatively little meaning."[13]

At the board meeting, Weiss displayed a different attitude, more in tune with the impatience of ACOA's black staffer members. He conceded that an important question was whether ACOA was "reformist" or "revolutionary." Weiss also admitted that in the past ACOA had been a "white-liberal organization, paternalistic towards the black community before realizing that black people had to work things out for themselves." Finally, Weiss said the question of Israel and the Middle East was outside ACOA's area of concern, but Israel's relationship with South Africa should be investigated and publicized.[14]

Other ACOA board and staff members contributed to the discussion of the type of organization ACOA was, or should be, as well as on the topic of what to do, if anything, about the Arab-Israeli conflict. Board member Blydon Jackson said that "the heart of the problem is that ACOA has a radical and black staff working for a white, liberal organization. But the staff has little role in the formation of policy and is cut off from this function." Another member of the board, Lydia A. Williams, noted that ACOA policy must come to terms and reflect the growing knowledge among blacks about Africa and Israel's "odd" role in the continent, "something that the black community has been aware of for a long time."[15] Nesbitt asserted that it was impossible for ACOA to ignore the Middle East. Board member Robert Van Lierop, who had just returned from a dramatic trip to Jordan, stated that Israel was a settler colony.[16] What was worse, he continued, was that some of those who signed Rustin's advertisement had refused to take public stances on African issues but were happy to do so for Israel. In the end it was decided to establish a mixed staff-board committee to investigate ways to change the decision-making process within ACOA and to discuss policy issue.[17] Once again, the Arab-Israeli conflict proved to be the springboard for presenting wider Black Power issues that confronted established liberal organizations dealing with African and Afro-American issues.

THE COMMUNIST PARTY USA

When Henry M. Winston published an article in November of 1970 titled "Black Americans and the Middle East Conflict," he was in a good position to write it. A black man born in 1911 in Mississippi, he joined the Young Communist League about 1930. The federal government later prosecuted him for sedition under the Smith Act and imprisoned him in 1956, and by the time he was released in 1961, he had become blind. Five years later he was elected national chair of the Communist Party USA. Winston's article compared the shared struggle of Palestinians, American blacks, and others suffering from imperialism by noting that "the struggle of the Arab people is an inseparable part of the fight of all peoples for liberation from imperialism. And this is indissolubly linked to the struggle of Black people in the U.S."[18]

Black support for the Palestinians in the 1970s also emerged within left-wing organizations outside the Black Power and civil rights movements. Winston and the rest of the leadership of the largely white Communist Party USA (CPUSA) expended great effort during and after 1967 to articulate the party's pro-Palestinian stance to the CPUSA rank and file, much of which was Jewish. Yet by the early 1970s it also began reaching out to black audiences.

Three years after Winston's article appeared, the CPUSA established a front organization to address Arab-Israeli issues in concert with issues of interest to blacks: the National Alliance Against Racist and Political Repression (NAARPR). The alliance grew out of the National Committee to Free Angela Davis, which had been formed in 1971 at the time that CPUSA member Angela Davis was arrested and tried for murder. Davis was an icon for both black and white activists of the 1960s generation. In 1969 California governor Ronald Reagan and the Regents of the University of California fired her from her teaching position at the University of California at Los Angeles because she was a communist. She later was reinstated but then terminated again the following year for other reasons. Davis then was arrested in October of 1970 and charged with murder in connection with a shootout outside a courtroom in northern California; she was acquitted in June of 1972.

The first NAARPR conference was held in Chicago less than one year later, in May of 1973. Davis became NAARPR's cochair, while fellow black party member Charlene Mitchell served as its executive secretary. Beyond its attempts to recruit militant blacks into party activity, the NAARPR was also significant in that its emergence marked the beginning of a new era in which the CPUSA began specifically addressing the issue of the Palestinians and championing their cause—as opposed simply to criticizing Israel and supporting a peaceful solution to the Arab-Israeli conflict, which it had been doing since the 1967 war.

Davis remained busy in her work for the NAARPR in the mid-1970s. She traveled to communist East Berlin for the Tenth World Festival of Youth and Students in July and August of 1973 and while there reportedly met Yasir Arafat. One year later, in August of 1974, she and the NAARPR issued a statement in support of the PLO and against Israeli jailing of Palestinians in the Occupied Territories.[19] Continuing to support Palestinians both inside and outside Israel and the Occupied Territories, Davis addressed a San Francisco press conference on October 10, 1976, alongside Tawfiq Zayyad, the communist mayor of

Nazareth, Israel's largest Arab city.[20] The NAARPR also sent a delegate to the Emergency International Conference in Solidarity with the People of Palestine and the National Lebanese Forces held in December of 1976 in Athens.[21] Communist support for the Palestinians offered a clear demonstration of the impact that Black Power stances on the Arab-Israeli conflict were having within the largely white political realm by the mid-1970s.

ARMED BLACK GUERRILLAS

On September 20, 1982, former Black Panther Sekou Odinga made a statement during the initial legal proceedings against him at the Rockland County Courthouse, thirty-four miles north of New York City, in which he denied the very legitimacy of the court to try him. Odinga was one of six militant defendants, three blacks and three whites, accused of the robbery of a Brinks Company armored car in October of 1981 that led to the deaths of two police officers and a Brinks guard in nearby Nyack, New York. He was, Odinga told the judge, a Muslim, a New Afrikan Freedom Fighter, and a prisoner of war.

Odinga also pointed out that the real issue that should be discussed in court that day was not his impending trial but "the massacre of the Palestinians"—a reference to the slaughter of at least one thousand Palestinians in the refugee camps of Sabra and Shatila a few days earlier in Beirut, Lebanon. Odinga also complained that prison guards had not allowed him and his fellow defendants to wear black armbands as a sign of mourning and solidarity with the Palestinian people. His lawyer, Chokwe Lumumba, joined in, asking Judge Robert J. Stolarik if his refusal to allow the defendants to wear armbands was "because you side with the Israelis in the Lebanese massacre?" Odinga and codefendants Judith Clark, David Gilbert, and Kuwasi Balagoon then refused to sit through the remainder of the proceedings of a court whose authority they rejected. The latter three shouted "Long live Palestine!" as they were escorted out of the courtroom.[22] Armed black militants and their white allies were still declaring their allegiance to the Palestinian cause even in the early 1980s, when most Black Power revolutionaries had long since stopped carrying out armed attacks on the Establishment. For Odinga and his comrades, support for the Palestinian struggle still constituted an essential part of their identity as revolutionaries at the dawn of the 1980s.

The origins of the New Afrikan Freedom Fighters extend back to a loose-knit armed underground black organization that grew out of the Black Panther Party's split in 1971: the Black Liberation Army (BLA). The BLA emerged in the open that year although its roots date to the mid-1960s and groups like the Deacons for Defense and Justice, the Revolutionary Action Movement, and the Black Panthers.[23] The BLA attracted, among others, former members of the Black Panther Party in New York City who were loyal to Eldridge Cleaver after the February 1971 factional rupture between Cleaver and Huey Newton.

This raises an interesting question: might Cleaver have been inspired to start an underground armed force like the BLA as a result of his contacts with al-Fateh in Algeria? Cleaver and the Black Panthers who lived in exile in Algiers certainly maintained a special affinity with al-Fateh. The day that Cleaver publicly opened his first office in Algiers in July of 1969, he delivered a statement in support of the Palestinians with an al-Fateh representative standing beside him. Cleaver and the BPP's international section in Algiers eventually were in daily contact with the Palestinians.[24] Kathleen Neal Cleaver confirmed that of all the revolutionary groups who maintained a presence in Algiers, the Panthers felt the closest to the Palestinians (along with Zimbabwean and South African groups) because the al-Fateh people spoke English and "had a knowledge of the United States and its devastating politics vis a vis their struggle."[25]

Regardless of whether the model of revolutionary warfare offered by al-Fateh is what motivated Eldridge Cleaver, it comes as no surprise that blacks who went on to become noteworthy BLA militants were solidly behind the PLO given their background in the pro-Palestinian world of the BPP. One famous BLA member was former Panther Zayd Malik Shakur (also known as Dedane Olugbala). Born James F. Coston, Shakur was a Muslim convert who spoke out publicly in support of the Palestinians while in the BPP. In May of 1970 he wrote, "It must be pointed out that the only right that the Zionist clique, headed by Golda Meir and Moshe Dayan, have to the land that they call Israel is a robber's right."[26] He later joined the BLA and was killed by the New Jersey state police during a shootout in May of 1973. Afterward, the FBI claimed that Shakur was doing more than just speaking out on behalf of the Palestinian cause. The bureau claimed it found the names and addresses of two Arabs, an Egyptian, and an Algerian, as well as the contact information of the PLO, in the car in which Shakur had been riding when he was killed. An FBI report claimed that "the material is considered particularly significant as it could relate to prior information received that Arab terrorists are training U.S. blacks in guerrilla operations and previous information concerning the BPP-CF's [Black Panther Party—Cleaver Faction] complicity in a terrorist plot in this country."[27] After a number of BLA militants died in battles with the police, the group largely melted away by the mid-1970s.

In the late 1970s the New Afrikan Freedom Fighters began to coalesce. Their leaders included Sekou Odinga. Odinga had an interesting connection with the Palestinians and the Arab world. Born Nathaniel Burns, he joined Malcolm X's Organization for Afro-American Unity and, later, both the Black Panthers and an early incarnation of the BLA. He fled the United States for Cuba in mid-1970 and ended up in Algeria with Eldridge Cleaver in August of that year. Odinga served as Cleaver's bodyguard and no doubt was familiar with the Palestinians from al-Fateh. Perhaps this is why, when he left Algeria in 1972, Odinga made his way back to underground life in the United States in order to continue the struggle—but apparently not before spending time in Lebanon, home to the PLO's headquarters.[28] Odinga and other militants like Mutulu Shakur later carried out a series of robberies in the late 1970s and early 1980s with help from white radicals. Their organizations were called various names, including the Revolutionary Armed Task Force of the Black Liberation Army and the New Afrikan Freedom Fighters.

As part of their ongoing commitment to armed revolutionary struggle within the United States, the New Afrikan Freedom Fighters continued the strong Black Power support for the Palestinians first expressed in the 1960s. This came out publicly in a communiqué that was issued in the name of the Revolutionary Armed Task Force of the Black Liberation Army on August 21, 1982, to mark the occasion of New Afrikan Freedom Fighters Day.[29] In addition to spelling out what the aims of the New Afrikan Freedom Fighters were and noting the black fighters' solidarity with the Palestinians, it contained a section on groups and struggles that the fighters considered allies in the fight against "U.S./Zionist/Apartheid brands of imperial domination." The PLO was one of them:

The P.L.O., F.L.N.C., S.W.A.P.O., and P.A.C. are engaged in life and death struggles to extricate their nations from imperialism's grip. So too are the fighting forces of New Afrika. We see that objectively there is an alliance between these anti-imperialist/

pro-national liberation forces. We must support one another morally, materially and politically and we must learn from one another's experiences. From the PLO we have learned the lesson of tenacious steadfast struggle. . . . *We have learned from them in the final analysis if we want to be free we must do it ourselves.* In this period of revolutionary struggle this lesson is invaluable.[30]

The militants' supporters outside of prison also hailed the Palestinian struggle. A group called the National Committee to Defend New Afrikan Freedom Fighters took the opportunity of the end of Israel's long siege of West Beirut and the subsequent Sabra-Shatila Massacre in the late summer of 1982 to make its own statement in support of the Palestinians. The committee may have been prompted to do so by the six persons on trial: in October of 1982 the FBI opened and read a letter that an imprisoned member of the group wrote to someone on the outside—probably in the committee—urging that a statement of support be sent to the PLO. It read: "As to the Palestinian struggle, I think it would be an excellent idea for the committee to send a statement of Solidarity and support, and if possible to fix it so we can establish closer ties with them. I'm sure it will be comforting to them to know that there are people in America who they have never been in official contact with that have been supporting their struggle for a very long time."[31]

The support committee did in fact issue a statement. "New Afrika and Palestine are linked in a common struggle," it stated in classic 1960s-style Black Power rhetoric, "against a common enemy—u.s.-led [*sic*] imperialism." The committee hailed the strategy of people's war exemplified by the PLO, and pointed out once again that the New Afrikan Freedom Fighters saw their struggle and that of the PLO as a "manifestation of the common enemy of the Palestinian and the New Afrikan people—imperialism led by the u.s.a. [*sic*]." The statement ended with "Death to Zionism and White Supremacy! Death to Imperialism! Victory to the PLO! Victory to the New Afrikan struggle for Land, Independence, and Socialism."[32] Fifteen years after SNCC's newsletter article, revolutionary black anti-imperialism was still alive.

The initial court proceedings against the New Afrikan Freedom Fighters afforded the defendants a public opportunity to assert their support for the Palestinian cause. During those preliminary hearings two other defendants besides Odinga offered statements in court criticizing Israel. One was David Gilbert. Born to a Jewish family, Gilbert joined Students for a Democratic

Society in the 1960s and later was a member of the Weather Underground Organization in the 1970s. After that he was associated with a group of white supporters of the New Afrikan Freedom Fighters and was one of three whites driving getaway vehicles the day of the Brinks robbery. He was put on trial for murder along with Odinga and the rest. In a statement delivered in court, Gilbert censured both America and Israel in the same sentence when he said, "The government that dropped napalm in Vietnam, that provides the cluster bombs used against civilians in Lebanon, and that trains the torturers in El Salvador calls us 'terrorists.' "[33]

Codefendant Kuwasi Balagoon's statement included this: "The United States, Israel, and South Africa stand as expanding imperialist settler states, rotten to their cores, from inception." Born Donald Weems, Balagoon joined the Black Panther Party in 1968 and stood trial in New York from 1969 to 1971 in the famous Panther 21 case. After his acquittal Balagoon became active in the BLA and the New Afrikan Freedom Fighters until his capture in October of 1981. When his actual trial began the next year, in July of 1983, Balagoon's opening statement once again criticized the American government for the fact that it "supports and aids the Israeli government in its massacres of Palestinian people and the theft of their homeland—just as the euro-americans [sic] stole this land."[34] Balagoon became an author after his eventual conviction. Among his writings were some about Israel and the Palestinians in which he argued that the Palestinians were in many ways like African Americans and the American Indians: the West Bank was a ghetto, and the refugee camps were reservations. Both American Indians and Palestinians were colonized peoples.[35]

Another famous group of armed, underground revolutionaries in the 1970s who waged war against the establishment, who supported the Palestinian cause, and who were well versed in the history of the Palestinian struggle were the militants of the Symbionese Liberation Army (SLA). The SLA emerged in late 1973 in the San Francisco Bay area and was not, strictly speaking, a black militant group like the New Afrikan Freedom Fighters. Although its leader was a black former prisoner, Donald DeFreeze, the rest of the small group were whites. One of them, Nancy Ling Perry, even adopted an Arabic nom de guerre—Fahizah (also Fayiza: the winner, the victor)—much like black nationalists sometimes had taken Arabic names. The SLA went on to commit several high-profile acts, including the famous February 1974 kidnapping of heiress Patty Hearst.

A number of the group subsequently died in a gun battle with Los Angeles police in May of 1974.

The SLA was another group waging armed guerrilla warfare in the United States in the 1970s that clearly was familiar with the Palestinian armed struggle. The first action that the group apparently planned sometime in the fall of 1973, but never carried out, was going to be an attack on a local office of the Avis car rental company in retaliation for the fact that the company allegedly supported several "fascist governments," including Israel.[36] Russell Little, one of the SLA's founders, commented on the group's familiarity with the Palestinian armed struggle: "We also read everything we would [sic] on the Tupamaros in Uruguay and urban guerrilla warfare in general as well as studying the actions of the Palestinians and Japanese Red Army guerrillas."[37] Gary Atwood, the divorced spouse of SLA member Angela Atwood, used to talk about Palestinian guerrillas with his friends and perhaps influenced his wife.[38] An SLA support group called the New World Liberation Front later wrote in 1975 about the "heroic Palestinian people": "US imperialist policy dictates that the Palestinians must be dealt with to create a 'suitable climate' for Amerikan [sic] capitalist Investment. Daring revolutionary tactics by Palestinian guerrillas have drawn world-wide support for their Just struggle against the US death order's oil barons that strangle poor people world-wide—Angola-Gulf, Vietnam-Shell, Middle East, etc."[39]

As the 1960s faded away, one dimension of that turbulent time remained vital for African Americans' understanding of their identity and political agendas in the United States: the Arab-Israeli conflict and its role as a vehicle for expressing black political stances and black visions of identity. By the 1970s even mainstream black voices were expressing support, or at least understanding, for the Palestinian cause, including those in the halls of power in Washington.

THE CONGRESSIONAL BLACK CAUCUS

When she spoke, people listened, and when people listened to Shirley Chisholm as she was running for president of the United States in 1972, they may have been surprised to hear her address the problem of the 1948 Palestinian refugees in a sympathetic way that directly compared them to the ghetto experience of black American life, with all its poverty, injustice, and explosions of violent anger: "A generation has grown up in the Palestinian ghetto, and, like the young who have survived their early years in our ghettos, these Palestinians have made clear that they will no longer tolerate the injustice of their condition. . . . Their acts of desperation in recent years have shocked us, perhaps unnecessarily, for we should have learned from our problems here at home the inevitable result of social injustice and poverty."[40]

These were strong words, but then Chisholm was not just any presidential candidate. In 1968 she became the first black woman ever elected to the United States House of Representatives. Three years later she helped form the Congressional Black Caucus (CBC). The CBC's origins extended back to 1969 and a group of black congressional officials from the Democratic Party called the Democratic Select Committee, which then changed its name to the Congressional Black Caucus in 1971 in order to become the official grouping of all black members of Congress. Black Power's belief that African Americans needed to have and maintain political power to advance their people's agenda had spread to the halls of power in Washington.

When Chisholm announced on January 25, 1972, that she was running for president on the Democratic Party ticket, she became the first black person ever to run for president from a major political party. Her voice mattered, and her voice indicated that the sympathy and support for the Palestinians had begun to take root among more mainstream blacks by the early 1970s—not just any mainstream blacks, but those running for president of the United States. The fact that Chisholm clearly felt that the situation in the Middle East was an important one can be seen in the fact that the second policy paper her campaign ever issued dealt with the Arab-Israeli conflict. In it she berated the Nixon administration for failing to address the Palestinian refugee problem: "Is it merely a coincidence that the Administration has done virtually nothing to help the Vietnamese refugees, the Pakistani refugees, and the Palestinian refugees while it is also eliminating aid to our poor in America?"[41]

The paper also underlined Chisholm's remarkably keen and sympathetic understanding of the Palestinians' plight. She noted that many people had "failed to see and understand the personal implications of that development [creation of Israel] on those human beings who had lived in Palestine prior to 1948, those people still referred to as the 'Palestinian refugees.'. . . While we must protect Israel's very existence against outside threat by giving her whatever assistance she truly needs, we must also finally launch a new effort to resolve the root cause of the Middle East conflict, the Palestine dispute." Part of any resolution of that dispute, she maintained, included "full representation for the Palestinians in all negotiations concerning the return or compensation for Palestinian Arab property; and immediate consideration of the problem of the lack of status of the several hundred thousand people who left Israeli held territory in 1948 and 1967."[42]

This was a powerful affirmation about the rights of the refugees, although her obvious human compassion did not extend to calling for some kind of political solution for the Palestinians such as establishment of an independent state. As a nationally recognized black congresswoman, Chisholm was also careful to distance herself from some of the more radical views on Israel emerging from the Black Power movement. Expressing support for the plight of Palestinian refugees was one thing; attacking Israel was quite another.

This was highlighted when the National Black Political Convention (NBPC) convened in Gary, Indiana, in March of 1972—just two months after she declared her candidacy for the presidency. The NBPC ended up adopting a plank on Israel that, even though it later was toned down, rankled members of the CBC. Chisholm was one of them. Both as a member of the CBC and as a presidential candidate, Chisholm could not afford to be seen as supportive of the NBPC plank. Nor, for that matter, did she actually believe what she thought it was saying. The month after the convention, Chisholm wrote, "While the Gary Convention resolution called for the dismantling of Israel, I have not and will not ever take such a radical and absurd position. I have always and will continue to stand firmly in favor of the right of existence for the State of Israel, and wish to be fully disassociated from the Gary position."[43] This was overkill: Chisholm either did not read the resolution carefully or purposely misstated it for political purposes, because nowhere in either the original or the final version of the statement on the Middle East did the NBPC call for what she described as "the dismantling of Israel."

As the group that brought together all the black members of the House of Representatives, the CBC epitomized the growth of mainstream black political power on the national level by the early 1970s. The experience of Chisholm and the NBPC showed that almost from the moment it was established, the CBC was thrust into taking stands on Israel, the Palestinians, and the Arab-Israeli conflict, much as other mainstream black groups had been forced to do prior to that.

What had started out as solidly pro-Israeli CBC positions began to become more nuanced, to the point that the CBC, too, began to embrace Palestinian rights, if not Palestinian aims and objectives. In 1972 the entire CBC disassociated itself from the NBPC's plank on Israel.[44] Representative Louis Stokes, chair of the caucus, issued a press release at the end of the convention that read: "As the black elected officials to the U.S. Congress, we affirm our position that we fully respect the right of the Jewish people to have their own state in their historical national homeland. We vigorously oppose the efforts of any group that would seek to weaken or undermine Israel's right to existence. . . . We pledge our continued support to the concept that Israel has the right to exist in peace as a nation."[45] During the October 1973 Arab-Israeli war, thirteen of the then fifteen members of the CBC—two shy of consensus—cosponsored a resolution in the House of Representatives urging President Nixon to rearm Israel as the fighting was still under way.[46]

Only two years after that, just ten of the seventeen members of the CBC wrote a letter objecting to UN efforts to expel Israel.[47] The following year, on April 14, 1976, the CBC issued the "Congressional Black Caucus Legislative Agenda." As part of that agenda, the CBC noted the following about the Middle East:

— It supported a new peace initiative "based on mutual recognition of Israeli and Palestinian rights";

— ". . . The Caucus believes that Israel must recognize that the Palestinian question is essentially a political one. The avoidance of the question of providing for a homeland for displaced Palestinians can only lead to another war . . .";

— "We believe that on the Palestinian side, the notion of replacing Israel with a secular state must be completely abandoned."[48]

The CBC had embraced the concept of Palestinian political rights wholeheartedly while still remaining fully supportive of Israel. Much had changed in just four years.

The CBC's eventual embrace of Palestinian national rights (although it still eschewed criticisms of Israel) by the mid-1970s was another indication of the degree to which Black Power's embrace of the Palestinian people in the 1960s had spread to become acceptable even to many mainstream blacks eleven years after SNCC's famous newsletter story. It seemed that African Americans working within the system now viewed mainstream black identity and political activity as fully compatible with acceptance of Palestinian human rights. The irony was that by that time, Black Power was largely a spent force. The fact that the drama of the Arab-Israeli conflict had reached into the black mainstream and even congressional black politics offers testimony to the extent to which Black Power stances on Palestine had transformed the politics of black identity in America starting in the 1960s.

CHAPTER 9

A SEAT AT THE TABLE

Bayard Rustin, Andrew Young, and Black Foreign Policy

WHEN BAYARD RUSTIN and his solidly pro-Israeli colleagues Roy Wilkins and A. Philip Randolph decided in 1975 that they needed once again to promote unlimited United States assistance to Israel, they decided to form a new black group to drum up support. Rustin wrote a "statement of principles" for the organization laying out their case. The document began by noting that the struggle of American blacks for racial equality had long been guided by a commitment to democracy, opposition to all forms of discrimination, and that the denial of equal rights to any minority threatened not only all minorities but democracy itself. It then articulated seven main points concerning Jews and the Arab-Israeli conflict and its impact on America. One asserted that Jews and blacks "have common interests in democracy and justice." These common interests were much stronger than any differences they may have. Indeed, the statement opined, "Jews . . . have been among the most staunch allies in the struggle for racial justice." Two other points attacked the Arab world. One of them denounced the Arab League's boycott of Israel and blacklist of persons and companies doing business in or on behalf of Israel. The other claimed that "Arab oil policies have had disastrous effects upon blacks in America and in Africa."[1]

Turning to Israel, the Statement of Principles upheld the Jewish state's right to exist and praised Israel for "her impressive social achievements." As for the Palestinians, Rustin and Randolph once again expressed "compassion" toward the refugees but anger at the Arab states for not resettling them. It continued: "We support the rights of the Palestinians to genuine self-determination," but without saying the words *independent state*, without saying where that self-determination would take place, or what *genuine* meant. Also, Palestinian self-determination could not come "at the expense of the rights of Jews to independence and statehood, and not at the command of economic blackmailers [a reference to the Arab oil boycott] or of terrorists [presumably, the PLO] who would force their own 'solution' at the point of a gun." The statement further denounced what it called "the so-called Palestinian Liberation Organization" by calling it an unelected, terrorist group. "Israel has consistently demonstrated the desire to make concessions in the interest of peace with her Arab neighbors," the statement opined, but not where concessions would threaten its very existence. The Arabs, by contrast, refuse to "accept the legitimacy of the state of Israel."[2] It was vintage Bayard Rustin.

RUSTIN REDUX

The mid-to-late 1970s witnessed Rustin working harder than ever to articulate his belief that blacks and Jews in the United States must work together and support one another's causes rather than focusing inward, engaging in the narrow politics of identity, and sinking into ethnic particularism. He believed in coalition politics and political action within the American system. In terms of his efforts among blacks, this meant embracing and promoting causes near and dear to Jewish Americans. Rustin believed this was good for blacks, good for Jews, and good for America.

Rustin also thought that support for Israel was good for American foreign policy. His vision of what was good for US interests overseas was becoming more and more right-wing. His views mirrored those of the Social Democrats USA, the political party he had chaired since 1972 that was moving further and further away from its left-wing origins and toward neoconservatism.[3] Rustin's championing of democracy and demonizing of the Soviet Union and its allies increased throughout the decade and led him to help establish the right-wing Committee on the Present Danger in 1976.

This hawkish foreign policy vision dovetailed perfectly with Rustin's robustly pro-Israeli sentiments. His faith in Israeli democracy knew no bounds, nor did his antipathy for Arab governments and the PLO. To him, they merely used Israel as an excuse to divert the Arab masses' attention away from more pressing problems. "Marx once said," Rustin wrote, "that religion is the opiate of the masses. In the Middle East, Israel is the opiate of the Arabs."[4] The Israel resolution adopted by the National Black Political Convention in March of 1972 furthered his desire to combat Black Power support for the Arabs and criticism of Israel and to generate a more pro-Israeli black body politic. The Gary resolution troubled him because of the "misrepresentations and distortions which enabled a conference of black people to even consider such a proposal."[5] He set out developing arguments designed to sway blacks away from residual Black Power sentiments and to start thinking positively about Israel.

By 1972 Rustin was using several familiar arguments—familiar in the sense that some Jewish critics of Black Power were using them also—when arguing why blacks should turn their backs on the condemnation of Israel first articulated by black militants in the late 1960s. These arguments were designed both to smear the Arab world and contradict the idea that the Arabs were fellow people of color fighting in the same progressive struggle as American blacks. For example, Rustin wanted black audiences to see through the "myth of Arab-African brotherhood." He touched on the raw nerve of slavery, claiming that Jews had never been slave traders while Arabs had. Second, he argued that the Arab states were not sending aid and technicians to black African countries like Israel was. Third, he claimed that Arab countries were helping to oppress black Africans: the Sudan persecuted blacks in the country's south, he opined, and Egypt supported Nigeria during the bloody Biafran secession and civil war. Finally, he scorned the notion that Arab and Palestinian society constituted a "revolutionary vanguard." In contradistinction to all this Rustin touted Israel as a progressive democracy.[6]

Rustin did feel some human if not political compassion for the Palestinian people. The refugees were individuals who were suffering from "severe" problems, he wrote in 1974, and he "deplore[d] the continued plight of the Palestinian refugees." He believed, however, that it was the Arab regimes that were perpetuating the refugee problem by refusing to resettle them with their respective territories. Never mind that the refugees themselves overwhelmingly rejected resettlement and demanded their right to return to Israel or that Israel categorically had refused to repatriate the refugees. For Rustin it was the Arab states, not Israel, who were primarily responsible for the plight of the refugees.[7] A month after Arafat addressed the United Nations General Assembly in November of 1974, Rustin was arguing that the Palestinians deserved "self-determination"—he steadfastly avoided the words *independent state*—because the PLO's official vision of a secular, democratic state in all of historic Palestine would spell the end of Israel as a Jewish state: "I believe that the Palestinian people have the right to a homeland, to self-determination, to the resolution of their state of uncertainty," Rustin wrote. Just where this "self-determination" would be exercised, he did not say.[8]

The Black Power movement continued to earn Rustin's condemnation in the 1970s for its stances on Israel. In a draft text titled "Israel: A Beleaguered Bastion of Democracy and Socialism," which he wrote sometime soon after his pro-Israeli advertisement appeared in the *New York Times*, Rustin claimed that many Americans, black and white, were surprised by his 1970 statement because they had been seduced by Black Power advocates into thinking that "the majority of black Americans were opposed to Israel's existence." His advertisement proved the opposite, he argued. Why had all those black American leaders lent their names to it? It was because it "represented an expression of solidarity with the *progressive ideals and values* which a nation like Israel represents." As he turned rightward—perhaps not so coincidentally as many whites were as well—Rustin was fighting his war over identity not with Black Power advocates themselves but by presenting his alternative vision of blacks and Jews defying ethnic particularism by working together for the good of Israel and American foreign policy.

In early 1975 Rustin once again thought that he needed to harness his energy and connections within the black mainstream in defense of Israel and in hopes of affecting American foreign policy. In late 1974 the PLO gained two important political victories when the Arab League recognized it as the "sole legitimate representative of the Palestinian people" and when the United Nations invited Arafat to address the General Assembly. Just four years after its mauling by Jordanian forces during the Black September fighting, the PLO had a new lease on life politically, if not militarily. Equally bad for Rustin, US-Israeli relations were once again testy, even in crisis by the spring of 1975. Another

Republican administration, that of President Gerald R. Ford, was pressuring Israel hard to make diplomatic concessions in the hopes that the United States could broker a second interim agreement between Egypt and Israel following the October 1973 Arab-Israeli war. The Ford administration was angry with Israel's refusal to go along with American plans and decided in March of 1975 to undertake a "reassessment" of relations with Israel. As part of this reassessment the government once again held up Israel's request to acquire top-of-the-line American aircraft. Israel and American Jewish organizations went on a public relations offensive much as they had in 1970.

Rustin decided to act by forming an organization that would assist in pressuring the Ford administration. He called it the Black Americans to Support Israel Committee (BASIC). The month that the administration spoke of a "reassessment" of United States policy toward Israel and then held up the aircraft to the Jewish state, Rustin met with a group of Jewish friends. They included, among others, Irwin Suall of the Anti-Defamation League, Rabbi Balfour Brickner, and the Jewish Labor Committee's Emanuel Muravchik. The men discussed whom in the black community they could invite to join.[9] Rustin then joined with the NAACP's Roy Wilkins and A. Philip Randolph to draw up a BASIC "Statement of Principles" that was shown to a number of prominent blacks in the spring of 1975.

Seventeen people endorsed the BASIC Statement of Principles at first, including three congressional representatives, some labor union officials, and others. By June of 1975, fifty people, plus Randolph and Rustin, had agreed to sponsor BASIC. Twenty of these had signed Rustin's advertisement five years earlier, in 1970. Among the new names were writer Ralph Ellison, musician Lionel Hampton (who agreed to serve as BASIC's treasurer), former CORE leader James Farmer, Representative Andrew Young, and Professor Pauli Murray, the civil rights activist who cofounded the National Organization of Women in 1966.

On April 24, 1975, Rustin held a coming-out party for BASIC at the New York City home of Robert Gilmore, treasurer of the A. Philip Randolph Institute. Rustin announced the formation of BASIC and stated what its goals would be. Minorities seeking justice must support democracy, he said, and therefore we as blacks support Israel. He was quick to add, "Our support of Israel does not mean that we do not support self-determination for the Palestinians." However, he continued, "we are not for the self-determination of the Palestinians if they are dedicated to the destruction of another people." Randolph added, "It will be a crime for anyone, especially the Blacks of America, not to support the just cause of Israel." Several prominent Israelis attended the reception, including the Israeli consul general in New York, David Rivlin; his subordinate, Yakov Levi; and the director general of the Israeli oil corporation Paz, Moshe Bitan.[10]

After spending the summer months building support, Rustin and several others held another press conference in New York on September 11, 1975, to announce the actual formation of BASIC. Flanking him were the aging Randolph, along with the dependably pro-Israel Roy Wilkins and New York City commissioner of human rights Eleanor Holmes Norton.[11] As he had done before, Rustin decided to publish an advertisement in the *New York Times* heralding the birth of the new group. Civil rights activist Arnold Aronson helped raise money. The advertisement, which cost $13,992, finally appeared in the November 23, 1975, edition of the *New York Times*.[12]

It repeated the "Statement of Principles" that Randolph, Rustin, and Wilkins had drawn up several months earlier and included a clip-out coupon that readers could use to send in donations or seek more information about BASIC. Besides listing the names of Randolph, Rustin, and Hampton, 214 other people signed the advertisement. They spanned the gamut of business leaders, labor leaders, clergymen, academics, politicians from all levels of government, attorneys, and the like. Civil rights figures included Ralph Abernathy, Daisy Bates, Julian Bond, Mrs. Medgar Evers, James Farmer, Ernest Green, Benjamin L. Hooks, Vernon E. Jordan Jr., Coretta Scott King, Martin Luther King Sr., Floyd McKissick, Rosa Parks, Wyatt Tee Walker, Roy Wilkins, and Andrew Young. From the world of sports came Hank Aaron, Arthur Ashe, and Roy Campanella. Musician Count Basie and his wife, Catherine, and writer Ralph Ellison added their signatures. So did a host of mayors from large cities, like Los Angeles's Tom Bradley and Atlanta's Maynard Jackson. Twelve members of Congress lent their names, including Representative William L. Clay, who had complained after the last time Rustin included his name in a pro-Israel advertisement. Cultural figures Harry Belafonte and Mrs. Louis Armstrong also had joined BASIC by September, but their names were not printed on the advertisement in November.[13]

At least two leading figures in the black community were approached in the initial attempt to garner supporters in the spring of 1975 but refused to lend their names. One was Jesse Jackson, who had worked with Martin Luther King Jr.'s Southern Christian Leadership Conference and was a significant player on his own right on the national black political scene. Jackson apparently thought that the best way to work for Arab-Israeli peace was in a less stridently pro-Israeli manner. According to Harry Fleischman of the American Jewish Committee, "Rev. Jesse Jackson refused to sign because he insisted that he has a different approach to create Jewish-Arab reconciliation." Another leader who declined to sign on to BASIC was John H. Johnson, publisher of *Jet*, *Ebony*, and *Black World/Negro Digest*, even though he had signed Rustin's first advertisement back in 1970. Johnson said, in Fleischman's words, that "he feared physical attack from the Black Muslims if he were to sign such a statement."[14]

After the advertisement was published, Rustin fully intended to have BASIC continue functioning toward the realization of its goals. This time it would be different from 1970, when he had published a statement in major newspapers and essentially left it at that. Armed with a $12,000 loan from the A. Philip Randolph Institute, Rustin formally registered BASIC as a social welfare organization with the Internal Revenue Service (IRS) on September 9, 1975. On the "statement of purpose" section of the application to the IRS, BASIC listed seven such purposes for the group: foster better understanding of Israel as a democracy; sponsor exchange visits of American blacks and Israelis; publish literature; make speakers who can discuss Israel available to black audiences; work for improved understanding between Israel and black Africa; work for Middle East peace; and "counter anti-Israel propaganda which characterizes the Israeli people and their government as racist, fascist, imperialist, and the like." This included, the application continued, "the widespread—and totally false—charge that Israel is an enemy of the emerging nations of Africa."[15]

Rustin and BASIC soldiered on into the late 1970s. For its first two years of existence after the advertisement appeared, BASIC planned activities with two objectives in mind: building support for Israel among blacks and helping them to understand the Arab-Israeli conflict. BASIC held press conferences and sponsored joint black-Jewish receptions for visiting Israeli officials. It had blacks speak at Jewish conferences and even became involved in issues unrelated to Israel and the Arab-Israeli conflict, such as participating in demonstrations on behalf of Soviet Jews. BASIC organized study trips to Israel for black leaders, such as the one it held in October of 1977, and gave a scholarship for a one-year study-abroad program starting in mid-1977 at The Hebrew University of Jerusalem to a third-year college student at St. Louis University, Sheila Lynch.[16] Rustin spoke at an Israel bonds fund-raiser in Sacramento, California, in April of 1977 held to honor a black AFL-CIO trade union leader. He said, "We have an obligation to defend democracy and Israel is the only democracy left in the Middle East."[17]

How successful were all of these efforts? That depended on how one viewed the situation. Two years into BASIC's existence, Rustin had reason to believe that his efforts had been in vain. In 1977 BASIC estimated that only 14 percent of American blacks were pro-Israel, compared with 17 percent who were "Third World oriented" and a full 69 percent who were uncommitted.[18] By that measure Rustin was losing his battle for black identity.

BASIC began experiencing other problems. One setback stemmed from the fact that it worked hard to convince members of its core constituency—blacks who were interested in democracy and justice in foreign affairs—that Israel was a progressive country kindly disposed toward black Africa. In April of 1976 South African prime minister John Vorster made this much more difficult by visiting Israel and meeting with Israeli prime minister Yitzhak Rabin. This meeting was tailor-made for Black Power advocates, who for years had railed at Israel's ties with the apartheid regime in Pretoria. It now was becoming exceedingly difficult for pro-Israeli acolytes like Rustin to ignore such ties and claim that Israel cared about black Africa when the bête noire of Africa and African support groups in the United States was cozying even further up to Israel.

Even Rustin sensed the danger. On August 27, 1976, he wrote Arthur Hertzberg, president of the American Jewish Committee, to complain about this. In his letter Rustin expressed his "deep sense of concern and disturbance." We in the black community, he wrote, support Israel for moral reasons and because Israel is a progressive, democratic society. Why, then, was Israel doing this?[19] The private letter indicates that Rustin was suffering from a serious case of myopia and naiveté. Israeli ties with South Africa were nothing new, as he surely had to have known, and his own long experience in real politik and coalition building should have made him aware that Israel and South Africa needed each other in more ways than one.

Other regional changes presented Rustin and BASIC with challenges, as well. In May of 1977 Israel's Labor Party failed to win the Knesset elections for the first time in Israel's history. The new governing party was now the right-wing Likud Party, led by the firebrand hardliner on Arab-Israeli affairs Menachem Begin. Begin's bellicose attitude toward the Arabs, his categorical refusal to contemplate withdrawing from any of the 1967 Occupied Territories, and his prickly attitude toward his detractors distressed some liberal American Jews. This complicated the formerly "united front" attitude of American Jews and Jewish organizations, let alone a black group like BASIC, when it came to supporting Israel. It also put Rustin in an odd place: as a dyed-in-the-wool supporter of Israel, he had to keep up his pro-Israeli efforts. But as a longtime socialist labor activist who was quite close to Israel's now-defeated Labor Party and the Histadrut labor federation, Rustin now had to contend with the Likud's hostility toward Labor, the Histadrut, and socialist politics in general. He also believed that Likud contained a "hard-line bloc" that was "inflexible," posing a challenge to Middle East peacemaking and did not mind saying so publicly.[20]

Another change with which BASIC had to contend was shifting American priorities in the Middle East. By mid-1978 Egypt was moving toward making peace with Israel and becoming an American ally, and Saudi Arabia was seeking to buy advanced American aircraft. Peace or no peace, the prospect of advanced American aircraft in Arab hands was of great concern to Israel and its supporters in the United States. When President Jimmy Carter therefore proposed selling military aircraft to Egypt, Saudi Arabia, *and to Israel*, the Israelis objected. Rustin joined with others like the *New Republic*'s Martin Peretz in forming the Emergency Committee for the Middle East to urge the United States to reject the arms deal "in order to give peace a chance in the Middle East." Following his marching orders, Rustin thus found himself in the odd position of for once encouraging the American government *not* to sell planes to Israel.[21]

The even more serious problem facing BASIC by 1977 was financial. The main reason for this was the dearth of contributions it received. Despite Rustin's efforts to impress potential Jewish donors in particular that some blacks were pro-Israeli after all, donations did not roll in at nearly the level he needed. This was because contributions to BASIC were not tax deductible under American tax law—always a major liability for any group soliciting funds in the United States. BASIC's mounting financial problems can be seen in the fact that for the fiscal year ending on August 31, 1977, BASIC's total income was $22,118, while its expenses totaled $29,462. At the end of that fiscal year the group was not only spending more than it received; it still owed the A. Philip Randolph Institute $18,783 that it had received in loans. Thereafter, BASIC stopped receiving or spending any money.[22] BASIC essentially was moribund after just two years of existence.

Rustin pressed on, and BASIC continued to function, barely, throughout the late 1970s and into the early 1980s, although black participation at meetings dwindled compared to Jewish participation. At the November 24, 1980, BASIC meeting in New York City, for example, Rustin and eight other blacks attended, whereas sixteen Jews were there.[23] By that point BASIC seemed more like an extension of the pro-Israeli establishment in the United States and less like a group of "black Americans in support of Israel." It was a testament to Rustin's inability to gain support among blacks for his vision of black-Jewish amity based around mutual support of Israel.

Also complicating Rustin's mission were events in the Middle East. The Israeli invasion of Lebanon that Prime Minister Begin ordered in June of 1982 prompted some new BASIC actions that suggested that Rustin was beginning to worry about the fallout over the war and the way it could rebound in the PLO's favor politically. Israel's encirclement of West Beirut as its forces tried to bombard besieged PLO fighters into submission, and the concomitant devastation wreaked on Lebanese and Palestinian civilians trapped in the city, was being broadcast daily on television channels all over the world throughout the summer of 1982. Israel was looking to some like an aggressor.

As early as two weeks after the invasion began, Rustin sent a telegram to Begin on June 21, 1982. Its guarded language seemed to suggest that Rustin was already worried about the negative political fallout for Israel if the Israelis continued the war. In the telegram Rustin encouraged Begin to begin shifting from Israel's overwhelmingly dominant military efforts to neutralize the PLO to political and diplomatic ones: "Now that the military threat to Galilee is ended, we in [the] Black Americans to Support Israel Committee are eager to support exhaustive diplomatic and political efforts to achieve both stability in Lebanon and peace with secure borders in Israel. Shalom, Bayard Rustin, President, B.A.S.I.C." Ever mindful of his efforts to show Jewish groups that blacks cared about Israel, Rustin made sure to send copies of the telegram to a number of Jewish groups in the United States. Whatever Rustin's intentions were in the telegram, Begin wrote back as if Rustin had congratulated him and

Israel for the invasion and was extending his full support. "Dear Friend," Begin wrote, "I thank you from the heart for your words of solidarity and support for Israel's just cause in carrying out Operation Peace for Galilee."[24]

If Israel was now perceived as a bully in 1982, many in the world conversely saw the embattled PLO as the underdog. When the PLO finally withdrew its battered forces from West Beirut that September, thanks to indirect American diplomacy, and American, French, and Italian troops entered to oversee the operation, the PLO managed to balance its obvious military defeat with the backhanded legitimacy it received from all the global attention. Thereafter, President Ronald Reagan soon issued a plan for a peaceful resolution of the Arab-Israeli conflict. Arafat even met with Pope John Paul II on September 15, 1982, shortly after leaving Beirut. All of these events elevated the PLO's profile and its potential role in a diplomatic solution to the conflict, giving even more legitimacy to it than it already had accrued in the 1970s. Rustin was concerned.

In October of 1982 he and BASIC's Charles Bloomstein wrote to Uri Bar-Ner of the Israeli consulate in New York about an idea they had to write a pamphlet on the PLO. Their purposes would be to show "that the P.L.O. should not be recognized by any Western democracy as representing the interests of the Palestinian people—and certainly not be accepted as the sole representative of the Palestinian people." Bloomstein and Rustin asked Bar-Ner to provide them with information to help them write the pamphlet, including a list of PLO terrorist activities in Israel and other countries, documented information about PLO behavior in Lebanon since 1970, and documented data about the PLO's training of terrorists seeking to attack countries other than Israel. The two seemed to want to write something showing how much the PLO's presence in Lebanon had presented a threat to the entire world. Rustin and Bloomstein also told Bar-Ner that after they had written the pamphlet, they would telephone him for his "reactions" to it. SNCC's use of Arab government propaganda and public relations material in 1967 had been roundly condemned in some quarters, but apparently Rustin had no qualms about resorting to such material as long as it came from Israeli sources.[25]

Rustin's desire to write a pamphlet denouncing the PLO reflected more than just an immediate need to contend with the group's high profile after Israel invaded Lebanon. It also reflected Rustin's long-held and deep hostility toward the PLO that predated the Israeli attack. His hatred of the PLO matched his hatred of Black Power. He often expressed this hostility in opinion pieces. After the PLO achieved two political victories in the fall of 1974—Arafat addressed the United Nations, and the Arab League recognized the PLO as the sole, legitimate representative of the Palestinian people—Rustin tried to parry these public relations successes by writing a December 1974 opinion piece titled "The PLO: Freedom Fighters or Terrorists?" In the piece Rustin argued that by calling the PLO freedom fighters instead of terrorists, the world had seriously warped words like *liberation, racism,* and *peace.* The best example of this was the "fundamental surrendering of political and humanitarian principles" on the part of the UN General Assembly when it enthusiastically greeted Arafat. What "legitimate struggle" was Arafat representing, Rustin asked? "It is a struggle being waged with the tactics of calculated violence, where military targets are avoided, but women, children, athletes, diplomats, airline passengers—the defenseless and uninvolved—are sought and struck down."[26]

He also dismissed the PLO's call for creating a secular, democratic state in Palestine. Rustin conceded that the Palestinians had a right to a homeland, to "self-determination," but so did the Jewish people. Whatever he may have thought of multiculturalism at home, Rustin clearly believed that ethnic segregation was what was called for in the Middle East. He ended his piece: "At a time when so many appear willing to accept lies as the truth, to reach dishonest conciliation with terrorists, to barter away the most basic ideals of justice and compassion, Israel more than ever deserves the support of people of good will and common decency."[27]

By 1983 Rustin still fervently supported Israel, but Begin's controversial tenure as prime minister had caused him to become fairly forthright in some of his criticisms of the Jewish state's actions. An example was a noteworthy opinion piece he authored that appeared in the August 4, 1983, *Los Angeles Times.* In the piece Rustin still accused the Arab world of being the main obstacle to Arab-Israeli peace by its stubborn refusal to accept Israel's right to exist. He lamented that American foreign policy was not more clear-sighted and that it was failing to exert the proper pressure on the Arabs to do so. Yet what was remarkable about the article was the forthrightness with which Rustin criticized three particular aspects of Israeli policy. The first was the construction of Jewish civilian settlements in the occupied Arab territories of the West Bank and Golan Heights (he did not mention Gaza). Rustin claimed that Israel's policy of building settlements was "misguided from the outset"—an interesting observation given that his Labor Party friends like Prime Ministers Levi Eshkol, Golda Meir, and Yitzhak Rabin had overseen the establishment of the first settlements.[28]

He also addressed "charges of Israeli mistreatment of Arab residents," which, he conceded, "regrettably are true." He did not specify whether he was referring to the 20 percent of Israeli citizens who were Palestinians, or the Palestinians subject to Israeli military rule in the West Bank and Gaza, although elsewhere in the piece he said that Israel could be faulted for treating "its Arab population as second-class citizens." Finally, and most remarkably, Rustin noted that another criticism that could be leveled against Israel is "that it has expanded its borders by conquest."[29] He offered excuses for all these blemishes: Israel had lived for decades with war and terrorism. Its human rights record was better than that of other countries faced with such pressures, but his criticisms were there nonetheless, in black and white, for all to read.

Despite this, pro-Israeli groups once again were thrilled by Rustin's piece. Chris Gersten, political director of the American Israel Public Affairs Committee (AIPAC), wrote to him saying, "Terrific article in the *L.A. Times*. I am pleased to have been able to circulate it around AIPAC." The national director of the Anti-Defamation League of B'nai B'rith, Nathan Perlmutter, sent him a note about the piece, saying, "Editorially it is useful, logically it is sound; and I have every intention of plagiarizing its reasoning." Finally, *Commentary* magazine's editor, Norman Podhoretz, wrote to Rustin and crowed, "I have just read your piece in the L.A. *Times* on the Arab-Israeli conflict, and my only comment is Bravo!"[30]

Four years and twenty days after his opinion piece appeared in the *Los Angeles Times*, Rustin died. He had come a long way in terms of owning up publicly to Israel's faults since he first began acting as "Israel's man in Harlem" in the late 1960s, although he remained firmly convinced in the justice of its cause and the need for Americans, black and white, to support the Jewish state. Rustin's reign as the undisputed champion of pro-Israeli activities among mainstream black civil rights leaders represented the most vigorous and long-lasting effort to counteract black support for the Palestinians at the expense of Israel. Rustin's hatred of the Black Power movement, its revolutionary internationalism, and its Third World identity politics drove him further and further into the arms of mainstream liberal, labor, and Jewish organizations that were fighting back against militant black denunciations of Israel. Rustin strove long and hard to demonstrate to Jewish allies that not all blacks accepted Black Power perspectives on Israel or the American system. This was part of his crusade to assure Jews that more moderate blacks still cared about their concerns and were still good Americans—not Third World radicals. It was a question of identity, and for Rustin that clearly meant locating black identity within the mainstream of political acceptability.

Bayard Rustin's tireless and ultimately failed efforts on behalf of Israel demonstrated that both 1960s-era Black Power positions on the Middle East and events in the Middle East in the 1970s had shifted the goalposts, and Rustin desperately tried to stay in the game playing by the old rules. The Palestinian problem and pro-Palestinian viewpoints had become part of mainstream American public discourse. By the time of his death in 1987, acceptance of the notion that the Palestinians deserved at least some type of national and human rights had come increasingly to be accepted in the American body politic, among both blacks and whites. Even Rustin was forced to concede that much. And given his concern for moving from "protest to politics," the changing black discourse about the Arab-Israeli conflict became increasingly clear in 1979 with the eruption of the Andrew Young Affair, the consequences of which caught many in the American mainstream by surprise by the torrent of black outpourings of understanding of, if not outright support for, the Palestinians.

ANDREW YOUNG AND THE ARAB-ISRAELI CONFLICT

The statement delivered to the United Nations Security Council on August 24, 1979, by the American ambassador to the United Nations, a man who just twenty-three days earlier had assumed the rotating position of president of the Security Council, was as remarkable as any of those assembled that day had ever heard. The man, Andrew Young, announced that he would be leaving his position on the Security Council because just days before he had resigned from his post as US representative to the United Nations. Having read the newspapers, no one seated around the table that day was surprised. The hushed delegates knew this moment had been coming; the die had been cast the previous month. For when Young walked out of the New York City apartment of the Kuwaiti ambassador to the United Nations on July 26, 1979, after secretly having met with the PLO's permanent observer to the United Nations, in defiance of a 1975 American governmental ban on any contacts with the PLO, Young had sealed his fate as the highest ranking black in the administration of President Jimmy Carter. Despite having been forced to resign some three weeks after that meeting, Young was hardly contrite in his final remarks to his Security Council colleagues. "So I leave this Council," he stated in his farewell address, "with no regrets for the fact that perhaps we broke the comfortable diplomatic channels and we violated some long-ago made agreements that are ridiculous."[31]

Despite Young's relatively graceful comments, all hell broke loose, and a major domestic scandal befell the Carter presidency revolving around blacks, Jews, and American policy in the Middle East. As the 1970s were coming to an end, the Arab-Israeli conflict still cast a shadow over black politics in America, as it had done in the previous decade. The conflict once again was a major feature in the black American political discourse and the search for place and identity within the country. Adding to that was black insistence that African American voices mattered just as much as those of any other ethnic group in terms of offering input into the directions American foreign policy should take.

Equally significant, the key actors in what came to be called the "Andrew Young Affair" in 1979 could hardly be described as Black Power radicals. The protagonists, in fact, were Christian ministers, congressional representatives, and leaders of mainstream black organizations. The question of the Palestinians and the Arab-Israeli conflict clearly had taken root within conventional national black politics in America that motivated not only revolutionary Third World–oriented blacks but also those seeking greater power and influence within American society. Black Power may have waned, but its demand that blacks had a right to speak about or with the Palestinians clearly had not. It was another example of the staying power of the Palestinian issue in American racial and identity politics.

Andrew Young in the 1970s was already a noted civil rights figure.[32] He had been Martin Luther King Jr.'s trusted associate in the Southern Christian Leadership Conference (SCLC) and knew something about the Arab-Israeli conflict. Young had spoken with many Israelis and Palestinians on his 1966 trip to the Middle East and was on good terms with pro-Israeli black stalwarts Bayard Rustin and A. Philip Randolph, even serving on the executive board of the A. Philip Randolph Institute. When Rustin's pro-Israeli advertisement ran in the *New York Times* in June of 1970, Young was running for Congress as a Democrat. He was asked to add his name to the statement by Samuel W. Williams, another figure in Atlanta's black community. Young apparently declined because his name did not end up appearing in the advertisement.[33]

Young issued his own two-page statement on Israel, as well, for he no doubt thought it expedient to release a supportive statement about Israel in advance of the elections in November of that year. The document advocated sending military aircraft to Israel, and it laid out for the public what he wanted them to know about his commitment to Israel. Young stressed three particular themes: his emotional attachment to Israel; his concern that as an ally, Israel could help stop the Soviet Union from gaining increased influence in the Middle East; and his belief that the Republican administration of President Richard Nixon was not fully committed to Israel, as evidenced by its "vacillation" and willingness to "dangle" the promise of aircraft in front of the Israelis to get them to adhere to American policies.

The statement affords a fascinating insight into what Young thought—or what he was willing to say publicly, at least—about Israel in 1970. It offered a ringing endorsement of a very mainstream, conservative cold war attitude about foreign policy:

The United States must support Israel for strategic reasons, as well as moral ones. The Middle East is a critical area for the security of the United States and especially for our European allies. If the entire area were to come under Russian influence, the Soviets could employ an economic stranglehold on Western Europe whenever they wished. For this reason it is vital to our own interest to guarantee Israel's survival as an outpost of democracy in the Middle East.

It is therefore imperative that the United States continue to do all that is necessary to maintain Israel's security as a nation. . . . [The United States and the West] should supply the Israelis with the necessary means to defend themselves. We ought not dangle aircraft in front of Israel's nose, hoping for greater fidelity to our policies. We must make a firm commitment to provide Israel with the fighter planes and technical and economic assistance it so urgently needs.[34]

As for the Palestinians, Young had learned of their plight from those Palestinians he had met in East Jerusalem in November of 1966. This, along with statements he made to Martin Luther King Jr. on June 8, 1967, to the effect that the Arab perspective on the situation rarely was heard in the United States, all indicate that he was well aware of the aspirations of the Palestinian people.[35] Young's statement therefore *did* mention them, although he argued that a solution to the refugee problem was resettling all of them to a new Palestinian state that would be carved somewhere out of the Arab world, not for Israel to allow them to return.

Young did not win the election but succeeded in 1972 and was a member of the House of Representatives by the time the United States Senate confirmed him as American ambassador to the United Nations on January 26, 1977. Young became the first black ever to hold that position and also became the highest ranking black official in the Carter administration.

THE FATEFUL MEETING WITH THE PLO

Two and one-half years later, in July of 1979, Young was faced with a dilemma. He was about to assume the position of UN Security Council president beginning on August 1. He also was informed that the council was set to discuss a report by the UN Division for Palestinian Rights and that the deliberations would lead to the submission of a draft of a Kuwaiti resolution calling for recognition of an independent Palestinian state. The American government was anxious to delay any such resolution being brought before the council and ordered Young to try to block it. After Young discussed the matter with some Arab UN ambassadors, they agreed to support his efforts to take the report off the Security Council's agenda provided that the PLO approved such a decision. Young faced a quandary: to advance American diplomatic needs, he would be forced to meet with the PLO's Permanent Observer to the United Nations, Zehdi Labib Terzi, and sound him out. Yet stemming from a September 1975 American pledge to Israel that the United States would not negotiate with the PLO until it recognized Israel's right to exist and accepted UN Security Council Resolutions 242 and 338, American diplomats were forbidden to negotiate with or even meet PLO representatives. Young decided to meet Terzi anyway, in secret.

On July 26, 1979, Young walked from his home in New York City to a party at the apartment of Kuwait's UN ambassador, Abdullah Bishara. Waiting among other guests, as planned, was Terzi. Young and Terzi quietly excused themselves from the other guests and discussed the matter in another room in the presence of both Bishara and Syria's UN ambassador, Hammoud Elchoufi. Thanks to Young's chat with Terzi, the PLO agreed to a postponement of the issue, and the Security Council took it off the agenda for three weeks.

Young thought he had succeeded, until *Time* magazine's bureau in Jerusalem, based apparently on Israeli intelligence sources, found out about the meeting and asked the State Department for comment before publishing the story. On being queried by the department about the press inquiry, Young said (apparently somewhat jokingly) that he indeed had met Terzi at Bishara's apartment, but accidentally, and the two did not discuss anything beyond social pleasantries. *Time* published the story. Israel sent a formal protest to the American government, claiming that Young's actions violated the 1975 agreement not to negotiate with the PLO. The die was cast.

American Jewish groups had already been angry with aspects of Carter's Middle East policy, notably statements made by Young earlier in the year that were seen as supportive of the PLO. Now they were further upset on learning that Carter's UN representative actually had met with a PLO official. Several Jewish groups issued strong statements, although only Joseph Sternstein, head of the American Zionist Federation, actually called for Young's dismissal. American Jewish Committee executive vice president Bertram Gold came close, hedging his language somewhat by saying, "If Andrew Young indeed did talk with the PLO on his own, he should be fired," leaving open the possibility that Young may have done so under orders from Carter.[36] Amid the outcry, Young's story quickly fell apart. According to Carter's published diaries, the president wrote on August 13, 1979, that "this [meeting with Terzi] is understandable because Andy is president of the Security Council." Carter's diary entry noted, however, that "when interrogated about it by the State Department he told them a lie. . . . This is an almost impossible problem to resolve without Andy leaving."[37]

On August 14 Carter and Secretary of State Cyrus Vance agreed that Young would have to resign and take the fall for the brouhaha. Young immediately wrote his letter of resignation, which he presented to Carter at a White House meeting the following afternoon. Carter's diary entry for that day reveals that he, too, thought that not being able to talk to the PLO was "ridiculous" but believed that America's reputation was at stake: "Andy was not penitent at all, saying he had done what he thought was right. It is absolutely ridiculous that we pledged under Kissinger and Nixon that we would not negotiate with the PLO; but our country's honor is at stake, and we will do the best we can. I instructed Cy [Young] and Zbig [National Security Adviser Zbigniew Brzezinski] not to make any more reassurances that we were not meeting with the PLO; if the Israelis couldn't trust us, they could find another 'trustworthy' partner."[38] Writing several decades later, Carter claimed that Young would have been allowed to stay had he not lied about the meeting with the PLO representative. Young ended up staying in his post for another month, until September 23, to give time for a replacement to be found.[39]

That was the background to Young's farewell statement to his UN Security Council colleagues on August 24, 1979. He held his head high during his remarks and expressed no regrets. Young began his statement by saying that he had not expected to leave the council, especially given the fact that he was its president at the time. "And yet," he continued, "I have no regrets for what has occurred; in fact, I see it as a part of a plan of the work of this Council, a part of the work of this Council which I intend to be associated with long after I have left you." He conceded that he knew what he was doing when he had met with Terzi and therefore had not been "set up by my Arab or Israeli friends. . . . I think that whatever happened leading to my resignation was something that I entered into very much with my eyes open," he continued, noting as well that his action was the culmination of "a fundamental disagreement with a policy, one that I sought to run from for two and a half years, for I never agreed with it." Therefore, despite the risk of his job, Young noted, "it was no great decision on my part to visit the home of my friend and to meet another friend."[40]

Young also took the opportunity to attack publicly the American government's prohibition on talking to the PLO, as well as certain policies of both Israel and the Arab world. He said, "I hope that in some small way it may have opened up a question to the American people that will call attention to some of the tragic history of our nation as a result of the refusal to communicate." Young continued: "And it was because I felt that not talking would contribute to violence and bloodshed that I thought the risks of talking to the PLO were nothing compared to the risk" of further violence. Turning his critical comments toward the Arabs and Israel, Young said that if it was "ridiculous," as he put it, for the United States or Israel not to talk to the PLO, it was equally ridiculous for some of those sitting on the council not to talk to Israel—a clear reference to Kuwait's ambassador, Abdullah Bishara. He admonished the Palestinians by saying that their attempts to destroy Israel had cost them moral capital but countered by saying that Israel had done the same through the violence it had wreaked in Lebanon, as well as "in the building of settlements where perhaps while affirming [Security Council Resolution] 242, the very act violates 242."[41]

Young continued to serve for another month after delivering his oration to the Security Council, officially leaving his post as US ambassador to the United Nations on September 23, 1979. As if to prove a point, Young went out of his way during the subsequent forty-eight hours to meet with PLO officials. He dined the very next evening, September 24, with top PLO officials Faruq Qaddumi and Shafiq al-Hut, who were visiting New York to attend the sessions of the UN General Assembly. The evening after that, September 25, Young attended a dinner that included Terzi.[42] He continued to insist that he had done nothing wrong, reiterating publicly a few days later what he had told his colleagues on the Security Council: "I really don't feel a bit sorry for anything that I have done. And could not say to anybody that given the same situation, I wouldn't do it again almost exactly the same way."[43]

That was hardly the end of the affair. The top black official in the Carter administration had been forced out over what many African Americans saw as his actions in response to a flawed policy vis-à-vis the Arab-Israeli conflict. Black leaders from across the political spectrum were livid. Some of the fiercest reactions came not from radicals but from mainstream black leaders from all levels of political life. Gary, Indiana, mayor Richard Hatcher called it a "forced resignation" and "an insult to black people." Benjamin Hooks, the executive director of the NAACP, said that Young was "a sacrificial lamb for circumstances beyond his control." Black anger increased when it was discovered that the American ambassador to Austria, Milton Wolf—an industrialist and prominent member of the Jewish community in Cleveland, Ohio—himself had held a total of three meetings with the PLO's Isam Sartawi several months earlier, in the spring of 1979. Two had been "social" meetings, but the third involved more substantial matters. More to the point, the Carter administration had known about them.[44] Why, black leaders asked, was a Jewish diplomat not forced out for talking to the PLO, but a black one was?

ERUPTION OF BLACK ANGER

On August 16, 1979—the day after Young resigned—a group of black leaders met in New York City. Among them were Coretta Scott King, Bayard Rustin, and Vernon Jordan—hardly pro-Palestinian activists. Yet they issued a statement that questioned the different treatments meted out to Wolf and Young, and they hoped that the incident would not harm black-Jewish relations. That proved to be wishful thinking. The Andrew Young Affair marked a return to the black-Jewish tensions over the Middle East. It also showed the staying power of the Question of Palestine among blacks as the 1970s drew to a close.[45]

Black sensitivities were worsened by the widespread perception that Carter had caved in to Jewish pressure to fire Young. Jesse Jackson noted a "tremendous tension in the air around the nation over the forced resignation," and he claimed that black-Jewish relations were "more tense than they've been in 25 years."[46] Joseph Lowery, head of the SCLC, weighed into the controversy, as well. Lowery spoke for many blacks when he addressed the perception that blacks were still in a subservient position to Jewish financial patrons who provided support for the civil rights movement but expected blacks to stay quiet about Israel. Lowery addressed Jews by saying, "If we have to maintain your friendship by refraining from speaking to Arabs, then that friendship must be reassessed."[47] In the wake of the Young affair sociologist Kenneth Clark said that blacks finally felt free to discuss black-Jewish relations more honestly, without fear of the withdrawal of Jewish financial support.[48] A major controversy about the Arab-Israeli conflict had broken out that enveloped mainstream black leaders.

A number of major public figures sprang into action. The small group that gathered in New York City on August 16, 1979, paved the way for the NAACP to issue an invitation to scores of others to attend a much larger meeting at the group's headquarters in New York on August 22. Some 230 persons ended up attending, including a number of "heavyweights" among black leaders. Besides the NAACP's executive director Benjamin L. Hooks, other major black civil rights and political figures included Joseph Lowery, Wyatt Tee Walker, and Walter Fauntroy of the SCLC; Vernon Jordan of the National Urban League; Jesse Jackson of Operation PUSH; Gary, Indiana, mayor Richard Hatcher; and Georgia state senator Julian Bond. Hooks opened the meeting by telling the assembled leaders, "Because of our background, heritage and tradition, there is a natural tendency for many black Americans, historically, to have tremendous sympathy with people who are deprived wherever they are." He added, "This is true of the Jewish people, the Arab people, the Palestinian people."[49]

Beyond the actual issue of the substance of Young's dismissal and the reasons behind it—the PLO, Israel, and Middle East negotiations—what was clearly uppermost on the minds of those in attendance was the manner in which Young was so abruptly fired and the speed with which Carter came to that decision. The assembled group unanimously adopted a statement at the conclusion of the meeting that said, among other things, "Black Americans strongly protest the callous, ruthless behavior of the United States State Department toward Mr. Young." The statement went further: "We demand once more to know why the American Ambassador to Austria was given a mere reminder about U.S. policy prohibiting meetings with the P.L.O. while Mr. Young was harshly reprimanded. We call upon the Carter Administration to account for this gross double standard."[50]

Another particularly sensitive black grievance that arose during the Young affair was the perception that blacks were being marginalized in terms of the country's foreign policy decision-making process. Many blacks thought that Young, a black man, had been attacked for daring to interpret what was in the best interests of American foreign policy, whereas other Americans from various ethnic backgrounds, notably Jews, felt perfectly free to interpret, discuss, lobby, and try to shape American foreign policy without sanction. This sentiment was reflected in several sharply worded phrases in the final statement. Noting that blacks had fought and died in all of America's wars, and would again were the United States to become involved in a war in the Middle East, the statement declared:

Nevertheless, the involvement of blacks and their concerns in foreign policy questions is repeatedly questioned. . . . Clearly, the stakes for minorities in the conduct of American foreign policy continues to be high. . . . Neither Jews, Italians, Germans, Irish, Chinese, British, French or whatever other ethnically or nationally identifiable group has any more right to be involved in the development of United States foreign policy than Americans of African descent. If there is any single area where the melting pot concept applies, it is with foreign affairs. For we either all pursue the common interests of this nation or help it sink separately.[51]

It also stridently stated: "We summarily reject the implication that anyone other than blacks themselves can determine their role in helping to shape and mold

American foreign policies which directly affect their lives."[52] The black leaders keenly resented being told by whites what issues lay within their purview to discuss. They would set their own agenda. Questions of race, identity, and place within America clearly animated those at the meeting, and the context once again dealt with the Arab-Israeli conflict.

The final statement also reflected the leaders' anger toward Israel and the American Jewish groups whose incitement, they believed, had been a major contributing factor in Young's dismissal. Turning to Israel and its demand that the United States not speak to the PLO, the assembled leaders said, "We join with Ambassador Andrew Young in rejecting the notion that any foreign nation should dictate the foreign policy of the United States." They also asserted that "Black America is also deeply concerned with the trade and military alliance that exists between Israel and the illegitimate regimes and oppressive racist regimes in South Africa and Southern Rhodesia." Turning their obvious anger on American Jewish groups, among others, the leaders stated that "the overreaction by the national news media, some of the Jewish community, the Carter Administration and some congressional leaders was a regrettable consequence of the double standard by which this nation judges its black leaders. . . . Blacks, however, were deeply affronted by the inherent arrogance in the attacks upon Ambassador Young by certain Jewish groups and the news media for his having dared to place the interests of the United States above all other considerations."[53]

Clearly, the Andrew Young Affair had touched a black nerve, one already made raw by past grievances and tensions, including black-Jewish friction over Middle East policy that in some ways had lain dormant since the heyday of Black Power several years earlier. Some high-profile African Americans, in fact, quickly began to mobilize for action that would illustrate dramatically the right of blacks to participate fully in the national discussion about America's Middle Eastern policy, even if that meant challenging the country's opposition to talking to the PLO. The fierce 1960s Black Power resentment against what black activists had believed was whites dictating to blacks what they could or could not say about the Middle East was being repeated now by more mainstream black leaders in 1979. They differed from Black Power activists in that they believed their identity was American, not Third World. Yet precisely because of that, they keenly resented what they saw as their marginalization from the realm of foreign policy. They were mad as hell and were not going to take it anymore.

CHAPTER 10

LOOKING OVER JORDAN

Joseph Lowery, Jesse Jackson, and Yasir Arafat

ON SEPTEMBER 20, 1979, a group of black ministers from the Southern Christian Leadership Conference (SCLC) held a meeting in Beirut, Lebanon, with PLO chair Yasir Arafat. The gathering lasted for three and one-half hours, during which the SCLC delegation proposed to Arafat that the PLO "recognize the sovereignty of Israel" and agree to both an immediate cease fire with Israeli forces in southern Lebanon and a wider "moratorium" on violence from the PLO anywhere. The first request was presented because, the SCLC argued, "the failure to recognize, or the rejection of its [Israel's] existence, constitutes futile defiance of world opinion and presents a formidable barrier to universal recognition of the role of the PLO in putting forth the legitimate claims of the Palestinian peoples." At the end of the meeting the delegation's Henry Gibson, a Methodist minister, offered a prayer in English, which was followed by an Arabic-language prayer delivered by a Roman Catholic priest. The Americans then linked arms with Arafat and sang the civil rights anthem "We Shall Overcome" as the cameras clicked.[1] African Americans once more were traveling to the Middle East and meeting with Arafat, but this time they were far more mainstream figures than the Black Power militants who had done so in the late 1960s and early 1970s.

THE SCLC'S "MIDDLE EAST PEACE INITIATIVE"

Andrew Young's resignation on August 15, 1979, happened to occur while the SCLC was holding its national convention in Norfolk, Virginia. Established by Martin Luther King Jr. and others, the SCLC now was led by another Protestant Christian clergyman, Joseph E. Lowery. Lowery became involved in the civil rights movement, helped King and Ralph Abernathy establish SCLC in 1957, and served as its first vice president. Lowery had known Young personally for many years because Young had worked as SCLC's executive director in the 1960s.

Lowery was furious about what had happened to Young, not just because of who he was and what he stood for—the top-ranking black in the Carter administration—but also because of the implications of his dismissal. What did it say about the ability of white Americans to accept the fact that black leaders were certainly as capable as anyone else of trying to bridge diplomatic gaps, including between Israel and the PLO? While speaking on the floor of the SCLC convention on August 17, 1979, two days after Young resigned, Lowery dramatically announced that he would carry on with Young's mission by personally meeting with both Israeli and PLO representatives to the United Nations in the near future. "We must carry on Andy Young's intent for building bridges of communication because it is morally correct, healthy and productive," Lowery stated.[2] It was the humble beginnings of what would come to be a major, and controversial, diplomatic effort by Lowery that within a month would lead him to the Middle East and the PLO leader, Yasir Arafat.

True to his word, Lowery was in New York within days to meet with both the Palestinian and Israeli ambassadors to the United Nations. He first met with the PLO's Zehdi Labib Terzi on August 20, 1979. Lowery and six others, including fellow SCLC ministers Walter E. Fauntroy and Wyatt Tee Walker, met with Terzi over lunch for two hours. Among other things, the group urged Terzi to tell Arafat that he should consider recognizing Israel and negotiating with it. Lowery gave a statement afterward in which he supported "the human rights of all Palestinians, the right of self-determination, involving, among other things, their homeland." Lowery described the meeting as "very interesting and communicative."[3]

The following day, the SCLC delegation met with Israeli UN ambassador Yehuda Blum. This time the two-and-one-half-hour meeting was less pleasant.

According to an agenda that the group members drew up prior to the meeting, they told Blum that they wished to "Reiterate our support of nationhood of Israel and human rights of all Israelis; Reiterate and clarify our support of human rights of all Palestinians (does not lessen support of human rights for all Israelis); Communicate concerns of Black American's [*sic*] about Israel's relations with South Africa . . . effect on relations with American blacks; Communicate our support and faith in non-violence as most vital means of resolving conflict and affecting [*sic*] change (discuss bombing raids—Lebanon).[4]

Blum responded by criticizing Lowery's statement of the previous day that called for Palestinian self-determination, telling him that he should have listened to both sides first. He also insisted that Israel would not negotiate with "the terrorist PLO," which was "bent on the destruction of Israel." Going straight for the jugular, Blum declared that any support the PLO could garner from meetings, such "could only discourage the peace process." When the delegation brought up Israel's trade ties with South Africa and Israeli bombardments of southern Lebanon, Blum deflected the questions with the usual diplomatic ripostes expected of someone in his position. Afterward, both sides told the press that the meeting had not been fruitful. "We missed each other somehow" is how one member of the SCLC group told a Jewish press service.[5]

After the two meetings, the SCLC delegation issued a press release emphasizing that Lowery and the others told both men that "the killing of innocent Palestinian and Israeli citizens both by bombs in garbage cans and bombs dropped from aircraft" must end. "The PLO cannot achieve its good intentions through violence any more than the Israeli [*sic*] can resolve the Palestinian problem by bombing Lebanon." The delegation told both sides that it had not come to negotiate "but to communicate the need for an end to the killing."[6]

On August 22, 1979, two days after Terzi met with Lowery and the others, Arafat formally invited them to visit Lebanon and meet with him at his headquarters in Beirut. Lowery leapt at the chance. He and nine others traveled to the Middle East four weeks later, hoping to visit both PLO and Israeli leaders as part of what they called the "SCLC Middle East Peace Initiative." SCLC's peace initiative specifically sought two things of all parties to the Arab-Israeli conflict, notably Israel and the PLO: "First, that each declare a moratorium on acts of violence. And second, that the PLO become a part of the Camp David peace process, with both Israel and the PLO prepared to recognize mutually all the rights of Israel and the Palestinians to peace within the secure and recognized borders of a homeland."[7]

The group arrived in Beirut on September 17, 1979. Leading the SCLC delegation were Lowery and Fauntroy, who served as SCLC's chair of the board and also was the congressional delegate from Washington, DC, in the House of Representatives. The delegation also included the seasoned civil rights veteran C. T. Vivian and several others. While in Lebanon, the group visited Palestinian schools, refugee camps, and hospitals in Beirut. According to press accounts, at one point Lowery donned a keffiyeh headdress made famous by the Palestinian guerrillas (and Arafat personally) and posed for pictures holding a toy gun handed to him by a boy in one of the refugee camps in Beirut. Fearful of the fallout from this rather undiplomatic act, were images of it to be published, the SCLC's Reverend Al Sampson and a PLO official seized the cameraman's film.[8] The group also traveled to South Lebanon, stopping by the town of Damur before heading to Nabatiyya and the PLO military position at the medieval Beaufort Castle, known in Arabic as Qal'at al-Shaqif. At one point Lowery suggested that Palestinian refugees should stage a civil rights–like march from Nabatiyya to the Israeli border.[9]

The visiting Americans were treated as dignitaries while in Lebanon and held meetings with top leaders such as President Elias Sarkis, Prime Minister Salim al-Hoss, and Foreign Minister Fuad Boutros. They also met with representatives of various political groups, from the Lebanese National Movement, which was friendly to the PLO, to Maronite Catholic political leaders Pierre Gemayel and Camille Chamoun, who very much were not. As members of the clergy, the SCLC group also met with representatives of the Middle East Council of Churches and the Islamic Council of Lebanon.[10]

The highlight of the trip was the delegation's meeting with Arafat in Beirut on September 20, 1979. The meeting lasted for three and one-half hours. It was then that the Americans proposed that the PLO issue a moratorium on all violent actions both in Lebanon and elsewhere. Lowery and the others explained it to Arafat this way: "Even with an understanding of the causes, we do not believe that the PLO can achieve its objectives through continued violence. Moreover, we believe that a moratorium on violence is a powerful initiative with the potential for dramatically shifting the moral advantage to [the Palestinian] side in the eyes of the world, and make possible some relief for those Palestinians now suffering from the violence of Israel."[11]

Arafat did not agree to the request to recognize Israel, and he refused to accept UN Security Council Resolution 242, which offered an indirect recognition of Israel. He was more circumspect on the request for a moratorium on violence, arguing that the two sides were not equal in that respect, but agreed to consider the idea.[12] Lowery also asked Arafat if he would come to America and address the first of what Lowery hoped would be several SCLC seminars on the Middle East (the Israeli press later quoted the American State Department as saying that if Arafat tried to obtain a visa to enter the United States, such a request would be denied).[13]

The reaction from the government of Israel to the idea of meeting with Lowery and his colleagues was markedly different, however. SCLC had asked Israeli officials in the United States before the group left if the delegation could visit Israel and meet with Israeli officials on their trip. They were anxious to meet with both sides, much as they had met with both Terzi and Blum in New York. On the last day of their mission to Lebanon, however, the delegates found out that Israeli foreign minister Moshe Dayan had advised Prime Minister Menachem Begin not to meet with the delegation. They then flew back to the United States without having traveled to Israel.[14]

Back home in the United States Lowery issued a statement: "We believe that our mission has been successful because we went as Children of God, carrying a message of peace through non-violence which was heard by many of the parties to the conflict . . . in Lebanon and the rest of the Middle East." Regarding Begin's refusal to meet with him and his colleagues, Lowery expressed his disappointment in no uncertain terms: "If the Israeli government does not wish to hear our proposals for a moratorium on violence, and to discuss our moral initiative, then the responsibility for the deficit is theirs. It shall in no way, however, deter us from the aggressive pursuit of peace with justice for all persons in the Middle East." He also announced that the SCLC intended to follow up on the trip with a series of educational fora in at least ten American cities and would try to meet with national leaders as well as UN Secretary General Kurt Waldheim.[15] Lowery clearly believed in what he was doing, but his announcement also was a clear jab at those he believed were trying to muzzle black participation in the making of American foreign policy.

Just over a week later, on October 1, 1979, Terzi sent the SCLC a telegram informing the group of several developments that occurred in the wake of the trip. First, he reported that twelve hours after the delegation left Beirut on September 21, the PLO announced a unilateral cease fire in southern Lebanon effective at 11:00 p.m. However, the Israeli air force soon shot down some Syrian aircraft, effectively ending the cease fire from the PLO's point of view. Later in the week, the SCLC received confirmation that the PLO had indeed declared a cease fire in southern Lebanon but that this did not cover Palestinian actions in the West Bank and Gaza. Second, regarding the SCLC's request that the PLO recognize Israel: Terzi's telegram stated that the PLO supported UN General Assembly Resolution 3236 on Palestinian self-determination and would support UN Security Council Resolution 242, which effectively would thereby be recognizing Israel, when 242 was paired together with 3236.

In light of these developments the SCLC perceived that Arafat had not fully accepted important components of its initiative. Disappointed, the SCLC decided on October 7 that that was not good enough. It therefore decided not to invite Arafat to come to the United States after all and to cancel its plans for a series of fora on the Middle East around the country. As Fauntroy said two weeks later, on October 15, "We cannot and will not reward that refusal."[16]

For all intents and purposes, then, the "SCLC Middle East Peace Initiative" was over almost as soon as it began. The group nonetheless considered it a success, particularly in demonstrating that American blacks had a constructive role to play in American foreign policy just like any other ethnic group did. The group summed up their efforts: "We were successful in illustrating by our mission that we take seriously the material costs to us as Black Americans in any area of the world where the U.S. has a vital stake and that we will not be silenced or excluded from participation in those decisions which affect our lives and the well-being of this country."[17]

For his part, Lowery waxed biblical in a speech called "All Children of Abraham," which he gave at the national conference of the Palestine Human Rights Campaign in Washington on September 21, 1979, the day he returned from Lebanon. In it, he stressed the personal ties he shared with the Middle East and its peoples by virtue of his Christian faith:

As a Christian, I lay claim to the Holy Land (Palestine, Israel) as part and parcel of the heritage of faith. My Jesus was born there, and in that lovely land he opened the gates of God through which millions have marched. . . . And while I may not, as Jews and Arabs do, call myself a direct, blood descendant of Abraham in the "begat" sense of the Book of Matthew, he is a father of my faith which is Judeo-Christian in its roots and fruits. So my brothers, the Jews, and my brothers the Palestinians are mine and I am theirs and no manner or matter of disavowal can change it.[18]

Black politics had moved in a different direction since the demise of Black Power militancy, but it still claimed a connection with the people of the Middle East.

Both as chair of the board of SCLC and as a sitting congressman, Walter Fauntroy was also visible in the days after the delegation returned. Fauntroy was a Baptist minister who began his work with SCLC in 1960 and later became chair of its board of directors. In 1971 he was elected to the House of Representatives as the nonvoting congressional delegate from the District of Columbia. Fauntroy admitted that he traveled to the Middle East for both religious and political reasons. "I went to Lebanon as a minister of the gospel, as an ambassador of goodwill, committed to a ministry of reconciliation," Fauntroy was quoted as saying. Yet he also pointed out that his search for peace served a more temporal purpose rooted in his life in the black community of Washington. He said that if a war ever broke out in the Middle East, black soldiers would be disproportionately affected. He was also quoted in the Jewish press as saying, "For me, Killing is Killing. Bombs dropping out of the sky are as terrifying as bombs in a shopping center. Whatever you call it, I want the killing to stop."[19]

On October 11, 1979, Fauntroy gave a report on the trip to his colleagues in Congress. While he said that he had traveled to the Middle East in his capacity as a minister and chair of the board of directors of SCLC, he nevertheless was a sitting congressman and used the prerogatives of that position to make his report. He frankly admitted that he and SCLC considered the state department's ban on talks with the PLO to be an "ill-conceived" policy. "We [SCLC] resolved to exert moral leadership with the strong support of a unified Black leadership in opposing what we consider to be an ill-conceived policy of our government—with respect to the Middle East," he said. "That policy presently prohibits any contact with the PLO." Continuing, Fauntroy noted that the American assumption that the PLO was just a terrorist group was wildly off the mark. "Our visit to these [PLO] facilities also gave striking evidence that the PLO is not the one-dimensional 'terrorist organization' we have been led to believe that it is, but contains all the infrastructure of a nation in exile."[20]

Fauntroy's report also took aim at another American government policy: supplying Israel with advanced weaponry that it used against Lebanese and Palestinian civilians. "To our outrage, we saw unmistaken evidence of the use of American weapons on non-military targets," his report stated. Fauntroy actually brought home pieces of American ordnance the group had found during its tour of southern Lebanon, and his report noted, "I have returned with shrapnel, parts of exploded shells and cluster bombs, which I lifted from the ruins of bombed-out Palestinian and Lebanese villages in Lebanon."[21] The trip clearly was leading to deepening SCLC sympathy with the Palestinians much beyond the nuanced SCLC position articulated in the late 1960s by Martin Luther King Jr.

JESSE JACKSON'S MISSION TO THE MIDDLE EAST

The issue of America's lack of relations with the PLO, and of black determination to play a role in Middle East policy, led another important civil rights leader to visit the Middle East as a result of the Andrew Young Affair: Jesse Jackson. In fact, there seemed to be a veritable race to see which black leader could get to Arafat first. Jackson was already a controversial figure among SCLC stalwarts by 1979, and there was no love lost between them. Jackson first began working with SCLC as a young man in 1965. The April 1968 murder of SCLC's Martin Luther King Jr. had left a void in terms of who would replace King as the "top" spokesperson for black Americans. Jesse Jackson had considerable ambitions in that direction, which brought him into conflict with King's replacement as SCLC president, Ralph Abernathy. Even King had noted Jackson's ambitions, and after King's death Abernathy was particularly leery of Jackson's intentions. Tensions came to a head in December of 1975, and Jackson left SCLC to form People United to Save Humanity (PUSH) in Chicago.

Now that Lowery was head of SCLC and Jackson was head of PUSH, the rivalry continued, although Walter Fauntroy's spokesman, Eldridge Spearman, denied to the press that there was a rivalry between SCLC and Jackson. "They are not in conflict," Spearman said.[22] But they clearly were. Both Jackson and Lowery had attended the August 22, 1979, meeting of black leaders at the NAACP headquarters in New York, which took place just forty-eight hours after Lowery had met with the PLO and Israeli representatives to the United Nations. Jackson, too, decided to initiate a public effort to provide a bridge between Israelis and Palestinians by meeting with Israeli and PLO representatives in the United States. This did not take place until mid-September, however, at which time Jackson met in Washington with the PLO's Terzi at the congressional office of Representative Paul Findley (R-IL) and with Israel's ambassador to the United States, Ephraim Evron.[23] By the time Jackson decided to travel to the Middle East, Lowery had already announced the upcoming SCLC trip. Jackson was playing catch-up.

The rivalry even extended to the national conference of the Palestine Human Rights Campaign, which was under way on September 21, 1979, the very day that Lowery returned from the SCLC trip and at which Lowery spoke. Jackson, too, addressed the gathering that day. He was just days from traveling to the Middle East himself. Jackson delivered a speech titled "The Challenge to Live in One World," in which he denounced the American policy prohibiting talks with the PLO: "The no-talk policy toward the PLO is ridiculous. The public has a right to know the whole story in the Middle East. . . . The national interest of the United States is jeopardized by a no-talk policy. A no-talk policy against *anybody* at the United Nations is an international absurdity. It is an affront to the civilized community. The most important link in civilization is communication; so we affirm communication." Jackson also addressed the wider black concern that the Andrew Young Affair represented an attempt to sideline blacks from the foreign policy process: "There is and has been for a long time a concerted effort to isolate Black Americans and challenge the audacity of black involvement in foreign affairs. Witness the experiences of Dr. [W. E. B.] Du Bois and his Pan African efforts; Paul Robeson and his social, economic, and political analysis made within an international context; and Dr. Martin Luther King, Jr.'s stand against the war in Vietnam. Black Americans have an interest in a just and lasting peace. . . . We have a stake in peace in the Middle East.[24]

Despite lagging behind Lowery and the SCLC in picking up the reigns of black diplomacy vis-à-vis Israel and the PLO, Jackson did have one leg up on Lowery: both his wife and a high-ranking official of Jackson's PUSH organization had already been to Lebanon and had met Arafat, just months before the Andrew Young Affair burst onto the scene. Even though he would arrive at Arafat's headquarters a full month after Lowery did, he would arrive as a known entity and with contacts. Jackson's wife, Jacqueline, had just recently visited Lebanon in June of 1979 in the company of the director of PUSH's international affairs department, Jack H. O'Dell. O'Dell had been around. Nearly twenty years Jesse Jackson's senior, O'Dell joined the Communist Party in 1950. He served as an adviser to Martin Luther King Jr. and SCLC beginning in 1961, but he left soon thereafter when President John F. Kennedy and others pressured King to dismiss O'Dell because he had been a communist. He then worked as an editor for the influential black journal *Freedomways* before working with Jackson and PUSH.

O'Dell and Jacqueline Jackson traveled to Lebanon at the invitation of the Association of Arab-American University Graduates. The group was in Lebanon from June 12 to June 20, 1979. While there, they visited medical facilities of the PLO's Palestine Red Crescent Society, as well as social and rehabilitation workshops of the PLO's Dar al-Sumud and SAMED organizations. They visited Palestinian refugee camps near Tyre and witnessed the damage inflicted by Israeli air raids on the town of Nabatiyya. In Beirut O'Dell and Ms. Jackson met with high-level Palestinian officials, including such senior figures as al-Fateh Central Committee member Salah Khalaf (Abu Iyad), PLO Political Department head Faruq Qaddumi, and Yasir Arafat himself. Ms. Jackson described Arafat as "a most moving individual." On their return she encouraged PUSH to become more involved with the Palestinians. Both she and O'Dell also met with then-American ambassador to the United Nations Andrew Young to communicate their findings. They reportedly urged him to make informal contacts with the PLO. It would be only about a month later that Young did just that by meeting with the PLO's Terzi in New York, setting the entire brouhaha in motion.[25]

O'Dell also returned a friend of the Palestinian cause. He later spoke of having supported the creation of Israel in 1948, something fully in line with the policy of the Communist Party, but "those of us who were present at the birth of Israel, and who went to rallies supporting it," he noted, "knew nothing of the Palestinians." He continued: "We thought that, given the great human rights traditions of the Jewish people, an answer to the Holocaust that took the form of a state in the Middle East would certainly play a positive role in the region. When we found that, wait a minute, there's folks there called Palestinians, who are people of color and Arab, some of us felt that we needed to be better acquainted with that."[26]

A year after his trip, O'Dell explained why he and other blacks identified with the Palestinians: "The response of Black Americans to the Palestinian appeal for justice is one of sensitive appreciation, for we too know what it is to be dispossessed, exploited, lied about, insulted and ignored." He also criticized American aid to Israel by comparing what that money could be used for if spent at home in the United States: "Our taxes are used to facilitate the wanton destruction of human life [by Israel]. The international community would obviously have more reason to respect the U.S. if that tax-money was being used to provide a decent public transportation system for the people of Watts, or to reopen the coal miner's [*sic*] medical clinics in Kentucky and West Virginia that have been closed for two years."[27]

With O'Dell and Jackson's wife recently having traveled to the region, Jesse Jackson announced shortly after his visits with Terzi and Evron in Washington that he, too, would act on behalf of black Americans to advance the cause of Middle East dialogue and peace by traveling to the Middle East. Jackson then flew to Israel, arriving on September 24, 1979—just three days after Lowery and the SCLC delegation arrived back in the United States from their trip to Lebanon. Jackson had requested a meeting with Prime Minister Menachem Begin during his visit with Evron in Washington. When Jackson and sixteen others arrived in Israel, he immediately found himself facing a firestorm of controversy. Evron had indeed passed along Jackson's request to meet with Begin. Perhaps still stinging from Begin's refusal to meet with Lowery earlier in the month, some Israeli politicians and diplomatic personnel were eager for Begin or someone else in the Israeli government to meet with Jackson in order to avoid having the government appear disrespectful in the eyes of American blacks. Begin still refused, but given the pressure for *someone* to do so, three top officials in the opposition Labor Party eventually agreed to meet with the visiting Americans: Shimon Peres, Yigal Allon, and Jerusalem mayor Teddy Kollek. Kollek led Jackson on a tour of Jerusalem's Old City and a hospital, where they comforted Israelis recently injured in a Palestinian attack.[28]

Jackson then traveled to the West Bank and met with Palestinians in the Qalandiya refugee camp on September 25, 1979. While there, Jackson said he felt a "sense of identification." "I know this camp," he said. "When I smell the stench of open sewers, this is nothing new to me. This is where I grew up." He applauded when some of the elderly refugees who gathered around him said that the PLO spoke in their name. The next day, Jackson traveled to Nablus, the biggest town in the West Bank, where he spoke before a gathering of several hundred people at the municipality building. He told those assembled there that the Palestinians should halt terrorism and adopt civil rights–style tactics instead. He also led the crowd in his trademark "I am somebody!" chant, and was carried aloft by youths shouting, "Jackson, Arafat!"[29]

The PUSH leader left Israel and the West Bank after three days, crossing into Jordan, where he visited a Palestinian refugee camp outside Amman on September 27, 1979. The following day he was in Lebanon, touring another refugee camp near Tyre and meeting with Palestinians in the seaside town of Damur before arriving in Beirut. The PLO welcomed him there with an honor guard, complete with band members playing bagpipes in their camouflage uniforms. Jackson met with Arafat for two hours, returning later for an evening meeting with the PLO leader. Jackson told Arafat that he needed to dispense with any talk of doing away with Israel and just come out and say clearly what it was that he really wanted. Arafat reportedly replied, "The West Bank and Gaza," in reference to the idea of establishing an independent Palestinian state just in those two parts of historic Palestine. Jackson responded, "Well, say that." As during Lowery's visit nine days earlier, Jackson was photographed with Arafat, awkwardly embracing him.[30]

From Beirut, Jackson flew to Cairo, where he met with Egyptian president Anwar al-Sadat, who six months earlier had signed the first peace treaty between an Arab state and Israel. Jackson returned to Beirut, reportedly carrying a message from Sadat to Arafat, whence he finally left to return to the United States on October 5, 1979. His exhausting schedule included a total of eleven days traveling to Egypt, Jordan, Lebanon, Syria (where he met with President Hafiz al-Asad), Israel, and the West Bank. The trip also took a physical toll on him: he twice fell ill, once having to be hospitalized in Beirut. While there, he received a special bedside visitor: Yasir Arafat.[31]

THE DRAMA CONTINUES

Back in the United States, the visits and diplomatic aims of both Lowery and Jackson were quickly overshadowed in the fall of 1979 by criticisms about black leaders meeting with PLO officials. It was a replay of the controversy back in August, when news of Young's secret meeting with Terzi first emerged. Charlotte Jacobson of the World Zionist Organization and the venerable rabbi and activist Joachim Prinz criticized Lowery's visit in letters published in the *New*

York Times in late September of 1979. SCLC also received many angry letters from Jews, especially those on the group's mailing list who had received its fall 1979 fund-raising letter.

Jews were not alone in criticizing the visits with Arafat. Some mainstream black leaders also took Lowery and Jackson to task. The NAACP's Benjamin Hooks was cautiously critical. James Farmer, former head of the Congress of Racial Equality in the 1960s, offered up another circumspect critique in a speech he gave on October 15, 1979: "I have also been troubled by recent statements of some black leaders regarding events in the Middle East. A passionate concern for the social, political and economic freedom of all peoples must of course, include the Palestinians. But that is not the issue. The issue here is, simply put, is [*sic*] whether a unilateral, pro-PLO stance, with its implied opposition to the nation of Israel, serves the cause of that freedom, or whether it might not escalate hostilities and limit the opportunity for a peaceful resolution of these long-standing conflicts."[32]

The National Urban League's Vernon Jordan laid into Lowery and Jackson. Calling their actions "ill-considered flirtation with terrorist groups devoted to the extermination of Israel," Jordan insisted that "the Black civil rights movement is based on non-violent moral principles. It has nothing in common with groups whose claims to legitimacy are compromised by cold-blooded murder of innocent civilians and school children." He also denounced the trips as a "sideshow" that diverted attention from the real issues that mattered to blacks: "In the past several weeks we've seen more concern exhibited about Palestinian refugee camps than about American ghettos. We've seen more concern about the PLO's goals than about Black America's aspirations for equality. And we've seen more concern about Yasser Arafat's future than about the future of millions of little black children growing up in poverty."[33]

In response to the uproar Lowery and Jackson each reacted in his own style. For his part, Jackson pithily defended himself against the charge that by merely meeting with Arafat, he was supporting or endorsing PLO violence. Nearly two years later, when Jackson looked back, he said, "My talking with Mr. Arafat should not be construed as endorsing terrorism any more than Dr. King's talking with President Johnson should have been seen as endorsing U.S. terrorism in Vietnam."[34] Lowery waxed diplomatic in a statement he released on October 16, 1979. Responding to the criticisms of Jordan and others, he said that the SCLC already had heard much of what they had to say during meetings it had held with Jewish leaders. We agree with them, and with the Jewish leaders, the statement noted, that Israel must "be secure in her nationhood." Lowery's statement opined that where they differed with Rustin and Jordan was on the policies of the government of Israeli prime minister Menachem Begin. He stated that SCLC urged them to challenge the Begin government to recognize the human rights of the Palestinians.[35]

If Lowery was restrained in his comments, SCLC board member Wyatt Tee Walker was not. A writer, activist, and minister, Walker was strong-willed and ready to speak as he lived—without fear. He had helped Martin Luther King Jr. found SCLC and served as its first full-time executive director from 1960 to 1964. Walker first visited Israel and the West Bank in 1976 with a group of black clergy and described discovering things about the Arab-Israeli conflict that the mainstream media omitted. He would return frequently thereafter as a firm believer that the Palestinian people needed justice.[36] For example, even before the SCLC trip had taken place, Walker told a gathering at his congregation at the Canaan Baptist Church of Christ on August 21, 1979, "All you have to do is visit a refugee camp one time and you will know that the Palestinians are the niggers of the Middle East. The Palestinians deserve justice in the Middle East."[37]

Later that month, Walker reacted to Vernon Jordan's sharp criticism of Lowery and the SCLC trip by writing his own strong comments in an open letter to the National Urban League leader. The letter was later adopted by the Progressive National Baptist Convention, a group of black Baptists formed in 1961 by Martin Luther King Jr. and others who parted ways with more conservative Baptists. Jordan's denunciation, Walker wrote, "brought an end to the masquerade of the Urban League as a civil rights organization and of you as a civil rights leader."[38]

BLACK SUPPORT FOR SCLC AND JACKSON

A number of religious and secular black organizations jumped into the fray. While not always explicitly defending the trips and visits with Arafat, they contributed to the growing chorus of black groups demanding that blacks be included in the discussions about the nature and direction of American foreign policy, as well as adding their voices to calls for dialogue and negotiations as

the way to solve the Arab-Israeli conflict. Black religious organizations and figures adopted official stances in this direction. In fact, some weighed in shortly
before the Young affair broke out. Ralph Abernathy, for example, endorsed a
call in early 1979 for the State Department to dispatch a fact-finding mission
to the Occupied Territories to investigate allegations of violations of Palestinian human rights by Israeli security forces.[39]

The Black Theology Project also had addressed the Palestinian issue just days
before the Young affair erupted. The project was an interfaith organization that
grew out of an initiative of the National Council of Churches. It was established
in 1976 and was led by Sister Shawn Copeland, the Reverend Charles Spivey,
and the Reverend Muhammad Kenyatta. At its third national convention in
Cleveland, the group adopted a resolution on the Palestinians on August 4, 1979.
The Reverend Frederick Douglass Kirkpatrick, who was also a musician and,
before he embraced nonviolence, one of the founders of the armed civil rights
protection force called the Deacons for Defense and Justice, served as chair.
Those who attended the meeting approved a forceful resolution that equated
the Palestinians' struggle with that of oppressed blacks in southern Africa:

As black Christians committed to the fight for liberation of the oppressed whether
they be in South Africa, Israel, the occupied Arab territories, or in the U.S., we see
the essence of the struggle of the Palestinian people as the same struggle for freedom
of our Black Brothers and Sisters in southern Africa. . . . The indigenous people of
both lands have been displaced by violence or forced to live as oppressed people in
their own countries. The human rights of the indigenous people of Southern Africa
are violated because of *apartheid*, and the human rights of the indigenous Palestinian
Arabs, Christian and Moslem, are violated because of Zionism.[40]

It sounded like vintage 1960s Black Power internationalism. The resolution
also expressed support for Palestinian national independence and the "right of
return to their homeland," noting that "there can never be peace in the Middle
East until the Palestinian people can regain their inalienable rights and live as
a free people in their homeland." The theologians' statement ended with a call
for ending American support to Israel and South Africa: "Therefore, as Black
Christians in the U.S.A., we are opposed to the United States' providing aid
to South Africa and Israel as long as these two regimes violate human rights,
international laws, and those basic ethical principles enunciated in the Holy

Scriptures of Christian, Jewish, and Islamic faiths. . . . We oppose U.S. military and economic aid to Israel."[41]

More Black Christian groups affirmed their support for the Palestinian struggle as well, an interesting change inasmuch as the Nation of Islam and other Muslims had been the ones championing the Palestinians just a decade earlier. One such group was the National Black Pastors' Conference. The conference was a new group established in 1979 by William Augustus Jones, who at the time was president of the Progressive National Baptist Convention, to bring together black clergy persons from both the Protestant and Roman Catholic traditions. At the conference's first national meeting in Detroit, a five-day affair that ended on November 16, 1979, the approximately one thousand members of the clergy assembled there adopted resolutions calling for recognition of the PLO, the internationalization of Jerusalem, and condemnation of Israel's "persistent denial of human rights to the Arab inhabitants of occupied territories." They also called on Israel to refrain from bombing southern Lebanon and to withdraw from the Occupied Territories.[42]

After the conference in Detroit, the National Black Pastors' Conference decided that it, too, would dispatch a delegation to Lebanon to meet with the PLO. The group toured various PLO institutions and issued a joint statement with it in Beirut on February 14, 1980. The declaration noted that the delegation "observed striking similarities between the Palestinian refugee camps and the urban ghettos of the United States" and that it and the PLO "recognize[d] the black masses in the United States as an oppressed people." The two sides then enunciated several principles, among which were "their commitment to and solidarity in their common struggle against racism and oppression" and their desire to "condemn Israel as an international outlaw because of its repeated violations of United Nations resolutions and its support of the racist regimes in southern Africa."[43]

The groundswell of black support for Lowery and Jackson grew when secular black organizations also joined the call for a new American approach to the Palestinians and the Arab-Israeli conflict. One such organization was TransAfrica, an advocacy group established to raise awareness of Americans about Africa and the African diaspora. Established in July of 1977, TransAfrica played a leading role in the antiapartheid struggle in the United States. The group sent a letter to President Jimmy Carter after the Andrew Young Affair that stated, "We hope that the country will now seize upon this first opportunity we have had in our national discourse openly and fully to consider on their own merits the issues of the rights of the Palestinian people," as well as, it noted obliquely, "the role of whatever organizational or individual spokesmen they may freely choose to put forward to represent their interests."

TransAfrica then put forth in clear, strong terms the reasons why it believed that Americans had not dealt forthrightly with the Palestinian question in the past: "For whatever reason, Israel and its most ardent supporters have been able virtually to dictate the terms of reference of such a debate, and have allowed Israel unilaterally to compound its political and territorial ambitions with its legitimate security needs, and to define the Palestinian issue as one of refugees. Each sovereign state has a right to define its own policies, but that does not mean that Americans have to follow them slavishly, still less to finance their implementation."[44] TransAfrica's letter to Carter also offered a reasoned, politically and historically based statement of support for the PLO, even while accepting Israel's right to exist.

Another black organization contributing to the growing calls for changing American policy toward the PLO and the Middle East was the venerable NAACP. In September of 1979 the NAACP board of directors called for negotiations. Despite Benjamin Hooks's critiques of the visits made by Lowery and Jackson to the PLO headquarters, the statement noted that the United States government should not shut out or otherwise limit the participation in the peace process of any "bona fide Middle East entity"—an indirect but unmistakably obvious reference to the PLO. The NAACP also called on the Carter administration to reexamine the government's 1975 understanding with Israel that the United States would not talk to the PLO and supported self-determination and a homeland for the Palestinians.[45] This represented a sea change since the days when Roy Wilkins mounted his forceful defense of Israel at the NAACP in the 1960s. It was another example indicating that what had been considered radical thinking about the Arab-Israeli conflict among blacks in the 1960s had become more mainstream by the late 1970s.

For a few months from the late summer of 1979 through the spring of 1980, it seemed like black Americans from across the political spectrum were rushing to meet Arafat on his home turf. Some did so in solidarity with Young, some to burnish their own foreign policy credentials, some for these and other reasons. Even figures formerly associated with the Black Power movement did so, as well, although their trips generally occurred under the media radar given that the movement had largely faded from public consciousness by that time. Stokely Carmichael went to Lebanon in the summer of 1979 to meet with PLO officials. The PLO invited Black Panther Party leader Huey Newton to do so as well. Traveling in April of 1980, he, too, posed for the requisite photograph with Arafat. It was ironic that two of the most famous early Black Power supporters of the Palestinians and critics of Israel were sidelined by the media as it focused on mainstream black leaders who traveled to meet with Arafat. It was another testament to how far the American political landscape had shifted since the heady days of Black Power in 1967.

The Andrew Young Affair and the meetings with the PLO also engendered a solidly pro-Israeli, anti-PLO tour of the region on the part of at least one senior black leader. The venerable Bayard Rustin once again stepped up to the plate to take a spirited lead in Israel's defense. At age sixty-seven Rustin was still adamant not only about Israel's virtues but in his desperate need for America's blacks to support the Jewish state, reject the PLO, and thereby remain true, in his opinion, to the civil rights–era partnership with American Jews. He had just been on a two-week visit to former Nazi concentration camps in Poland and the Soviet Union, but to counteract the negative impact on both the Israeli government and American Jews that was caused by the Middle Eastern trips made by SCLC and PUSH, Rustin very quickly rounded up some black political allies and set off on his own trip—but only to Israel, not Lebanon. Shortly before departing the United States, Rustin said, "Speaking for myself, I want to make it clear to the Israelis that there are great numbers of Black people who want the United States to give Israel whatever support it needs."[46] The delegation was headed by William S. Pollard, director of the civil rights department of the powerful AFL-CIO labor union. Other delegates included the National Urban League's vice president, Ron Brown, and the NAACP's Althea Simmons. They were guests of the Histadrut, the Israeli labor federation.

This time, the Israeli leadership was only too happy to meet with the visiting black Americans, in marked contrast to its attitude toward the visits of Lowery and Jackson the previous month. The group arrived in Israel in mid-October of 1979, and Prime Minister Menachem Begin himself met with the delegation in Jerusalem on October 17. If Rustin thought his stalwart support for Israel over the years meant that Begin might be amenable to hearing the group's ideas about constructive Israeli steps toward peace, the prime minister quickly disabused him of such hopes. When the group expressed its concerns about the Israeli government's decision of a few days earlier to expand settlement building in the Occupied Territories, Begin would have none of it. He retorted, "Jewish settlements in this land are no obstacle to peace." Afterward, Pollard reaffirmed Rustin's long-standing goal by saying, "We want to cement the relationship between blacks and Jews and Israel."[47] The degree to which Rustin succeeded over the years in his struggle to forge a safe-and-sane, mainstream black identity by vigorously championing Israel was questionable and offered further evidence of the staying power of the Arab-Israeli conflict as an animating force among people of color in their efforts at forging their identity and vision of political struggle within America.

The various trips to the Middle East made by mainstream blacks in the wake of the Andrew Young Affair showed that the Arab-Israeli conflict remained a lightning rod for expressions of black grievances and concern about identity, place, and political action in America at the dawn of the 1980s. The Palestinian question provided the spark for a revival of the 1960s-era demand that blacks be able to develop and pursue their own analyses of international issues and American foreign policy questions without being challenged or held back by whites, including erstwhile liberal supporters. Just like SNCC had done more than a decade earlier, groups like the SCLC insisted in the wake of the Young affair that black Americans had just as much right to independent thinking and action in the realm of foreign affairs as any other ethnic group. If Jews could claim a stake in America's attitudes toward the Arab-Israeli conflict, then so could blacks. Nothing less than the very political identity and freedom of movement of American blacks was at stake in the drama that unfolded after Young's resignation in 1979.

Perhaps the most significant takeaway from the affair and the black responses to it was just how much understanding of the plight of the Palestinian people had moved from the radical fringes to the mainstream of black American politics since SNCC first made its case publicly twelve years earlier. Black Power was essentially dead and gone by the waning years of the Carter presidency, yet its belief that the Palestinians were a fellow people of color that deserved their support, not to mention its vision for robust black participation in foreign policy matters dealing with the Middle East, remained.

EPILOGUE

BLACK STANFORD UNIVERSITY STUDENT Kristian Davis Bailey was shocked to discover when he visited the West Bank in the summer of 2013 that Palestinians there had painted a tribute to Trayvon Martin—the black American youth shot and killed in Sanford, Florida, in February of 2012 under controversial circumstances—on the large separation wall built around the West Bank by Israeli occupation forces. Then, in August of 2014, Palestinians issued a statement of solidarity with the family of Michael Brown, a young black man shot and killed by a white police officer that month in Ferguson, Missouri. Other Palestinians began sending tweets to black protestors confronting police in Ferguson, advising them how to combat the effects of police tear gas and other practical lessons they themselves had learned from clashes with the Israeli army and border police. Like some of the black protestors in America, they were noticing the parallels between their experience with security forces and that of faraway African Americans. One young man in the West Bank village of Bil'in sent a photo showing him holding a sign reading, "The Palestinian people know what it means to be shot while unarmed because of your ethnicity."[1]

Palestinian students visited Ferguson a few months later, in November of 2014, and returned to organize events explaining the struggle of Black Americans.

A delegation of American activists associated with groups like Black Lives Matter and Dream Defenders visited the West Bank in turn in January of 2015. Kristian Davis Bailey then joined with another young black activist, Khury Petersen-Smith, in drafting a statement in November of 2015 titled "2015 Black Solidarity Statement with Palestine," which was signed by more than one thousand noted black activists, scholars, and others—including Black Lives Matter cofounder Patrisse Cullors, as well as three persons who had signed Paul Boutelle's 1970 COBATAME statement in the *New York Times* forty-five years earlier titled "An Appeal by Black Americans Against United States Support of the Zionist Government of Israel."

Bailey and Petersen-Smith were clear about the links between the African American and Palestinian experiences when they wrote the statement. "The foundation of the Israeli state came through the ethnic cleansing of Palestinians," noted Petersen-Smith. "While there are differences between Israel and the U.S., we see parallels with a country that was founded on the enslavement of black people and where anti-black racism remains at the heart of U.S. society centuries later." Baily concurred and directly referenced the example set by the 1960s black freedom struggle: "Malcolm X, Martin Luther King Jr. and the Black Panther Party taught us that internationalism is a central part of our liberation here. This statement seeks to honor the legacy of black internationalism and the historic solidarity between black and Palestinian struggles as our movements enter a new chapter."[2]

Present-day black support for the Palestinians has not been restricted to the political; it also is being seen on a cultural level. Various black rap/hip hop musicians, for example, are drawing comparisons between their own liberation struggle and that of the Palestinians. Jasiri X produced a song and video titled "Checkpoint" after he witnessed Israeli checkpoints during his January 2014 trip to the West Bank. They reminded him of how he and other blacks had to deal with the New York City Police Department's controversial "stop and frisk" policy back in the United States: "In Hebron it was very reminiscent of being a young black man in the inner city. Here you're a person of color so I'm just going to assume you are a criminal, stop you, frisk you, and assume you are doing criminal activity. It was really the same treatment I saw with Palestinians and African refugees. Automatically, if you are Palestinian I am just going to assume you are a criminal and treat you as such, especially from what I saw at checkpoints."[3]

Rappers Boots Riley and Talib Kweli are two other black artists who have come out strongly on the side of the Palestinians. At a September 2012 concert, for example, Kweli and the other half of the duo known as Black Star, Mos Def, held their fists in the air and shouted, "Let's get free just like the Palestinians." The two had been writing songs referencing the Palestinian struggle as far back as 1998. Even before that, Method Man released the song "P.L.O. Style" in November of 1994. When asked years later to explain the reference to the PLO, he stated, "They're freedom fighters and we felt like we were fighting for our freedom every day, too, where we lived at."[4] The phrase "P.L.O. Style" has even crept into urban slang as a term for an unorthodox, wild-and-crazy way of doing things.

All of these twenty-first-century examples of African Americans expressing support for the Palestinians and basing their own identity and political programs on a global anti-imperialist discourse of liberation illustrate the lasting power of the notion first articulated in the 1960s and 1970s: for blacks, Palestine was a kindred country of color struggling to be free from occupation. This conceptualization implies that if African Americans and Palestinians are "of color," then their oppressors conversely are "white." Does this contemporary conjuring up of 1960s-era expressions of a global racial divide by black activists still work today?

Aside from what these activists of color themselves may think, white American supporters of tough immigration policy, "Blue Lives Matter," and border walls might suggest that the idea of a color divide is still very much with us indeed. Whether coded or not, their present-day discourse also is racialized: whites vs. others, people of color who must be kept at bay. Some Israelis also agree. Menachem Shalev, a press officer at the Israeli consulate in New York, told an American journalist in 1986 that when dealing with American journalists, he always stressed that "we are just like you, an essentially white, European people."[5] Complaining about the influx of Muslim African migrants into Israel many years later, Interior Minister Eli Yishai stated something similar in June of 2012 when he opined that "Muslims that arrive here do not even believe that this country belongs to us, to the white man."[6] The color divide prophesied in the twentieth century by W. E. B. Du Bois and Malcolm X seems as relevant as ever, and some African Americans feel they are on the same side of that divide as the Palestinians five decades after Black Power first championed their cause in the 1960s.

Black Power and Palestine has shown that the Arab-Israeli conflict was intimately connected with how the black freedom struggle played itself out in America during the 1960s and 1970s inasmuch as black groups' stances toward that conflict reflected and deepened their own respective attitudes toward race, politics, identity, and foreign policy in America. For blacks, what position to adopt on Israel and the Palestinians at that time signified much more than just an ideological stance on a faraway foreign policy issue. It also signified how they viewed themselves and their place in America. They accordingly reacted to the Arab-Israeli conflict with a fervor that reflected a deep sensitivity to these questions.

The 1960s marked the first time that Americans heard serious anti-Israeli and pro-Palestinian viewpoints in public. The impact of this development was significant beyond questions of race in America, both in the short and long terms. The short-term impacts included deepening the connections between Black Power advocates in America and the wider anti-imperialist movements of the Global 1960s overseas. Black activists traveled to the Middle East and in return obtained the blessings and support of the PLO. Support for the Palestinians also contributed to formulation of a domestic black revolutionary culture by which blacks could portray themselves and subvert the dominant white American cultural hegemony.[7]

Black Power's pro-Palestinianism also helped heighten the friction between young black militants and their elders in the civil rights movement, whose success depended on their ability to generate mainstream liberal support, both moral and financial, for a domestic agenda that did not include dismantling the American system. Black-Jewish relations also were strained by the vocal attacks on Israel made by activists in SNCC, the Black Panther Party, and at the 1967 National Conference for New Politics in Chicago, not to mention the renewed friction that resulted from the Andrew Young Affair in 1979, which led to further intercommunal recrimination and suspicion from which black-Jewish relations have never quite recovered.

Another short-term impact was that the Palestinian Problem achieved greater visibility with the American body politic after it was first discussed publicly by Black Power advocates in the late 1960s. It quickly rose to become a marker of the revolutionary Left as opposed to liberal reformers during that tumultuous decade: those committed to what they viewed as real revolutionary change both at home and abroad saw supporting the Palestinians in their struggle against Israel and Zionism as a litmus test of true radicalism. It marked entrance into the Global 1960s by linking the domestic Left with one of the most notable Third World struggles of the time.

Longer term, African Americans' embrace of the Palestinian discourse of national liberation led to permanent changes in American political culture. By the time of the Andrew Young Affair in 1979, expressing support for the Palestinians and meeting with the PLO had become the realm of mainstream black groups like congressional officials and Christian ministers. Nor was this normalization of the Palestinian discourse of liberation restricted to blacks: white human rights activists, peace groups, and religious denominations increasingly asserted pro-Palestinian viewpoints beginning in the 1970s. Indeed, although uttering pro-Palestinian sentiments may still be controversial in the twenty-first century, the act is hardly seen as revolutionary. The fact that the Palestinian problem has remained on America's political radar in the fifty years since it was first placed there by Black Power in the 1960s stands as a testament to the staying power of this phenomenon.

Another longer-term impact has been the ongoing political backlash against this discourse of Palestinian liberation. The visceral anger first focused on Black Power positions on Israel by blacks like Bayard Rustin and by Jews of various political persuasions has never subsided. Highly organized pro-Zionist campaigns seeking to bolster Israel and its reputation in the United States emerged almost immediately in the late 1960s and continue to this day. Such efforts have included, inter alia, "monitoring" groups, academics, and activities deemed pro-Palestinian and redefining anti-Zionism as a new form of anti-Semitism. These efforts also dovetailed with the neoconservative movement that emerged in the 1970s, for which Israel has held a special place in its pantheon of virtuous states. Palestine solidarity has never been stronger in America than it is today, but the same also can be said of pro-Israeli sentiment and political activity.

The understandings of the conflict recently expressed by modern-day black Americans like Kristian Davis Bailey, Khury Petersen-Smith, Talib Kweli, and Jasiri X stem from the sentiments first articulated in the 1960s. Wyatt Tee Walker, Martin Luther King Jr.'s confidant in the Southern Christian Leadership Conference, said in 1979, "All you have to do is visit a refugee camp one time and you will know that the Palestinians are the niggers of the Middle East."[8]

The fact that more than one thousand people signed the "2015 Black Solidarity Statement with Palestine" suggests that Walker's racialized understanding of the Palestinian problem is still relevant for black American activists today. Palestine solidarity is indeed still alive among peoples of color in America who identify viscerally with the Palestinians' struggle. Palestine remains for them, as first expressed in the 1960s and 1970s, a country of color.

ACKNOWLEDGMENTS

I am indebted to a number of persons who assisted me over the course of years of researching and writing this book. I am especially grateful for the many people I interviewed. Some of them, notably Abdeen Jabara and Nick Medvecky, offered detailed recollections and went out of their way to help me by providing photographs, documents, and additional contacts. Many thanks go out to the various librarians and archival staff who worked with me in institutions in this country and abroad.

I particularly would like to acknowledge the hardworking staff of Randolph-Macon College, who do so much for the professors here for so little reward and acknowledgment in return. This includes the wonderful staff of the McGraw-Page Library, under the leadership of Director Virginia Young and, later, Nancy Falciani-White, who helped me obtain books and microfilms via interlibrary loan and otherwise assisted me. Staff members include Emily Bourne, Megan Hodge, James Murray, Scarlett Mustain, Laurie Preston, Kelli Salmon, Judee Showalter, Lynda Wright, and Lily Zhang. Outside the library I wish to thank Mimi Carter, who made countless photocopies of various drafts of the manuscript, just as student assistants Shuyan Zhan, Paige Weaver, and Tori Santiago Troutman helped me with various research assignments. Special thanks go to Brenda Woody and Princess Tunstall, who kept the history department's building in order, notably my sometimes cluttered office.

Off campus I benefited immensely from the keen talents of Kate Wahl, Leah Pennywark, Anne Fuzellier Jain, and Stephanie Adams at Stanford University Press and appreciated the comments of the anonymous peer reviewers and the copy editor, Joe Abbott. I would like to acknowledge Ma'agan and Hallel Forman; ask your father why. As always, I remain grateful to various friends and family members for their hospitality, love, and support.

Finally, I gratefully acknowledge the financial support of the Walter Williams Craigie Teaching Fund, the Rashkind Family Endowment, and the Committee on Faculty Development at Randolph-Macon College, as well as the Maurice Mednick Memorial Fellowship of the Virginia Foundation for Independent Colleges.

ABBREVIATIONS

ACOAR	American Committee on Africa Records
AJCA	American Jewish Committee Archives
AJCOA	American Jewish Committee Online Archives
APR	Papers of A. Philip Randolph
AYP	Andrew Young Papers
BRP	Bayard Rustin Papers
ECP	Eldridge Cleaver Papers
HPNC	Huey P. Newton Foundation Collection
ISA	Israel State Archives
JFP	James Forman Papers
KCOA	King Center Online Archives
K-LF	King-Levison File
NAACPP	National Association for the Advancement of Colored People Papers
SCLCM	Southern Christian Leadership Conference Microfilmed Records
SNCCP	Student Nonviolent Coordinating Committee Papers

NOTES

PROLOGUE

1. Paul Jacobs, "Watts vs. Israel: Black Nationalists and an Israeli Diplomat," *Commonweal*, March 1, 1968, 649–51, 654.

2. Stokely Carmichael and Charles V. Hamilton, *Black Power: The Politics of Liberation in America* (New York: Vintage, 1967), 179.

3. The text of the speech is available in George Breitman, ed., *Malcolm X Speaks: Selected Speeches and Statements* (New York: Grove, 1990), 3–17; and at the History Is a Weapon website: www.historyisaweapon.com/defcon1/malcgrass.html.

CHAPTER 1

1. Regarding the idea that black Americans were permanent exiles, Malcolm X said in 1964, "Everything that came out of Europe, every blue-eyed thing, is already an American. And as long as you and I have been over here, we aren't Americans yet." Lewis V. Baldwin and Amiri YaSin Al-Hadid, *Between Cross and Crescent: Christian and Muslim Perspectives on Malcolm and Martin* (Gainesville: University Press of Florida, 2002), 317.

2. Stokely Carmichael (Kwame Ture), *Stokely Speaks: From Black Power to Pan-Africanism* (Chicago: Lawrence Hill, 2007), 134–35.

3. See Yvonne D. Newsome, "Transnationalism in Black-Jewish Conflict: A Study of Global Identification Among Established Americans," *Race and Society* 4 (2001): 89–107.

4. Louis A. DeCaro Jr. *On the Side of My People: A Religious Life of Malcolm X* (New York: New York University Press, 1996), 150, 153; E. U. Essien-Udom, *Black Nationalism: A Search for an Identity in America* (1962; Chicago: University of Chicago Press, 1995), 238; C. Eric Lincoln, *The Black Muslims in America* (Boston: Beacon, 1961), 26, 170.

5. *New York Amsterdam News*, May 3, 1958, quoted in Lincoln, *Black Muslims in America*, 172, 96; see also the *Los Angeles Herald Dispatch*, April 10, 1958, cited in Karl Evanzz, *The Messenger: The Rise and Fall of Elijah Muhammad* (New York: Pantheon, 1999), 185–86; and Manning Marable, *Malcolm X: A Life of Reinvention* (New York: Viking, 2011), 149n517.

6. There is practically nothing in the historical record about Malcolm's trip to the holy city; I could find only one reference, in a file that the Federal Bureau of Investigation (FBI) kept on Malcolm X. See FBI File 100-399321 (Malcolm X Little), "FBI New

York Office Report," May 17, 1960, https://vault.fbi.gov/malcolm-little-malcolm-x/
malcolm-little-malcolm-x-hq-file-05-of-27.

7. FBI File 105-24822, sec. 10 (Elijah Muhammad), document: SAC, WFO to Director, FBI, memorandum, June 1, 1965, https://vault.fbi.gov/elijah-muhammad/elijah-muhammad -part-10-of-20/view.

8. Quoted in George Breitman, ed., *Malcolm X Speaks: Selected Speeches and Statements* (New York: Grove, 1990), 47.

9. Ibid., 48, 49–50.

10. Ibid., 5, 10.

11. Ibid., 36.

12. *Pittsburgh Courier*, August 15, 1959, cited in Lincoln, *Black Muslims in America*, 225.

13. Lincoln, *Black Muslims in America*, 166.

14. "Playboy Interview: Malcolm X," *Playboy*, May 1963, 53–63.

15. Malcolm X, *The Autobiography of Malcolm X*, with the assistance of Alex Haley (New York: Ballantine, 1973), 345; Marable, *Malcolm X*, 310.

16. *Egyptian Gazette*, August 23, 1964, http://malcolmxfiles.blogspot.com/2013/07/ speech-to-second-african-summit.html.

17. The Egyptians had maintained a military occupation of Gaza since 1948 but were willing to let him travel there just as they earlier had arranged for the famous Argentine revolutionary figure Ernesto "Che" Guevara to visit Gaza in June of 1959, no doubt in the hopes that it would further hone their pro-Palestinian sentiments.

18. Malcolm X Collection: Papers, 1948–1965, box 5, folder 14: Public Meetings, 1963–64 (microfilm roll 5), document: typed copy of Malcolm's travel diary, entries for Sept. 4–6, 1964, New York Public Library, Schomburg Center for Research in Black Culture.

19. Muhammad Ahmad (Maxwell Stanford Jr.), *We Will Return in the Whirlwind: Black Radical Organizations, 1960–1975* (Chicago: Charles H. Kerr, 2007), 31.

20. Malcolm X, "Zionist Logic," *Egyptian Gazette*, Sept. 17, 1964.

21. Ibid.

22. Ibid.

23. Breitman, *Malcolm X Speaks*, 89.

24. Ibid., 130.

25. Julian Bond, "SNCC: What We Did," at *Like the Dew*, April 27, 2010, http://like thedew.com/2010/04/27/sncc-what-we-did.

26. Breitman, *Malcolm X Speaks*, 85.

27. *The Student Nonviolent Coordinating Committee Papers, 1959–1972* (Sanford, NC: Microfilming Corporation of America, 1981), microfilm (hereafter SNCCP): Subgroup A: Atlanta Office, 1959–1972, ser. 3, Staff Meetings, 1960–68, reel 3, sec. 1: Minutes, Aug. 1, '60–Oct. 30, '68, "Press Release" (May 1967).

28. Casey King and Linda Barrett Osborne, *Oh, Freedom! Kids Talk About the Civil Rights Movement with the People Who Made It Happen* (New York: Alfred A. Knopf, 1997), 94–96.

29. Courtland Cox, telephone interview by the author, Oct. 15, 2015.

30. Stokely Carmichael, with Ekwueme Michael Thelwell, *Ready for Revolution: The Life and Struggles of Stokely Carmichael (Kwame Ture)* (New York: Scribner, 2003), 558–59 (emphasis in original).

31. Don Jelinek, "SNCC: Vietnam, Israel, & Violence," interview by Bruce Hartford, 2005, www.crmvet.org/nars/jelinek.htm#snccvietnam.

32. American Jewish Committee, *Arab Appeals to American Public Opinion* (New York: American Jewish Committee, Institute of Human Relations, 1969), 9.

33. SNCCP, Subgroup A: Atlanta Office, 1959–1972, ser. 3, Staff Meetings, 1960–68, reel 3, sec. 1: Minutes, Aug. 1, '60–Oct. 30, '68, "Research Department to Staff" (June 5, 1967).

34. Clayborne Carson, "Blacks and Jews in the Civil Rights Movement: The Case of SNCC," in *Bridges and Boundaries: African Americans and American Jews*, ed. Jack Salzman, Adina Back, and Gretchen Sullivan Sorin (New York: George Braziller, in association with the Jewish Museum, 1992), 42–43.

35. SNCCP, Subgroup A: Atlanta Office, 1959–1972, ser. 3, Staff Meetings, 1960–68, reel 3, sec. 1: Minutes, Aug. 1, '60–Oct. 30, '68, "National Office Report" (May 5, 1967), by Fay D. Bellamy.

36. Carmichael, *Ready for Revolution*, 558–59.

37. Two such SNCC staffers were Kathleen Neal and Philip Hutchings. See the interview with Kathleen Neal Cleaver, Sept. 16, 2011, conducted for the Civil Rights History Project under contract to the Smithsonian Institution's National Museum of African American History and Culture: https://cdn.loc.gov/service/afc/afc2010039/afc2010039_crhp0051_cleaver_transcript/afc2010039_crhp0051_cleaver_transcript.pdf. See also the interview with Philip Hutchings, Sept. 1, 2011, conducted for the same project: https://cdn.loc.gov/service/afc/afc2010039/afc2010039_crhp0042_hutchings_transcript/afc2010039_crhp0042_hutchings_transcript.pdf.

38. Karen Edmonds Spellman, telephone interview by the author, Sept. 24, 2015.

39. Ibid.

40. Carmichael, *Ready for Revolution*, 560.

41. James Forman, *The Making of Black Revolutionaries: A Personal Account* (New York: Macmillan, 1972), 494.

42. Ibid., 494–96.

43. Ibid., 496 (emphasis in original).

44. "The Palestine Problem: Test Your Knowledge," *SNCC Newsletter* 1, no. 2 (June–July 1967): 4.

45. Ibid., 5.

46. Ibid.

47. Ibid. (all-caps preserved from original).

48. Ibid.

49. Philip Hutchings, interview (see note 37 above).

50. See Cynthia A. Young, *Soul Power: Culture, Radicalism, and the Making of a U.S. Third World Left* (Durham, NC: Duke University Press, 2006); and Melani McAlister, *Epic Encounters: Culture, Media, and U.S. Interests in the Middle East, 1945–2000* (Berkeley: University of California Press, 2001).

51. McAlister, *Epic Encounters*, 115; Newsome, "Transnationalism in Black-Jewish Conflict," 89–107.

52. E. U. Essien-Udom, "From *Black Nationalism: A Search for Identity*," in *Racism: A Casebook*, ed. Frederick R. Lapides and David J. Burrows (New York: Thomas Y. Crowell,

1971), 167. Essien-Udom's *Black Nationalism: A Search for Identity* was originally published by the University of Chicago Press in 1962.

53. Frantz Fanon, *The Wretched of the Earth*, trans. Constance Farrington (New York: Grove, 1968), 213.

54. Simon Hall, "On the Tail of the Panther: Black Power and the 1967 Convention of the National Conference for New Politics," *Journal of American Studies* 37, no. 1 (2003): 61; Swarthmore College Peace Collection, Papers of David McReynolds, ser. 1, box 12, Business Correspondence, Aug. 1967 (3), advertisement in *New Politics News* (emphasis in original).

55. Hall, "On the Tail of the Panther," 67.

56. The committee had been formed in June of 1967 by an Old Left Marxist party, the Workers World Party. See Mike Rubin, *An Israeli Worker's Answer to M. S. Arnoni* (New York: Ad Hoc Committee on the Middle East, 1968).

57. Carson, "Blacks and Jews in the Civil Rights Movement," 45.

58. Sid Lens, "The New Politics Convention: Confusion and Promise," *New Politics* 6, no. 1 (1967): 10.

59. American Jewish Committee Archives, Bertram H. Gold Executive Papers, Black-Jewish Relations File (1967), document: King to Abram, Sept. 28, 1967.

60. Federal Bureau of Investigation, *The Martin Luther King, Jr., FBI File*, pt. 2, *The King-Levison File*, ed. August Meier and John H. Bracey Jr. (Frederick, MD: University Publications of America, 1987), microfilm: reel 7, 602, conversation of Sept. 19, 1967, and reel 7, 610, conversation of Sept. 21, 1967.

61. Frank Lynn, "New Left Hits Israel, Viet War, Draft," *Newsday*, Sept. 5, 1967.

CHAPTER 2

1. Gene Roberts, "S.N.C.C. Charges Israel Atrocities," *New York Times*, August 15, 1967.

2. "Anti-Semitic Attack in Organ of Extremist Negro Organization Evokes Jewish Protests," *Jewish Telegraphic Agency*, August 16, 1967, 1, http://pdfs.jta.org/1967/1967-08-16_158.pdf.

3. American Jewish Committee (AJC) online archives (hereafter AJCOA), Subject Files Collection, file: Race Relations/Jewish-Negro Relations, Correspondence and Reports on Jewish-Negro Relations (6), document: "Jewish Contributions to Negro Welfare," Feb. 27, 1942.

4. See, e.g., James Baldwin, "The Harlem Ghetto, Winter 1948: The Vicious Circle of Frustration and Prejudice," *Commentary*, Feb. 1948, 165–70.

5. A June 1958 report drawn up for the American Jewish Committee about black attitudes toward Jews in Newark, New Jersey, offers an insightful and early examination of these complaints. See AJCOA, AJC Subject Files Collection, file: Race Relations/Jewish-Negro Relations, Correspondence and Reports on Jewish-Negro Relations (6), document: Kellner to Dawidowicz, June 9, 1958.

6. C. Eric Lincoln, *The Black Muslims in America* (Boston: Beacon, 1961), 167.

7. James Baldwin, "Negroes Are Anti-Semitic Because They Are Anti-White," *New York Times*, April 9, 1967.

8. AJCOA, file: The Many Faces of Anti-Semitism, 1967, document [book]: Rose Feitelson and George Salomon, *The Many Faces of Anti-Semitism*, foreword by Nathan Glazer (n.p.: American Jewish Committee, 1967), 29.

9. See Baraka's own retrospective explanation of some of these poems in "Confessions of a Former Anti-Semite," *Village Voice*, Dec. 17–23, 1980, 18–22.

10. Baldwin, "Negroes Are Anti-Semitic."

11. Ibid.

12. Norman Podhoretz, "My Negro Problem—and Ours," *Commentary*, Feb. 1, 1963, 93–101.

13. Seymour Martin Lipset, "'The Socialism of Fools': The Left, the Jews, and Israel," *Encounter*, Dec. 1969, 31.

14. Ibid.

15. Karen Edmonds Spellman, telephone interview by the author, Sept. 24, 2015.

16. Charles Cobb Jr., telephone interview by the author, Sept. 16, 2015.

17. Courtland Cox, telephone interview by the author, Oct. 15, 2015.

18. Roberts, "S.N.C.C. Charges Israel Atrocities."

19. *The Student Nonviolent Coordinating Committee Papers, 1959–1972* (Sanford, NC: Microfilming Corporation of America, 1981), microfilm (hereafter SNCCP): Subgroup B: New York, ser. 2, International Affairs Commission, reel 51, sec. 36: Middle East Crisis, document: "The Big Lie Gets Bigger and Dirtier."

20. *Chicago Daily Defender*, August 17, 1967, cited in Keith P. Feldman, "Racing the Question: Israel/Palestine and U.S. Imperial Culture" (PhD diss., University of Washington, 2008), 185.

21. SNCCP, Subgroup B: New York, ser. 2, International Affairs Commission, reel 51, sec. 36: Middle East Crisis, document: "The Middle-East Crisis." This press release is also found in United States Library of Congress, James Forman Papers (JFP), Student Nonviolent Coordinating Committee file, 1950–2003, box 45, file: Press, General, 1961–68.

22. SNCCP, Subgroup B: New York, ser. 2, International Affairs Commission, reel 51, sec. 36: Middle East Crisis, document: "The Middle-East Crisis." This press release is also found in JFP, Student Nonviolent Coordinating Committee file, 1950–2003, box 45, file: Press, General, 1961–68.

23. Clayborne Carson, "Blacks and Jews in the Civil Rights Movement: The Case of SNCC." In *Bridges and Boundaries: African Americans and American Jews*, ed. Jack Salzman, Adina Back, and Gretchen Sullivan Sorin (New York: George Braziller, in association with the Jewish Museum, 1992), 43; see also Clayborne Carson "Blacks and Jews in the Civil Rights Movement: The Case of SNCC," in Maurianne Adams and John Bracey, *Strangers & Neighbors: Relations Between Blacks & Jews in the United States* (Amherst: University of Massachusetts Press, 1999), 583.

24. Douglas Robinson, "New Carmichael Trip," *New York Times*, August 19, 1967.

25. H. Rap Brown, *Die Nigger Die!* (New York: Dial, 1969), 44.

26. Robinson, "New Carmichael Trip."

27. "Anti-Semitic Attack in Organ of Extremist Negro Organization Evokes Jewish Protests," Jewish Telegraphic Agency, August 16, 1967, www.jta.org/1967/08/16/archive/anti-semitic-attack-in-organ-of-extremist-negro-organization-evokes-jewish-protests.

28. "How Racists, Black and White, Used Arab Propaganda Sources," *Facts* 17, no. 5 (1967): 421–32.

29. *Do You Know? Twenty Basic Questions About the Palestine Problem* (Beirut: Palestine Liberation Organization Research Center, 1965).

30. Izzat Tannous, *The Enraging Story of Palestine and Its People* (New York: Palestine Liberation Organization, 1965).

31. SNCCP, Subgroup B: New York, ser. 2, International Affairs Commission, reel 51, sec. 36: Middle East Crisis, document: unsigned and undated memorandum.

32. SNCCP, Subgroup A: Atlanta Office, 1959–1972, ser. 4, Executive Secretary Files, reel 11, "Stanley Wise," sec. 424: SNCC Press Releases, 1/27/67–3/15/70, document: "Suggested Response to Questions Dealing with SNCC and Israel."

33. Editor's note, *SNCC Newsletter* (Sept.–Oct. 1967).

34. Mary Hamilton, "SNCC Leader Asks for Guns," *National Guardian*, Sept. 9, 1967.

35. Editorial, "SNCC and the Arab-Israeli Conflict," *The Movement* 3, no. 9 (Sept. 1967): 2.

36. Junebug Jabo Jones, "The Mid-East and the Liberal Reaction," *SNCC Newsletter* (Sept.–Oct. 1967): 5–6.

37. Editorial, "SNCC and the Arab-Israeli Conflict."

38. Julius Lester, *SNCC Newsletter*, quoted in the *Atlanta Constitution*, Dec. 28, 1967, according to an FBI report of May 14, 1968: FBI file 100-6488 (p. 74 of 102), https://archive .org/stream/StudentNonviolentCoordinatingCommitteeSNCCFBIFiles/Student%20Nonvio lent%20Coordinating%20Committee%20%28SNCC%29%20FBI%20FILES/sncc2b#page/ n73/mode/2up/search/atlanta+constitution.

39. SNCCP, Subgroup B: New York, ser. 2, International Affairs Commission, reel 51, sec. 36: Middle East Crisis, document: "The Big Lie Gets Bigger and Dirtier."

40. Editorial, "SNCC and the Arab-Israeli Conflict."

41. Dorothy Zellner, telephone interview by the author, Feb. 28, 2012.

42. Cleveland Sellers, *The River of No Return: The Autobiography of a Black Militant and the Life and Death of SNCC* (Jackson: University Press of Mississippi, 1990), 203.

43. "Selected Racial Developments and Disturbances," Dec. 1, 1967, FBI document reproduced online in Gale Cengage's Declassified Documents Reference System, https:// www.gale.com/c/us-declassified-documents-online (subscription required).

44. Sellers, *The River of No Return*, 203.

45. Stokely Carmichael, with Ekwueme Michael Thelwell, *Ready for Revolution: The Life and Times of Stokely Carmichael (Kwame Ture)* (New York: Scribner, 2003), 560–61.

46. James Forman, *The Making of Black Revolutionaries: A Personal Account* (New York: Macmillan, 1972), 496–97.

47. Stokely Carmichael [Kwame Ture], *Stokely Speaks: From Black Power to Pan Africanism* (Chicago: Lawrence Hill, 2007), 199.

48. CIA memorandum, Nov. 1, 1967, reproduced in Gale Cengage Declassified Documents Reference System online, www.gale.com/c/us-declassified-documents-online (subscription required).

49. JFP, box 18, Correspondence, Nov.-Dec. 1967, document: Carmichael to "Black Brother" [James Forman?], Sept. 1, 1967.

50. CIA memorandum, Nov. 1, 1967, reproduced in Gale Cengage Declassified Documents Reference System online, www.gale.com/c/us-declassified-documents-online (subscription required). See also *National Guardian*, Sept. 16, 1967.

51. Robert G. Weisbord, *Bittersweet Encounter: The Afro-Americans and the American Jews* (Westport, CT: Negro Universities Press, 1970), 101.

52. Randa Khalidi al-Fattal, interview by the author, Beirut, Lebanon, June 24, 2012.

53. Carmichael, *Stokely Speaks*, 161.

54. JFP, box 18, Correspondence, Nov.-Dec. 1967, document: Carmichael to Minor, Oct. 25, 1967.

55. Ibid., document: Carmichael to Ethel [Minor], Sept. 24, 1967 (emphasis in original).

56. "Drawing Lessons: H. Rap Brown and Stokely Carmichael Addresses at Newton Rally." Transcript of Feb. 17, 1968, speeches based on the sound recording of the Pacifica Radio/UC Berkeley Social Activism Sound Recording Project, www.lib.berkeley.edu/MRC/carmichael.html.

57. Carmichael, *Stokely Speaks*, 139, 143.

58. Forman, *The Making of Black Revolutionaries*, 494.

59. AJCOA, Bertram H. Gold Executive Papers, Black Manifesto File (1967), document: "Total Control as the Only Solution to the Economic Problems of Black People" (April 26, 1969).

60. James Forman, *1967: High Tide of Black Resistance* (n.p: n.p., [1967?]), 1.

61. Forman, *The Making of Black Revolutionaries*, 496–97.

62. Frantz Fanon, *The Wretched of the Earth*, trans. Constance Farrington (New York: Grove, 1968), 36.

CHAPTER 3

1. *National Association for the Advancement of Colored People Papers* (hereafter NAACPP), pt. 28, *Special Subject Files, 1966–1970: Series A: "Africa" through "Poor People's Campaign"* (Bethesda, MD: University Publications of America, 2001), microfilm: reel 21, group 4, ser. A, Administrative File, General Office File, group 4, box A-44, Leagues and Organizations, Con–Cu [1966–1969], document: Decter to "Dear Friend," May 31, 1967; ibid., Wilkins to Decter, June 1, 1967.

2. Ibid., reel 14, group 4, ser. A, Administrative File, General Office File, group 4, box A-36, Israel, 1967, document: "Special Notice, Israel-Arab Dispute."

3. Ibid., documents: Wilkin's telegram, June 6, 1967; "Special Notice" (n.d.); Darden to Wilkins, telegram, June 7, 1967; "Replies Received re Poll of Entire Board" (n.d.). I could not locate a statement in the historical record.

4. Malcolm X, "The Black Revolution (April 8, 1964)," http://malcolmxfiles.blogspot .ca/2013/07/the-black-revolution-april-8-1964.html.

5. NAACPP, reel 14, group 4, ser. A, Administrative File, General Office File, group 4, box A-36, Israel, 1967, document: Draft statement on the War.

6. American Jewish Congress, *Israel, Africa, Colonialism and Racism: A Reply to Certain Slanders* (New York: American Jewish Congress, Commission on International Affairs, 1967), 11.

7. NAACPP, pt. 28: Special Subject Files, 1966–1970, reel 14, group 4, ser. A, Administrative Files, General Office File, group 4, box A-36, Israel, 1967, document: Wilkins to Rittenberg, July 18, 1967.

8. Ibid., reel 15, group 4, ser. A, Administrative Files, General Office File, group 4, box A-37, Jews, 1966–1969, document: "Statement by NAACP Executive Director Roy Wilkins," August 17, 1967.

9. "Prejudiced Negroes Scored by Wilkins," *New York Times*, Nov. 11, 1967.

10. Kathleen Teltsch, "S.N.C.C. Criticized for Israel Stand; Rights Leaders Score Attack on Jews as 'Anti-Semitism,'" *New York Times*, August 16, 1967.

11. *Israel Horizons and Labour Israel* 17, no. 7 (August–September 1969): 17–18. The journal was published by Americans for Progressive Israel—Hashomer Hatzair.

12. "Whitney Young Rejects Myth of Arab-Black Amity; Calls for U.S. Aid to Israel," Jewish Telegraphic Agency, Nov. 2, 1970, www.jta.org/1970/11/02/archive/whitney-young-rejects-myth-of-arab-black-amity-calls-for-u-s-aid-to-israel.

13. Thomas A. Johnson, "McKissick Derides Nonviolent Ghetto Protests," *New York Times*, August 18, 1967.

14. "CORE Executive Repudiates 'New Politics' Attack on Israel," Jewish Telegraphic Agency, Sept. 7, 1967, www.jta.org/1967/09/07/archive/core-executive-repudiates-new-politics-attack-on-israel.

15. *Long Beach (CA) Press Telegram*, Feb. 14, 1969.

16. *Black Panther*, Feb. 28, 1970.

17. C. Gerald Fraser, "CORE Head Assails Arab Guerrillas," *New York Times*, Sept. 17, 1970.

18. Daniel Levine, *Bayard Rustin and the Civil Rights Movement* (New Brunswick, NJ: Rutgers University Press, 1999), 225.

19. David McReynolds, telephone interview by the author, Dec. 20, 2010.

20. Ibid.

21. Eugene Guerrero, telephone interview by the author, May 27, 2011.

22. Teltsch, "S.N.C.C. Criticized for Israel Stand."

23. "Jacques Torczyner and Rep. Podell Assail US and French Middle East Policies," Jewish Telegraphic Agency, Jan. 25, 1970, www.jta.org/1970/01/26/archive/jacques-torczyner-and-rep-podell-assail-us-and-french-middle-east-policies.

24. *The Bayard Rustin Papers*, ed. John H. Bracey Jr. and August Meier (Frederick, MD: University Publications of America, 1988), microfilm (hereafter BRP): Subject Files, reel 15: Black Americans for U.S. Support to Israel, 1970 ad—Pre-BASIC, document: Randolph letter, June 12, 1970; BRP, Subject Files, reel 15: Black Americans for U.S. Support to Israel, 1970 ad—Pre-BASIC, document: "Black Americans Urge Support to Israel," press release, June 26, 1970.

25. "An Appeal by Black Americans for United States Support to Israel," *New York Times*, June 28, 1970, advertisement.

26. Ibid. (emphasis in original).

27. Ibid.

28. BRP, Subject File, reel 18: Jews and Anti-Semitism, document: "Israel: A Beleaguered Bastion of Democracy and Socialism" (emphasis in original).

29. Henry M. Winston, "Black Americans and the Middle East Conflict," *World Marxist Review*, Nov. 1970, 13.

30. BRP, Subject File, reel 14, Black Americans for U.S. Support to Israel, Subgroup: Support Letters [1970], document: Kenen to Rustin, July 1, 1970.

31. BRP, Subject Files, reel 14, Black Americans for U.S. Support to Israel, Subgroup: Golda Meir [1970], document: Rustin to Meir, July 7, 1970.

32. "Lewis of SNCC Angered over Pro-Zionist Ad," *Muhammad Speaks*, July 24, 1970.

33. BRP, reel 14, Black Americans for U.S. Support to Israel, Subgroup: Correspondence [1970], document: Rustin to Silberman, Sept. 21, 1970; "Black Leaders Muddy Middle East Waters," *San Francisco Sun Reporter*, July 18, 1970, repr. in *Daily World*, July 28, 1970.

34. BRP, Subject Files, box 9, reel 16, Black Americans for U.S. Support to Israel, Subgroup: Hostile Letters—Israeli Ad, document: Browne to BASIC, June 29, 1970.

35. Ibid., document: Grimes and Nixon to Rustin, n.d.

36. *St. Louis American*, August 13, 1970 (emphasis in original); text found in *Black World* 19, no. 12 (1970): 40–41. It is also found in BRP, Subject File, reel 15, Black Americans for U.S. Support to Israel [1970], Subfile: Ad—Pre-BASIC.

37. "An Appeal to Reason: A Message to the Negroes Who Support Israel," *Blacknews* 1, no. 18 (1970): 11–12.

38. BRP, Subject Files, box 9, reel 16, Black Americans for U.S. Support to Israel, Subgroup: Hostile Letters—Israeli Ad, document: Harlem Council for Economic Development, Bulletin no. 224 (July 4, 1970).

CHAPTER 4

1. Federal Bureau of Investigation, *The Martin Luther King, Jr., FBI File*, pt. 2, *The King-Levison File* (hereafter K-LF), edited by August Meier and John H. Bracey Jr. (Frederick, MD: University Publications of America, 1987), microfilm: reel 7, 447–52, conversation of July 24, 1967.

2. Ibid.

3. Clayborne Carson, senior ed., *The Papers of Martin Luther King, Jr.*, vol. 6, *Advocate of the Social Gospel, September 1948–March 1963*, ed. Susan Carson, Susan Englander, Troy Jackson, and Gerald L. Smith (Berkeley: University of California Press, 2007), 323.

4. For an excerpt of the speech see "Martin Luther King's Last Speech: 'I've Been to the Mountaintop,'" www.youtube.com/watch?v=Oehry1JC9Rk.

5. Vicken Kalbian, interview by the author, Winchester, VA, July 14, 2011.

6. Ibid.

7. *Time*, Feb. 18, 1957.

8. Dr. Kalbian would not indicate what ailment was afflicting King, nor did I ask him. When relating the story, however, he mentioned that most of the American tourists and dignitaries he treated in Jerusalem were suffering from various sorts of travelers' ailments.

9. Kalbian, interview.

10. Clayborne Carson, senior ed., *The Papers of Martin Luther King, Jr.*, vol. 5, *Threshold of a New Decade, January 1959–December 1960*, ed. Tenisha Armstrong, Susan Carson, Adrienne Clay, and Kieran Taylor (Berkeley: University of California Press, 2005), 169, 176.

11. Ibid., 169–76.

12. *Records of the Southern Christian Leadership Conference, 1954–1970* (microfilm) (hereafter SCLCM) (Bethesda, MD: University Publications of America, 1995), pt. 1, Records of the President's Office, ser. 1, Correspondence, 1958–1968, subseries 3, Secondary Correspondence, 1958, 1960–1967, reel 9, 12:27, Sept. 1964, document: Krech to King, Oct. 9, 1964.

13. Israel, Prime Minister's Office, Israel State Archives (hereafter ISA), file RG 93.8/MFA/6531/8, document: Dover to Bar-On, August 14, 1962.

14. ISA, file RG 93.8/MFA/6531/8, document: Ilan to King, Feb. 27, 1963; see also Marc Schneier, "Remembering Martin Luther King's Ties to Israel," *Chicago Jewish News*, Jan. 15, 2010.

15. ISA, file RG 93.8/MFA/6531/8, documents: Harmon to King, March 30, 1965; Engel to King, June 2, 1965; King to Engel, July 12, 1965. See also SCLCM, pt. 1, Records of the President's

Office, ser. 1, Correspondence, 1958–1968, subseries 1, Primary Correspondence, 1958–1960, reel 1, 2:6, April-May 1966; Harman to King, May 19, 1966; and SCLCM, pt. 2, Records of the Executive Director and Treasurer, subgroup 2, Executive Director, ser. 4, Andrew Young, subseries 1, Correspondence, reel 7, 42:6, American Jewish Committee—Israel Trip, 1966–67.

16. The King Center online archives (hereafter KCOA), Fortson to King, June 29, 1966; Draft letter by Ray, April 28, 1967; press release: "The Martin Luther King Holy Land Pilgrimage," May 15, 1967; pamphlet: "Dr. Martin Luther King, Jr., Invites YOU to Join Him on a Pilgrimage to the Holy Land in November 1967." The latter pamphlet can also be found at Emory University, Robert W. Woodruff Library, Southern Christian Leadership Conference Records, Printed Material, Printed Material by SCLC, subseries 17.1, box 798, folder 6.

17. SCLCM, pt. 2, Records of the Executive Director and Treasurer, subgroup 2, Executive Director, ser. 4, Andrew Young, subseries 1, Correspondence, reel 7, 42:6, American Jewish Committee—Israel Trip, 1966–67, documents: Engel to Young, June 8, 1966, and Dec. 12, 1966, itinerary.

18. Vicken Kalbian, interview by the author, Winchester, VA, May 21, 2011.

19. Ibid; SCLCM, pt. 2, Records of the Executive Director and Treasurer, subgroup 2, Executive Director, ser. 4, Andrew Young, subseries 1, Correspondence, reel 7, 42:6, American Jewish Committee—Israel Trip, 1966–67, document: Young to King, Dec. 12, 1966; see also K-LF, reel 6, 436, conversation of Dec. 1, 1966.

20. K-LF, reel 6, 412–13, conversation of Nov. 23, 1966.

21. Ibid., 434–37, conversation of Dec. 1, 1966.

22. KCOA, document: Burns to King, Jan. 23, 1967.

23. Ibid., documents: Ray to "Dear Friend," July 17, 1967; transcript of tape recording with Mr. Hanna Nazzal, June 21, 1967.

24. Silberman's group placed a second pro-Israeli advertisement in the *New York Times* three days later.

25. Americans for Democracy in the Middle East, "The Moral Responsibility in the Middle East," *New York Times*, June 4, 1967 (advertisement).

26. Murray Friedman, with the assistance of Peter Binzen, *What Went Wrong? The Creation and Collapse of the Black-Jewish Alliance* (New York: Free Press, 1995), 250–51; K-LF, reel 7, 287, 290, conversation of June 6, 1967.

27. K-LF, reel 7, 290, conversation of June 6, 1967.

28. United States Department of Justice, Federal Bureau of Investigation (FBI) online archives, file 100-392452, document: Director, FBI to Attorney General, Sept. 22, 1967, 2B; file 100-111181, document: summary of telephone conversations held by Stanley Levison; K-LF, reel 7, 295–99, conversation of June 8, 1967; K-LF, reel 7, 309, conversation of June 11, 1967.

29. K-LF, reel 6, 435, conversation of Dec. 1, 1966.

30. K-LF, reel 7, 295, conversation of June 8, 1967.

31. KCOA, draft of telegram by H. Wachtel, June 18, 1967.

32. KCOA, "MLK Interview," *Issues and Answers*, ABC, June 18, 1967.

33. K-LF, reel 7, 274, conversation of May 31, 1967; K-LF, reel 7, 291, conversation of June 6, 1967.

34. K-LF, reel 7, 333, conversation of June 15, 1967.

35. K-LF, reel 17, 447–52, conversation of July 24, 1967.

36. KCOA, Burns to King, Jan. 23, 1967; King to Ray, Sept. 6, 1967; King to Ben Ari, Sept. 22, 1967.

37. K-LF, reel 7, 544, conversation of August 24, 1967. Like fellow *Ramparts* co-owner Martin Peretz, Russell soon sold his shares in the magazine because he was angry that an editorial the magazine ran was not pro-Israeli enough for his taste.

38. K-LF, reel 7, 290–91, conversation of June 6, 1967.

39. AJCOA, Bertram H. Gold Executive Papers, Black-Jewish Relations File (1967), document: King to Abram, Sept. 28, 1967 (emphasis in original).

40. KCOA, document: "Anti-Semitism, Israel, and SCLC: A Statement on Press Distortions" (1967) (emphases in original).

41. KCOA, document: Walker to King, August 24, 1967. Walker later shifted his allegiance and became quite pro-Palestinian.

42. Quoted in Marshall Frady, *Jesse: The Life and Pilgrimage of Jesse Jackson* (New York: Random House, 1996), 347.

43. James Washington, ed., *A Testament of Hope: The Essential Writings and Speeches of Martin Luther King, Jr.* (New York: Harper One, 1990), 670–71.

44. Fadi Kiblawi and Will Youmans, "Desperation and Drastic Measures: The Use and Abuse of Martin Luther King Jr. by Israel's Apologists," *Counterpunch*, Jan. 17–18, 2004, http://willzuzak.ca/lp/morgan/morgan01.html. See also the January 22, 2002, statement issued by the pro-Israeli group CAMERA, the Committee for Accuracy in Middle East Reporting: www.camera.org/index.asp?x_article=369&x_context=8. The letter allegedly written by King is found in Marc Schneier, *Shared Dreams: Martin Luther King, Jr. and the Jewish Community* (Woodstock, VT: Jewish Lights, 1999).

CHAPTER 5

1. Askia Muhammad Touré, "A Song in Blood and Tears," *Negro Digest/Black World*, Nov. 1971, 20.

2. Emory Douglas, "On Revolutionary Culture," in *New Black Voices: An Anthology of Contemporary Afro-American Literature*, ed. Abraham Chapman (New York: Penguin, 1972), 490.

3. William L. Van Deburg, *New Day in Babylon: The Black Power Movement and American Culture, 1965–1975* (Chicago: University of Chicago Press, 1992), 27.

4. For treatments of the Black Arts Movement see Amy Abugo Ongiri, *Spectacular Blackness: The Cultural Politics of the Black Power Movement and the Search for a Black Aesthetic* (Charlottesville: University of Virginia Press, 2010); and James Edward Smethhurst, *The Black Arts Movement: Literary Nationalism in the 1960s and 1970s* (Chapel Hill: University of North Carolina Press, 2006).

5. William Jelani Cobb, ed., *The Essential Harold Cruse: A Reader* (New York: Palgrave, 2002), 76–77.

6. Harold Cruse, *Rebellion or Revolution?* (New York: William Morrow, 1968), 75.

7. Cobb, *The Essential Harold Cruse*, 83 (emphasis in original).

8. He later added *Imamu*, the Kiswahili variant of the Arabic *imam* as his title, thereby becoming Imamu Amiri Baraka.

9. Charles Anderson, "Finger Pop'in," in *Black Fire: An Anthology of Afro-American Writing*, ed. Amiri Baraka and Larry Neal (1968; Baltimore: Black Classic Press, 2007). The

"monster" that was put on the stage and used by Israel to buy bombs to use against Egypt was Nazi war criminal Adolph Eichmann, who was captured by Israeli secret agents in Argentina in May of 1960 and put on trial in Israel.

10. *Unity and Struggle,* Oct.–Dec. 1974; *Unity and Struggle* Nov. 1975.

11. The establishment by SNCC of a political party called the Black Panthers in Lowndes County, Alabama, occurred even before the formation of the famous Black Panther Party for Self-Defense on the West Coast.

12. Lawrence P. Neal, "Black Power in the International Context," in *Black Power Revolt: A Collection of Essays,* ed. Floyd B. Barbour (Boston: Porter Sargent, 1968), 143.

13. Haki R. Madhubuti, *Groundwork: New and Selected Poems of Don L. Lee/Haki R. Madhubuti from 1966–1996* (Chicago: Third World Press, 1996), 88.

14. "See Sammy Run in the Wrong Direction," in ibid, 104–5 (emphasis and brackets in original).

15. Hoyt W. Fuller, "Algiers Journal," *Negro Digest/Black World,* Oct. 1969, 84 (ellipses and italics in the original).

16. Hoyt W. Fuller, "Possible Israeli Attack on Africa?" *Negro Digest/Black World,* July 1973, 89.

17. Kiarri Cheatwood, "Stokely Speaks," *Negro Digest/Black World,* Nov. 1974, 83.

18. Hoyt W. Fuller, "Oil, Pressure and Black Lives and Loyalties," *Negro Digest/Black World,* Feb. 1975, 79.

19. Ronald Walters, "The Future of Pan-Africanism," *Negro Digest/Black World,* Oct. 1975, 4.

20. For an analysis sympathetic to the claim that Fuller was pushed out for his stance on Zionism, see Woodie King, *The Impact of Race: Theater and Culture* (New York: Applause Theatre and Cinema Books, 2003), 174. For an opinion that disputes this claim, see Jerry Gafio Watts, *Amiri Baraka: The Politics and Art of a Black Intellectual* (New York: New York University Press, 2001), 215.

21. Shirley Graham Du Bois, "Confrontation in the Middle East," *Black Scholar,* Nov. 1973, 32–37.

22. W. E. B. Du Bois's own views on the Arab-Israeli conflict changed over time. Despite his initial admiration of Zionism during the first half of the twentieth century, Du Bois later became disenchanted with Israel. After the 1956 Suez War he published a poem titled "Suez" in December of that year in which he called Israelis "the shock troops of two knaves/Who steal the Negros' land." The poem also advised the West: "Beware, white world, that great black hand/Which Nasser's power waves." The poem was published in *Mainstream* 9, no. 11 (1956). See Melani McAlister, *Epic Encounters: Culture, Media, and U.S. Interests in the Middle East, 1945–2000* (Berkeley: University of California Press, 2001), 85.

23. "Why I Left America: Conversation: Ida Lewis and James Baldwin," in *New Black Voices: An Anthology of Contemporary Afro-American Literature,* ed. Abraham Chapman (New York: Penguin, 1972), 412. *The Fire Next Time* was a major book Baldwin published in 1962 that described a coming explosion of racial unrest in America.

24. "Why Nasser and the New World Sees America as the Number One Villain," *Muhammad Speaks,* June 2, 1967, 3.

25. "Arabs: By Proxy the West Sows New Colonialism in Our Midst," *Muhammad Speaks,* June 23, 1967, 2.

26. Charles Simmons, personal communication, Sept. 11, 2013.

27. Nick Medvecky, "Revolution Until Victory—Palestine al-Fatah," *Inner City Voice* 2, no. 2 (1969): 5–6, 17.

28. Nick Medvecky, personal communication, April 9, 2011.

29. Wayne State University, Walter P. Reuther Library, Manuscripts and Records Collection, Dan Georgakas Collection, Papers, 1958–1980, ser. 1: Subject Files, box 1, folder 8: BSP Correspondence, document: Watson to Such, n.d. (emphasis in original).

30. "How the Palestinian People Were Driven from Their Lands," *African World* 3, no. 24 (1973): n.p.; "A Reply to Muhammad Speaks," *African World* 4, no. 5 (1974): 9, 29.

31. "The Israeli Land Grab," *Jihad News* (volume and issue not indicated but believed to be vol. 1, no. 3 [October 1973]).

32. "The Middle East: An Editorial Comment," *Jihad News* (volume and issue not indicated but believed to be vol. 1, no. 3 [October 1973]).

33. Naseer Aruri and Edmund Ghareeb, eds., *Enemy of the Sun: Poetry of Palestinian Resistance* (Washington: Drum and Spear Press, 1970).

34. Charles Cobb Jr., telephone interview by the author, Sept. 16, 2015.

35. Courtland Cox, telephone interview by the author, Oct. 15, 2015.

36. Ibid.

37. Aruri and Ghareeb, *Enemy of the Sun*, xv.

38. *Black Nationalism and the Revolutionary Action Movement: The Papers of Muhammad Ahmad (Max Stanford)*, Archives Unbound Series, Gale Cengage, file: Black Power Conference 1968, 1969, document: *Black Power Conference Reports*, "Politics, Minority Report, Omar Ahmed," 9: http://gdc.gale.com/archivesunbound/archives-unbound-black-nationalism-and-the-revolutionary-action-movement-the-papers-of-muhammad-ahmad-max-stanford/ (subscription required).

39. Resolution, as contained in Arnold Forster and Benjamin R. Epstein, *The New Anti-Semitism* (New York: McGraw-Hill, 1974), 197.

40. "Sub-resolution on Israel Adopted by the Continuations Committee of the National Black Political Convention, March 24, 1972," in ibid., 198–99.

41. Paul Delaney, "Black Convention Eases Busing and Israeli Stands," *New York Times*, May 20, 1972.

42. Congressional Black Caucus press release, March 21, 1972, cited in William L. Clay, *Just Permanent Interests: Black Americans in Congress, 1870–1991* (New York: Harper Collins, 2000), 209.

43. Boutelle later changed his name to Kwame Montsho Ajamu Somburu.

44. Kwame Somburu (formerly Paul Boutelle), telephone interview by the author, Oct. 19, 2010.

45. COBATAME, "An Appeal by Black Americans Against United States Support of the Zionist Government of Israel," *New York Times*, Nov. 1, 1970, advertisement (all-caps in original).

46. *The Black Power Movement*, pt. 2, *The Papers of Robert F. Williams*, ed. John H. Bracey Jr. and Sharon Harley (Bethesda, MD: University Publications of America, 2000), microfilm: reel 4, group 1, ser. 1, Correspondence, 1956–1979, Correspondence, July–December 1970, document: Boutelle to "Dear Friend," Dec. 22, 1970.

47. University of Utah, J. Willard Marriott Library, Special Collections, Fayez Sayigh Papers, box 233, folder 2, document: "Proposals for a Book or Pamphlet to Be Titled 'Black Americans, Jews and the Middle East Crisis.'"

CHAPTER 6

1. Eric Pace, "Cleaver Is Cheered in Algiers as He Denounces Israel as an American Puppet," *New York Times*, July 23, 1969; Kathleen Neal Cleaver, "Back to Africa: The Evolution of the International Section of the Black Panther Party (1969–1972)," in *The Black Panther Party [Reconsidered]*, ed. Charles E. Jones (Baltimore: Black Classic Press, 1998), 213.

2. Eldridge Cleaver, *Soul on Ice* (New York: Dell, 1968), 111.

3. *Peking Review*, June 9, 1967, repr. in *Black Panther*, July 20, 1967.

4. "Israel Military Aggression: Mao Condemns U.S.-Israeli Link," *Black Panther*, Nov. 16, 1968.

5. P. Schoner, "Palestine Guerillas vs Israeli Pigs," *Black Panther*, Jan. 4, 1969.

6. See the *Black Panther*, April 20, 1969. The paper did not give a date for the rally.

7. As counted by the FBI. See Federal Bureau of Investigation, "The Fedayeen Impact— Middle East and United States," June 1970, 39.

8. Dhoruba bin Wahad, interview by Hard Knock Radio, August 1, 2014, www.youtube .com/watch?v=atZVqscw6PI.

9. According to Cleaver, this turned out to be untrue; the Algerians were not insisting that he leave, but the Cubans had their own reasons for wanting him to leave for Jordan. See Eldridge Cleaver and Henry Louis Gates Jr., "Eldridge Cleaver on Ice," in "The Anniversary Issue: Selections from Transition, 1961–1976," special issue, *Transition* 75/76 (1997): 304; Cleaver, "Back to Africa," 218–19. See also Frank J. Rafalko, *MH/CHAOS: The CIA's Campaign Against the Radical New Left and the Black Panthers* (Annapolis, MD: Naval Institute Press, 2011), 100–104.

10. Pace, "Cleaver Is Cheered"; Cleaver, "Back to Africa," 213; "Cleaver, Panthers Cheered in Algeria," *Black Panther*, July 26, 1969.

11. Kathleen Cleaver, personal communication, March 19, 2015.

12. Al-Fateh, "To Our African Brothers," *Black Panther*, October 11, 1969. Al-Fateh's statement can also be found at University of California, Berkeley, Bancroft Library, Social History Collection, ser. 6, Miscellaneous: 1954–82, container 27, reel 100, folder 14: Arab-Israeli Conflict, 1969–73.

13. Cleaver and Gates, "Eldridge Cleaver on Ice," 307.

14. "Conference on Palestine," *Black Panther*, Jan. 17, 1970.

15. University of California at Berkeley, Bancroft Library. Eldridge Cleaver Papers BANC MSS91/213/C (hereafter ECP), carton 5, folder 9, document: "Black Panther Party Statement on Palestine," Sept. 18, 1970.

16. ECP, carton 5, folder 46, Black Panther Party Daily Reports, document: Daily Reports of February 12 and 19, 1971.

17. Statement of the Black Panther Party to Palestinian Student Conference, Kuwait, Feb. 13–17, 1971, in Arnold Forster and Benjamin R. Epstein, *The New Anti-Semitism* (New York: McGraw-Hill, 1974), 204.

18. *Black Panther*, July 5, 1969, quoted in United States House of Representatives, *The*

Black Panther Party: Its Origins and Development as Reflected in Its Official Weekly Newspaper, "The Black Panther Black Community News Service," Staff Study by the Committee on Internal Security, Oct. 6, 1970 (Washington: US Government Printing Office, 1970), 55.

19. Connie Matthews, "Will Racism or International Proletarian Solidarity Conquer?" *Black Panther,* April 25, 1970. The author would like to thank Robyn Spencer for providing me with a copy of this particular issue of the *Black Panther.*

20. "Yasser Arafat—Commander of Al Fat'h, Palestine: Voices of Rebellion," *Black Panther,* Dec. 20, 1969.

21. *Berkeley Barb,* August 15, 1969, cited in American Jewish Congress, "The Black Panther Party: The Anti-Semitic and Anti-Israel Component," 5 (Document contained in *FBI Files on Black Extremist Organizations,* pt. 1, *COINTELPRO Files on Black Hate Groups and Investigation of the Deacons of Defense and Justice,* ed. Robert E. Lester (A UPA Collection from LexisNexis, 2005), microfilm: reel 5, COINTELPRO Black Extremist File 100-448006, sec. 20 (June–August 1970).

22. Rita Freed, "Panthers: Vanguard Supporters of Arab Liberation," *Workers World,* May 1, 1970, repr. in *Free Palestine* 2, no. 2 (1970): n.p.; Steve D. McCutcheon, "Selections from a Panther Diary," in *The Black Panther Party [Reconsidered],* ed. Charles E. Jones (Baltimore: Black Classic Press, 1998), 125.

23. Cleaver, "Back to Africa," 223–24.

24. Huey P. Newton, *To Die for the People: The Writings of Huey P. Newton* (New York: Random House, 1972), 201. This was an interesting statement given that most Palestinian guerrillas were not socialists at all.

25. "Zionism (Kosher Nationalism) + Imperialism = Fascism," *Black Panther,* Jan. 3, 1970; the article is dated August 30, 1969, however, and may have been written by one of the Panthers in Algeria.

26. Emory Douglas, "On Revolutionary Culture," in *New Black Voices: An Anthology of Contemporary Afro-American Literature,* ed. Abraham Chapman (New York: Penguin, 1972), 489–90.

27. *Black Panther,* March 21, 1970, n.p.

28. Gary Yanker, *Prop Art: Over 1000 Contemporary Political Posters* (New York: Darien House, 1972), 76.

29. The BPP used the experiences of other Third World revolutionaries besides Palestinians in formulating a new, revolutionary identity for blacks. Rychetta Watkins has noted how the Black Panthers created an identity that intersected with that of Asian revolutionaries. See her *Black Power, Yellow Power, and the Making of Revolutionary Identities* (Jackson: University Press of Mississippi, 2012).

30. Stokely Carmichael and Charles V. Hamilton, *Black Power: The Politics of Liberation* (New York: Vintage, 1967), 17.

31. Newton, *To Die for the People,* 193–99. The book gives the date of the press conference as September 5, 1970, but according to an FBI transcription of a radio broadcast of the event, it took place on August 26, 1970. See file 105-165429 (Huey Percy Newton), document: SAC, San Francisco to Director, Sept. 14, 1970.

32. Newton, *To Die for the People,* 195–96.

33. Much has been written about COINTELPRO. See, e.g., Nelson Blackstock, *COIN-*

TELPRO: The FBI's Secret War on Political Freedom (New York: Pathfinder, 1988); and John Drabble, "Fighting Black Power–New Left Coalitions: Covert FBI Media Campaigns and American Cultural Discourse, 1967–1971," *European Journal of American Culture* 27, no. 2 (2008): 65–91. For an official United States Senate study of COINTELPRO in general, and its activities against the Black Panther Party in particular, see United States Senate Select Committee (Church Committee), *Final Report of the Select Committee to Investigate Governmental Operations with Respect to Intelligence Activities* (popularly known as the Church Committee Report) (Washington: US Government Printing Office, 1976), https://archive.org/details/ChurchCommittee_FullReport.

34. Elaine Brown interview, in *The Black Power Mixtape, 1967–1975*, dir. Göran Hugo Olsson (San Francisco: Independent Television Service, 2011).

35. *Black Nationalism and the Revolutionary Action Movement: The Papers of Muhammad Ahmad (Max Stanford)*, Archives Unbound Series, Gale Cengage, file: Black Panthers—Recollections, document: interview with Austin Allen, 43–44.

36. Akbar Muhammad Ahmad, *We Will Return in the Whirlwind: Black Radical Organizations 1960–1975* (Chicago: Charles H. Kerr, 2007), 207–8.

37. By the early 1980s Horowitz's politics had veered sharply right.

38. David Horowitz, *Radical Son: A Generational Odyssey* (New York: Touchstone, 1998), 227–28.

39. Du Bois interviewed Malcolm X for the *Egyptian Gazette* when the latter was in Egypt.

40. Huey P. Newton Foundation Papers, Stanford University, Hoover Institution, ser. 2, Black Panther Party Records, subseries 9, Manuscripts, box 58, folder 7, Black Panther Party Position Paper on the Middle East, 1974, document: Du Bois to Newton, May 2, 1974.

41. Editorial, "For Human Rights in the Middle East," *Black Panther*, May 25, 1974.

42. This and the following quotations are from "The Issue Is Not Territory: Black Panther Party Position Paper on the Middle East Conflict," *Black Panther*, May 25, 1974.

43. Elaine Brown, *A Taste of Power: A Black Woman's Story* (New York: Pantheon, 1992), 254–55.

44. Ibid.

45. Hugh Pearson, *The Shadow of the Panther: Huey Newton and the Price of Black Power in America* (Reading, MA: Addison-Wesley, 1994), 292.

46. Emory Douglas, interview by Block Report Radio, May 25, 2015, www.stashmedia.tv/emory-douglas-art-black-panthers.

47. "Toward Peace in the Middle East," *Black Panther*, July 1980, repr. in *The Black Panther Intercommunal News Service, 1967–1980*, ed. David Hilliard (New York: Atria, 2007), 146–49.

48. Mumia Abu-Jamal, *We Want Freedom: A Life in the Black Panther Party* (Cambridge, MA: South End Press, 2004), 113.

CHAPTER 7

1. Sami Shalom Chetrit, "The Black Panthers in Israel—The First and Last Social Intifada in Israel," *Manifesta Journal*, no. 15 (n.d.): www.manifestajournal.org/issues/i-forgot-remember-forget/black-panthers-israel-first-and-last-social-intifada-israel#. See also Israel State Archives, RG 77/A56/5, Minutes of Meeting of April 18, 1971 (in Hebrew): www.golda.gov.il/archive/home/he/1/1150633350/1199352757/panterim-_part1.PDF.pdf.

2. *Al ha-Mishmar*, Jan. 13, 1971, cited in Oz Frankel, "The Black Panthers of Israel and the Politics of the Radical Analogy," in *Black Power Beyond Borders: The Global Dimensions of the Black Power Movement*, ed. Nico Slate (New York: Palgrave Macmillan, 2012), 81.

3. *Israeleft* 6 (Nov. 1972), repr. in Shalom Cohen and Kokhavi Shemesh, "The Origin and Development of the Israeli Black Panther Movement," *Middle East Research and Information Project (MERIP)*, no. 49 (July 1976): 21.

4. Yosef Waksmann, "The Panthers Dream to Fight Together with the Arabs Against the Establishment," in *Ma'ariv*, April 11, 1972, repr. in *Documents from Israel, 1967–1973: Readings for a Critique of Zionism*, ed. Uri Davis and Norton Mezvinsky (London: Ithaca Press, 1975), 122.

5. Michel Warschawski, *On the Border*, trans. Levi Laub (Cambridge, MA: South End, 2005), 42. The man may have been Shimshon Wigoder.

6. The informant may have been Ya'akov Elbaz, one of the delegation that met Prime Minister Golda Meir in April of 1971 but who, according to the research of historian Oz Frankel, was in fact a police informant. The Matzpen activist in question may once again have been "Shimshon." Frankel, "The Black Panthers of Israel," 89.

7. Sami Shalom Chetrit, *Intra-Jewish Conflict in Israel: White Jews, Black Jews* (London: Routledge, 2010), 109. There is a street in East Jerusalem named after Kies.

8. Meir often is quoted today as having said, in Hebrew, "Hem lo bahurim nehmadim" ("They are not nice guys"). An alley in today's Musrara district of West Jerusalem is named "Hem Lo Nehmadim Alley" to commemorate the Panthers and Meir's statement of disgust. In fact, her actual words were a different, slightly more formal way to say the same thing: "hem einam bahurim nehmadim." This is evident from a film clip of her press conference: "Black Panthers Israel," www.youtube.com/watch?v=oc17wBfFreE.

9. *Yediot Aharonot*, June 1, 1971, cited in Frankel, "The Black Panthers of Israel," 97.

10. Chetrit, *Intra-Jewish Conflict in Israel*, 110.

11. Frankel writes of how the Israeli Panthers' identification with the BPP in America "fused Israeli and American history." See Frankel, "The Black Panthers of Israel," 102.

12. Sami Shalom Chetrit, "30 Years to the Black Panthers in Israel," www.authorsden.com/visit/viewArticle.asp?id=6831.

13. Waksmann, "Panthers Dream to Fight," 120.

14. Kokhavi Shemesh, "This Is My Opinion," *Matzpen*, Jan. 1973, repr. in *Documents from Israel, 1967–1973: Readings for a Critique of Zionism*, ed. Uri Davis and Norton Mezvinsky (London: Ithaca Press, 1975), 115–16.

15. Yale University, Beinicke Rare Book and Manuscript Library, Leon F. Litwack Collection of Berkeley, California, Protest Literature, ser. 1, files, box 2, folder 29, document: "Zionism, Western Imperialism, and the Liberation of Palestine."

16. American Jewish Committee, *Arab Appeals to American Public Opinion* (New York: American Jewish Committee, Institute of Human Relations, 1969), 9.

17. *The Student Nonviolent Coordinating Committee Papers, 1959–1972* (Sanford, NC: Microfilming Corporation of America, 1981), microfilm: Subgroup B: New York, ser. 2, International Affairs Commission, reel 51, sec. 36: Middle East Crisis, document: Elmessiri to Forman, Sept. 20, 1967, and attached "Resolutions"; *Muhammad Speaks*, Sept. 8, 1967.

18. Stokely Carmichael [Kwame Ture], *Stokely Speaks: From Black Power to Pan Africanism* (Chicago: Lawrence Hill, 2007), 142–43.

19. "Randa Khalidi on Palestinians, Black Panthers and Dramaturgy," *Daily Star*, Feb. 16, 2013, www.dailystar.com.lb/Culture/Performance/2013/Feb-16/206682-randa-khalidi-on -palestinians-black-panthers-and-dramaturgy.ashx (subscription required).

20. Richard P. Stevens, *Zionism, South Africa and Apartheid: The Paradoxical Triangle* (Beirut: PLO Research Center, 1969), 37.

21. "The Sky's the Limit," *Black Panther*, Oct. 24, 1970 (emphasis in original); see also Sgt. Pepper, "Oy Veh," *Berkeley Barb*, Jan. 30–Feb. 6, 1970.

22. Diane C. Fujino, *Heartbeat of Struggle: The Revolutionary Life of Yuri Kochiyama* (Minneapolis: University of Minnesota Press, 2005), 160.

23. "Ali Belts Zionism," Jewish Telegraphic Agency, March 8, 1974.

24. Ibid.; and *Black Panther*, March 18, 1974.

25. Gerald Early, "Muhammad Ali as Third-World Hero," *Ideas from the National Humanities Center* 9, no. 1 (2002): 1–35.

26. National Archives and Records Administration, RG 59, P-Reel Printouts, box 20B, document: P740020 0786, Beirut to Secretary of State, March 7, 1974.

27. In 1979 Boutelle changed his name to Kwame Montsho Ajamu Somburu.

28. Ibrahim Shukrallah of the Arab League paid for the transportation, and the group's expenses in the Middle East were covered by the General Union of Palestine Students.

29. Kwame Somburu (formerly Paul Boutelle), telephone interview by the author, Oct. 19, 2010; Randa Khalidi al-Fattal, interview by the author, Beirut, Lebanon, June 24, 2012.

30. Quoted in *al-Fateh*, Sept. 29, 1970.

31. "No Easy Victories Interview: Robert Van Lierop," interview by William Minter, New York, April 16, 2004, *No Easy Victories: African Liberation and American Activists Over a Half Century, 1950–2000*, ed. William Minter, Gail Hovey, and Charles Cobb, www.no easyvictories.org/interviews/int07_vanlierop.php; David Raab, *Terror in Black September: The First Eyewitness Account of the Infamous 1970 Hijackings* (New York: Palgrave Macmillan, 2007), 135–37, 172–73; Associated Press, "Air Hostages Cheer Release," *Pittsburgh Post-Gazette*, Sept. 28, 1970.

32. "El Fatah Investigated," *Near East Report*, May 14, 1969.

33. *Newsweek*, Aug. 18, 1969; see also *Near East Report*, Oct. 29, 1969; C. C. Aronsfeld, "New Left Germans and El Fatah," *Jewish Frontier*, Oct. 1969, 21–23.

34. Federal Bureau of Investigation, "The Fedayeen Impact—Middle East and United States," June 1970, iii, www.governmentattic.org/2docs/FBI_Monograph_Fedayeen-Impact _1970.pdf.

35. CIA Intelligence Report, "ESAU L: The Fedayeen (Annex to ESAU XLVIII: Fedayeen— 'Men of Sacrifice')," Jan. 1971, 25, http://www.theblackvault.com/documents/esau-49.pdf.

36. FBI, "The Fedayeen Terrorist—A Profile," June 1970. The document contained the man's name, but it was redacted in the version that the FBI declassified in 2008. See www .governmentattic.org/docs/FBI_Monograph_Fedayeen_Terrorist_June-1970.pdf.

37. FBI, "The Fedayeen Impact," 51.

38. See Rita Freed, "Panthers: Vanguard Supporters of Arab Liberation," *Workers World*, May 1, 1970, repr. in *Free Palestine* 2, no. 2 (1970): n.p.; Steve D. McCutcheon, "Selections from a Panther Diary," in *The Black Panther Party [Reconsidered]*, ed. Charles E. Jones (Baltimore: Black Classic Press, 1998), 125.

39. "The Black Panthers," *Facts* [Anti-Defamation League] 19, no. 2 (1970): 514. A classified June 1970 FBI report also mentioned this alleged incident. See FBI, "The Fedayeen Impact," 26; Eric Pace, "Arab Guerrillas Seek Other Militants' Aid," *New York Times*, August 27, 1970.

40. FBI, "The Fedayeen Impact," 26, 43.

41. Frank J. Rafalko, *MH/CHAOS: The CIA's Campaign Against the Radical New Left and the Black Panthers* (Annapolis, MD: Naval Institute Press, 2011), 120.

42. FBI, "The Fedayeen Impact," 43, 50.

43. FBI file 65-73268, document: 65-73268-115, FBI to President, May 14, 1970, and attached FBI Intelligence Letter of May 14, 1970, published by Paperless Archive Collection, DVD-ROM, disc 2, "FBI-Nixon Intelligence Letter Program, FBI Files."

44. FBI, "The Fedayeen Impact," iii, 38, 43.

45. Pace, "Arab Guerrillas."

46. FBI Files on "Operation Boulder," file 105-233838, document: 105-233838-2662, Director, FBI, to Attorney General, Feb. 22, 1974, http://intelfiles.egoplex.com/Operation-Boulder-SM.pdf.

47. "Al-Nasr li'l-Sha'b al-Filastini—al-Fuhud al-Sud" [Victory to the Palestinian People—The Black Panthers], *Al-Fateh*, August 30, 1970.

48. "Randa Khalidi on Palestinians, Black Panthers and Dramaturgy."

49. See, e.g., FBI domestic intelligence division document, "Memorandum for Inspector Miller Re: Administrative Memoranda and/or Work Papers," August 31, 1972, 168, https://archive.org/details/foia_FBI_Domestic_Intelligence_Division-HQ-4.

50. Osborn to executive secretary, CIA Management Committee, May 16, 1973. This document is on page 283 of the "Family Jewels" as published online by the CIA at www.foia.cia.gov/sites/default/files/document_conversions/89801/DOC_0001451843.pdf. It is also available at https://archive.org/details/CIA-Family-Jewels. The "Family Jewels" were some seven hundred pages of CIA documents that were generated by CIA employees in 1973 after receiving a directive from Director of Central Intelligence James Schlesinger asking his staff for reports on any CIA activities that may have been inconsistent with the agency's charter. Schlesinger requested this in light of Watergate-era revelations about illegal CIA activities.

CHAPTER 8

1. For more on Rustin's letter see Chapter 3.

2. *The Bayard Rustin Papers* (hereafter BRP), ed. John H. Bracey Jr. and August Meier (Frederick, MD: University Publications of America, 1988), microfilm: Subject Files, reel 14, "Black Americans for U.S. Support to Israel," subgroup: American Committee on Africa [1970], document: Hightower to Stokes, July 28, 1970. Hightower's letter can also be found in the *American Committee on Africa Records*, pt. 1, *ACOA Executive Committee Minutes and National Office Memoranda, 1952–1975* (hereafter ACOAR), ed. John Bracey Jr. and August Meier (Bethesda, MD: University Publications of America, 1991), microfilm: ser. 1, Administration, box 1, reel 3, interoffice memoranda, Aug.–Sept. 1970, document: Hightower to Diggs, July 28, 1970. See also ibid., interoffice memoranda, June–July 1970, document: Hightower to Musukwa, July 30, 1970, and other memoranda.

3. "Ticker Tape U.S.A.," *Jet*, August 27, 1970.

4. ACOAR, ser. 1, Administration, box 2, reel 6, Steering Committee Minutes, 1970–71, document: Minutes of August 6, 1970 Steering Committee Meeting.

5. ACOAR, ser. 1, Administration, box 1, reel 3, interoffice memoranda, Aug.–Sept. 1970, document: Weiss to Hightower, August 7, 1970; see also ibid., Hooper to ACOA executive board, August 17, 1970.

6. Ibid., Weiss to Hightower, August 7, 1970.

7. BRP, reel 14, Black Americans for U.S. Support to Israel, subgroup: American Committee on Africa [1970], document: Rustin to "Dear Friend," August 28, 1970; the letter is also found in ibid., subgroup: Memos to Signatories [1970].

8. ACOAR, ser. 1, Administration, box 1, reel 3, interoffice memoranda, Aug.–Sept. 1970, document: Nesbitt to ACOA Staff and Board, Sept. 14, 1970.

9. Ibid., document: Stevens to ACOA Staff and Board, Sept. 27, 1970.

10. Ibid.

11. Ibid.

12. Ibid.

13. ACOAR, ser. 1, Administration, box 1, reel 3, interoffice memoranda, Aug.–Sept. 1970, document: Houser to Executive Board, Sept. 29, 1970.

14. Ibid., box 2, reel 5, Executive Committee Minutes, June–Dec. 1970, document: Minutes of ACOA Special Executive Board Meeting, Oct. 8, 1970.

15. Williams also cochaired the Committee of Black Americans for Truth About the Middle East, along with Paul Boutelle.

16. Van Lierop also was secretary treasurer of the Committee of Black Americans for Truth About the Middle East.

17. ACOAR, ser. 1, Administration, box 2, reel 5, Executive Committee Minutes, June–Dec. 1970, document: Minutes of ACOA Special Executive Board Meeting, Oct. 8, 1970.

18. Henry M. Winston, "Black Americans and the Middle East Conflict," *World Marxist Review*, Nov. 1970, 19, 23. The CPUSA reprinted an amended version of the article as a pamphlet. See Henry Winston, *Black Americans and the Middle East Conflict* (New York: New Outlook, 1970).

19. *People's World*, August 17, 1974, cited in Harvey Klehr, *Far Left of Center: The American Radical Left Today* (New Brunswick, NJ: Transaction, 1991), 52n30.

20. "Arab Mayor Claims 'Blockade' by Israel," *San Francisco Chronicle*, Oct. 15, 1976.

21. *People's World*, Feb. 12, 1977, cited in Klehr, *Far Left of Center*, 52n32.

22. James Feron, "Turmoil Continues at Brink's Hearing," *New York Times*, Sept. 21, 1981.

23. See Akinyele O. Umoja, "The Black Liberation Army and the Radical Legacy of the Black Panther Party," in *Black Power in the Belly of the Beast*, ed. Judson L. Jeffries (Urbana: University of Illinois Press, 2006), 224–51.

24. See a transcript of the press conference in the FBI's file on Huey Newton: file 105-165429 (Huey Percy Newton), document: SAC, San Francisco to Director, Sept. 14, 1970.

25. Kathleen Cleaver, personal communication, March 19, 2015.

26. "Zionist Attack on Harlem Office Foiled by Community," *Black Panther*, May 19, 1970.

27. FBI File 1126840-000—157-HQ-10555, sec. 15, May 16, 1973–May 25, 1973, Black Liberation Army Collection, FBI Library, Gale Cengage's "Archives Unbound" online documents series, document: Miller to Moore, May 17, 1973. The claim was probably a reference

to a February 1972 FBI claim that the Cleaver faction was trying to obtain weapons and ammunition for two or three al-Fateh operatives in the United States who were planning to attack an American airport somewhere in the eastern part of the country. Among other sources, see FBI domestic intelligence division document "Memorandum for Inspector Miller Re: Administrative Memoranda and/or Work Papers," August 31, 1972, 168, https://archive.org/details/foia_FBI_Domestic_Intelligence_Division-HQ-4.

28. Bryan Burrough, *Days of Rage: America's Radical Underground, the FBI, and the Forgotten Age of Revolutionary Violence* (New York: Penguin, 2015), 454.

29. It is not clear whether the document was drafted by Odinga and the others awaiting trial in New York or other militants still underground.

30. "Communiqué from the Revolutionary Armed Task Force of the Black Liberation Army," *Arm the Spirit*, no. 14 (1982): 16 (emphasis in original).

31. FBI File 1126840–000—157-HQ-10555, sec. 39, July 14, 1982–May 10, 1983, Black Liberation Army Collection, FBI Library, Gale Cengage's "Archives Unbound" online documents series, document: SAC Albany to Director, FBI, Nov. 17, 1982.

32. National Committee to Defend New Afrikan Freedom Fighters, "Zionism Is Racism: Palestine Will Win! New Afrika and Palestine Linked in a Common Struggle," *Arm the Spirit*, no. 14 (1982): 10, 14.

33. "Statement from David Gilbert," *Arm the Spirit*, no. 14 (1982): 9.

34. Kuwasi Balagoon, "Brink's Trial Opening Statement," Anarchist Library, http://theanarchistlibrary.org/library/kuwasi-balagoon-brink-s-trial-opening-statement.

35. "Why Isn't the Whole World Dancin'?" in Kuwasi Balagoon, *Kuwasi Balagoon, a Soldier's Story: Writings by a Revolutionary New Afrikan Anarchist* (Montreal: Solidarity, 2001), 88.

36. Burrough, *Days of Rage*, 279.

37. Freedom Archives, Symbionese Liberation Army (SLA) Collection, "The Last SLA Statement: An Interview with Russ, Joe, Bill and Emily," 37.

38. Mae Brussell, "Why was Patty Hearst Kidnapped?" *The Realist*, no. 98 (Feb. 1974): 5.

39. Freedom Archives, Symbionese Liberation Army (SLA) Collection, *Dragon Supplement*, Nov. 3, 1975.

40. American Jewish Committee online archives, Bertrand H. Gold Executive Papers, Black-Jewish Relations File (1972), document: "Shirley Chisholm Speaks Out: Presidential Campaign Position Paper No. 2, the Middle East Crisis."

41. Ibid.

42. Ibid.

43. Ibid., document: Chisholm to Mehdi, April 18, 1972.

44. Paul Delaney, "Black Convention Eases Busing and Israeli Stands," *New York Times*, May 20, 1972.

45. Congressional Black Caucus press release, March 21, 1972, cited in William L. Clay, *Just Permanent Interests: Black Americans in Congress, 1870–1991* (New York: Harper Collins, 2000), 209.

46. Bayard Rustin, "American Negroes and Israel," *The Crisis*, April 1974, 115.

47. Jake C. Miller, "Black Viewpoints on the Mid-East Conflict," *Journal of Palestine Studies* 10, no. 2 (1981): 39–40.

48. United States House of Representatives, *Congressional Record: Proceedings and*

Debates of the 94th Congress, 2nd Session (Washington: Government Printing Office, 1976), debates of April 14, 1976.

CHAPTER 9

1. *The Papers of A. Philip Randolph*, ed. John H. Bracey Jr. and August Meier (Bethesda, MD: University Publications of America, 1990), microfilm: Subject file, 1908–1973, box 23, reel 19: Israel, 1964–1975, document: "Black Americans to Support Israel Committee: Statement of Principles."

2. Ibid.

3. Rustin became chair of the Socialist Party of America in 1972. Later that year the party changed its name to the Social Democrats USA, a move that came in the midst of a three-way split within the party.

4. Bayard Rustin Papers (hereafter BRP), Subject file, reel 18: Jews and Anti-Semitism, document: "Israel: A Beleaguered Bastion of Democracy and Socialism."

5. Bayard Rustin, "Black Links to Israel," *Amsterdam News*, March 29, 1972. The article appeared in twenty-five other black papers, as well as twelve union papers.

6. Ibid.

7. Ibid.; "American Negroes and Israel," *The Crisis*, April 1974, 115–18; repr. in *Time on Two Crosses: The Collected Writings of Bayard Rustin*, ed. Devon W. Carrado and Donald Weise (San Francisco: Cleis, 2003), 319–26.

8. "American Negroes and Israel," *The Crisis*, April 1974, 115–18; "The PLO: Freedom Fighters or Terrorists?" *Miami Times*, Dec. 19, 1974.

9. American Jewish Committee Archives (hereafter AJCA), Bertram H. Gold Executive Papers, box 190, file: Race Relations: Black-Jewish, 1974–75, document: Fleischman to Area Directors, May 7, 1975.

10. "Randolph Initiates Committee of Black Americans to Support Israel," Jewish Telegraphic Agency, April 28, 1975.

11. AJCA, Bertram H. Gold Executive Papers, box 190, file: Race Relations: Black-Jewish, 1974–75, press release: "Leading Black Americans Affirm Support for Israel," Sept. 11 [1975].

12. Murray Friedman, with the assistance of Peter Binzen, *What Went Wrong? The Creation and Collapse of the Black-Jewish Alliance* (New York: Free Press, 1995), 321; BRP, reel 15, Subject Files, Black Americans to Support Israel Committee (BASIC), BASIC 501(c)(4) Application, document: IRS Form 1024, Application for Recognition of Exemption, Dec. 2, 1977.

13. "BASIC: Black Americans to Support Israel Committee," *New York Times*, Nov. 23, 1975, advertisement; AJCA, Bertram H. Gold Executive Papers, box 190, file: Race Relations: Black-Jewish, 1974–75, document: Black Americans to Support Israel Committee Members as of Sept. 9, 1975.

14. AJCA, Bertram H. Gold Executive Papers, box 190, file: Race Relations: Black-Jewish, 1974–75, document: Fleischman to Area Directors, May 7, 1975.

15. BRP, Subject Files, reel 15: Black Americans to Support Israel Committee (BASIC), 501 (c)(4) Application, document: IRS Form 1024, Application for Recognition of Exemption, Dec. 2, 1977.

16. Ibid., documents: handwritten notes about implementing an educational program through the A. Philip Randolph Educational Fund; ibid., Activities and Prospects.

17. "Dinners Honoring Black Unionists Net Some $1.4 M for Israel Bonds," Jewish Telegraphic Agency, April 5, 1977.

18. BRP, Subject Files, reel 15: Black Americans to Support Israel Committee (BASIC), Statement of Purpose, document: Statement of Purpose.

19. Bayard Rustin papers, cited in Michael G. Long, ed., *I Must Resist: Bayard Rustin's Life in Letters* (San Francisco: City Lights, 2012), 411–12.

20. See his comments in the opinion piece "Blacks and the PLO: Setting Back Peace and Civil Rights," *Washington Post*, Oct. 7, 1979.

21. "Senate in All-Day Debate on Middle East Planes Sale Deal," Jewish Telegraphic Agency, May 16, 1978.

22. BRP, Subject Files, reel 15: Black Americans to Support Israel Committee (BASIC), BASIC Taxes, document: Gessay to BASIC, Jan. 5, 1978; Black Americans in Support of Israel Committee, Inc., Balance Sheet, August 31, 1977; Rustin to Shaffer, Nov. 8, 1985.

23. BRP, Subject Files, reel 15: Black Americans to Support Israel Committee (BASIC), Meetings (BASIC), document: BASIC Meeting, Nov. 24, 1980.

24. BRP, Subject Files, reel 15: Black Americans to Support Israel Committee (BASIC), BASIC 1982—Telegram to Begin re: Lebanon, documents: Mailgram of Rustin to Perlmutter, June 21, 1982, and Begin to Rustin, June 25, 1982.

25. Ibid., PLO pamphlet, document: Bloomstein and Rustin to Bar-Ner, Oct. 19, 1982.

26. Bayard Rustin, "The PLO: Freedom Fighters or Terrorists?" *Miami Times*, Dec. 19, 1974.

27. Rustin, "The PLO: Freedom Fighters or Terrorists?"

28. Bayard Rustin, "Arabs Must Be Persuaded to Bend; Peace Won't Be Achieved Until They Recognize Israel," *Los Angeles Times*, August 4, 1983.

29. Ibid.

30. BRP, Subject Files, reel 15: Black Americans for U.S. Support to Israel, BASIC Op-Ed. piece on Israel, documents: Gersten to Rustin, August 10, 1983; Perlmutter to Rustin, August 10, 1983; Podhoretz to Rustin, August 9, 1983.

31. Andrew J. Young Papers (hereafter AYP), ser. 4B: Correspondence, box 201, folder 6, document: "Ambassador Andrew Young's Personal Statement to the United Nations Security Council, August 24, 1979," Auburn Avenue Research Library on African American Culture and History, Atlanta, GA.

32. See my abbreviated biography of Young in Chapter 4.

33. AYP, ser. 3: Community Relations Commission and Congress, 1964–80, box 65, folder 8, document: Williams to Young, July 31, 1970.

34. BRP, Subject Files, reel 14: Black Americans for U.S. Support to Israel, subgroup: Correspondence [1970], document: Andrew Young, "Statement on Israel," September 1970. The document is also located at AYP, ser. 2: Southern Christian Leadership Conference and Civil Rights, 1957–2003, box 68, folder 4.

35. See Chapter 4 for more about his 1966 trip to Israel and East Jerusalem.

36. "Jewish Leaders, Congressmen Call for Dismissal of Young," Jewish Telegraphic Agency, August 16, 1979.

37. Jimmy Carter, *White House Diary* (New York: Farrar, Straus and Giroux, 2010), 351 (diary entry for August 14, 1979).

38. Ibid., 352 (diary entry for August 15, 1979).

39. Ibid.

40. AYP, ser. 4B: Correspondence, box 201, folder 6, document: "Ambassador Andrew Young's Personal Statement to the United Nations Security Council, August 24, 1979."

41. Ibid.

42. *Jerusalem Post*, Sept. 27, 1979.

43. "The Fall of Andy Young," *Time*, August 27, 1979.

44. Ronald Walters, "The Resignation of Andrew Young: What Does It Mean?" *New Directions: The Howard University Magazine*, Fall 1979, 7.

45. Ibid., 10.

46. Quoted in "The Fall of Andy Young."

47. *Washington Star*, August 16, 1979, cited in Walters, "The Resignation of Andrew Young," 10, 12.

48. Walters, "The Resignation of Andrew Young," 12.

49. "NAACP Sponsors Black Leadership Meeting," *The Crisis*, Nov. 1979, 365, 367.

50. Ibid.

51. James Zogby and Jack O'Dell, eds., *Afro-Americans Stand Up for Middle East Peace* (Washington: Palestine Human Rights Campaign, 1980), xii.

52. "NAACP Sponsors Black Leadership Meeting," 366.

53. Ibid., 366, 368, 370, 371.

CHAPTER 10

1. *Jerusalem Post*, Sept. 28, 1979; see also Paul Findley, *They Dare to Speak Out: People and Institutions Confront Israel's Lobby* (Westport, CT: Lawrence Hill, 1985), 61.

2. Emory University, Robert W. Woodruff Library, Manuscripts, Archives, and Rare Book Library, Southern Christian Leadership Conference Records (hereafter SCLCR), series: Department of Communications, Press Releases, 1963–2010, box 377, file 10, document: "SCLC Seeks World Peace" (undated, but August 1979).

3. "Black Leaders Meet PLO Leader," Jewish Telegraphic Agency, August 21, 1979.

4. American Jewish Committee Archives, Bertram H. Gold Executive Papers, box 189, file: Race Relations, 1978–79, document: Southern Christian Leadership Conference Agenda, August 21, 1979.

5. "Blum to Black Leaders: Any Encouragement to the PLO Will Discourage the Peace Process," Jewish Telegraphic Agency, August 22, 1979.

6. SCLCR, series: Department of Communications, Press Releases, 1963–2010, box 377, file 10, document: "SCLC Meets with PLO and Israeli Leaders" (undated, but August 1979).

7. Comments of Delegate Walter E. Fauntroy (D-DC) to House of Representatives, Oct. 11, 1979. "SCLC Fact-Finding Mission to Lebanon," *Journal of Palestine Studies* 10, no. 2 (1981): 159.

8. "Black Delegation Meets Lebanese Premier," *Spokane Daily Chronicle*, Sept. 19, 1979.

9. Ronald W. Walters, "The Black Initiatives in the Middle East," *Journal of Palestine Studies* 10, no. 2 (1981): 5–6. Walters was part of the SCLC delegation to Lebanon; see also Carla Hall, "The Peaceful Preacher and the Palestinians: Joseph Lowery's Divine Mission to the Middle East," *Palestine Digest* 9, no. 6 (1979): 4–5; and *Washington Post*, Sept. 20, 1979.

10. Walters, "Black Initiatives," 5–6; Hall, "The Peaceful Preacher," 4–5; *Washington Post*, Sept. 20, 1979; "SCLC Fact-Finding Mission to Lebanon," 68.

11. Walters, "Black Initiatives," 5 (brackets in original).

12. Ibid., 9.

13. Jake C. Miller, "Black Viewpoints on the Mid-East Conflict," *Journal of Palestine Studies* 10, no. 2 (1981): 44; *Jerusalem Post*, Sept. 24, 1979.

14. *Jerusalem Post*, Sept. 24, 1979.

15. SCLCR, series: Office of the President Records, Joseph E. Lowery Files, box 136, file 32, document: "Statement by Dr. Lowery Following SCLC's Middle East Peace Initiative."

16. SCLCR, series: Department of Communications, Press Releases, 1963–2010, box 377, file 10, document: "PLO Calls for Cease Fire After Meeting with SCLC," Oct. 5, 1979; "SCLC Fact-Finding Mission to Lebanon," 157–68; University of Michigan, Bentley Historical Library, Abdeen Jabara Papers, box 9, folder: Activities—Black/Arab Coalition, 1979–1983, document: "Statement of the Honorable Walter E. Fauntry [*sic*] (D-DC) Regarding Criticism of the SCLC Middle East Peace Initiative," Oct. 15, 1979.

17. James Zogby and Jack O'Dell, eds., *Afro-Americans Stand Up for Middle East Peace* (Washington: Palestine Human Rights Campaign, 1980), 9.

18. Joseph Lowery, "All Children of Abraham," in ibid., 16.

19. Simeon Booker, "Rep. Fauntroy Follows in Dr. M. L. King's Footsteps for Born-Again Politics," *Jet*, Nov. 1, 1979, 6–7; "Jordan Denounces Black Leaders Who Have Voiced Support for the PLO," Jewish Telegraphic Agency, Oct. 17, 1979.

20. Zogby and O'Dell, *Afro-Americans Stand Up*, 7–9.

21. Ibid.

22. "SCLC Delegation in Mideast to Meet Arafat and 'Hopefully' Begin," Jewish Telegraphic Agency, Sept. 18, 1979.

23. Ibid.

24. Zogby and O'Dell, *Afro-Americans Stand Up*, 13–14 (emphasis in original).

25. *Palestine: P.L.O. Information Bulletin* 5, no. 12 (1979); Karin L. Stanford, *Beyond the Boundaries: Reverend Jesse Jackson in International Affairs* (Albany: State University of New York Press, 1997), 56–57; Nikhil Pal Singh, *Climbin' Jacob's Ladder: The Black Freedom Movement Writings of Jack O'Dell* (Berkeley: University of California Press, 2010), 43; Marshall Frady, *Jesse: The Life and Pilgrimage of Jesse Jackson*, 1st pbk. ed. (New York: Simon and Schuster, 2006), 164–65.

26. Quoted in Singh, *Climbin' Jacob's Ladder*, 44.

27. Zogby and O'Dell, *Afro-Americans Stand Up*, 3, 5.

28. *Jerusalem Post*, Sept. 26 and 27, 1979.

29. *Jerusalem Post*, Sept. 27, 1979; Frady, *Jesse*, 297–98 (pbk. ed.).

30. Frady, *Jesse*, 439 (emphasis in original).

31. Stanford, *Beyond the Boundaries*, 59.

32. BRP, Subject File, 1942–1987, reel 15: Black Americans to Support Israel Cte. (BASIC), Black-Jewish Relations, document: "Excerpts from the Address of James Farmer at the Conference of the National Association of Human Rights Workers (NAHRW), Portland, Main, October 15, 1979."

33. "Jordan Denounces Black Leaders Who Have Voiced Support for the PLO," Jewish Telegraphic Agency, Oct. 17, 1979; Booker, "Rep. Fauntroy," 8; "SCLC, PUSH Leaders Hit by Other Black Leaders for Meetings with PLO," *Jet*, Nov. 1, 1979.

34. "Interview with the Rev. Jesse Jackson," *Ebony*, June 1981, 158.

35. SCLCR, series: Department of Communications, Press Releases, 1963–2010, box 377, file 10, document: "Statement by Dr. Joseph E. Lowery: Reaction to Criticism of Black Leaders," Oct. 16, 1979.

36. Wyatt Tee Walker, *A Prophet from Harlem Speaks: Sermons and Essays* (New York: Martin Luther King Fellows Press, 1997), 67; Wilfred Arnett Moore, "Wyatt Tee Walker: Theologian, Civil Rights Activist, and Former Chief of Staff to Martin Luther King, Jr." (PhD diss., Fuller Theological Seminary, 2009), 134–35.

37. "Black Leaders Continue to Discuss the Mideast Issue," Jewish Telegraphic Agency, August 23, 1979.

38. "SCLC, PUSH Leaders Hit by Other Black Leaders for Meetings with PLO," *Jet*, Nov. 1, 1979, 9.

39. The call was issued by the Palestine Human Rights Campaign at a press conference in Washington on February 9, 1979. See "State Dept. Report on Israel Seen as More Balanced Than Media Reports," Jewish Telegraphic Agency, Feb. 12, 1979.

40. "Resolution on Palestinian Rights and Middle East Peace," in *Afro-Americans Stand Up for Middle East Peace*, ed. James Zogby and Jack O'Dell (Washington: Palestine Human Rights Campaign, 1980), 25–26.

41. Ibid., 26.

42. "Black Clergy Unites for Voice in Foreign Policy," *Jet*, Dec. 13, 1979, 18.

43. "The Palestine Liberation Organization and the Black Pastors' Conference," in *Afro-Americans Stand Up for Middle East Peace*, ed. James Zogby and Jack O'Dell (Washington: Palestine Human Rights Campaign, 1980), 32–33.

44. "Message to the President on the Resignation of Ambassador Andrew Young and on United States Relations with the Middle East and Africa," in *Afro-Americans Stand Up for Middle East Peace*, ed. James Zogby and Jack O'Dell (Washington: Palestine Human Rights Campaign, 1980), 35–37.

45. BRP, Subject File, 1947–1987, reel 15: Black Americans to Support Israel Committee (BASIC), Black-Jewish Relations, document: NAACP statement; see also John Herbers, "Leaders of 2 Black Groups Seek Amity with Jews on P.L.O. Issue," *New York Times*, Oct. 12, 1979.

46. "Black-Jewish Relations: U.S. Civil Rights Leaders to Visit Israel; 2 Civil Rights Leaders Rap Blacks," Jewish Telegraphic Agency, Oct. 15, 1979.

47. "U.S. Black Delegation Promises to Work to Improve Relations with Jews," Jewish Telegraphic Agency, Oct. 18, 1979.

EPILOGUE

1. Bassem Masri, "The Fascinating Story of How the Ferguson-Palestine Solidarity Movement Came Together," Alternet, Feb. 18, 2015, www.alternet.org/activism/frontline-ferguson-protester-and-palestinian-american-bassem-masri-how-ferguson2palestine.

2. Quoted in David Palumbo-Liu, "Black Americans Send Clear Message to Palestinians: 'Now Is the Time for Palestinian Liberation, Just as Now Is the Time for Our Own

in the United States," Salon, August 18, 2015, www.salon.com/2015/08/18/black_activists_
send_clear_message_to_palestinians_now_is_the_time_for_palestinian_liberation_just_as_
now_is_the_time_for_our_own_in_the_united_states/.

3. Jasiri X, "'This Is Apartheid': Rapper Jasiri X on Visit to Palestine," interview by Amira Asad, Electronic Intifada, https://electronicintifada.net/content/
apartheid-rapper-jasiri-x-visit-palestine/13149.

4. "Method Man Talks 'P.L.O. Style,'" Feb. 16, 2015, www.youtube.com/watch
?v=nhOQ19IQxeA.

5. Robert I. Friedman, "Confessions of an Israeli Press Officer," *Mother Jones* 12, no.
2 (1987): 24.

6. Dana Weiler-Polak, "Israel Enacts Law Allowing Authorities to Detain Illegal Migrants for Up to 3 Years," *Haaretz* (English-language internet edition), June 3, 2012, www
.haaretz.com/israel-s-new-infiltrators-law-comes-into-effect-1.5167886.

7. William L. Van Deburg, *New Day in Babylon: The Black Power Movement and American Culture, 1965-1975* (Chicago: University of Chicago Press, 1992), 27.

8. "Black Leaders Continue to Discuss the Mideast Issue," Jewish Telegraphic Agency,
August 23, 1979.

BIBLIOGRAPHY

PRIMARY SOURCES
Archival Holdings
American Jewish Committee Archives, New York. Bertram H. Gold Executive Papers.
American Jewish Committee Archives, New York. Interreligious Affairs Collection.
Auburn Avenue Research Library on African American Culture and History, Atlanta, Georgia: Andrew J. Young Papers.
Duke University, Rare Book, Manuscript, and Special Collections Library, Durham, North Carolina: Social Democrats, USA Records.
Emory University, Robert W. Woodruff Library, Manuscripts, Archives, and Rare Book Library, Atlanta, Georgia: Harvey Klehr Papers.
Emory University, Robert W. Woodruff Library, Manuscripts, Archives, and Rare Book Library, Atlanta, Georgia: Southern Christian Leadership Conference Papers.
Freedom Archives, San Francisco, California, and online: Anti-Zionism Collection.
Freedom Archives, San Francisco, California, and online: Black Liberation Army Collection.
Freedom Archives, San Francisco, California, and online: Colin Edwards Collection.
Freedom Archives, San Francisco, California, and online: Symbionese Liberation Army Collection.
Library of Congress, Washington, DC: James Forman Papers.
McMaster University, Mills Memorial Library, Hamilton, Ontario, Canada: Bertrand Russell Archives.
Morehouse College, Atlanta, Georgia: Martin Luther King Jr. Collection.
National Archives and Records Administration, College Park, Maryland: State Department Central Files, Post Records.
New York Public Library, Schomburg Center for Research in Black Culture: Malcolm X Collection.
Stanford University, Hoover Institution, Palo Alto, California: Huey P. Newton Foundation Papers.
Stanford University, Hoover Institution, Palo Alto, California: New Left Collection.
Swarthmore College Peace Collection, Swarthmore, Pennsylvania: Papers of David McReynolds.
University of California, Berkeley, Bancroft Library, Eldridge Cleaver Papers.
University of California, Berkeley, Bancroft Library, Social History Collection.

University of Michigan, Ann Arbor: Bentley Historical Library, Abdeen Jabara Papers.
University of Utah, Salt Lake City: J. Willard Marriott Library, Special Collections, Fayez
     Sayigh Papers.
Wayne State University, Detroit, Michigan: Walter P. Reuther Library, Manuscripts and
     Records Collection, Dan Georgakas Collection.
Yale University, New Haven, Connecticut, Beinicke Rare Book and Manuscript Library,
     Leon F. Litwack Collection of Berkeley, California, Protest Literature.

Archival Collections on Microfilm, CD-ROM, and/or Online
American Jewish Committee online archives. http://ajcarchives.org/main.php.
The Bayard Rustin Papers. Edited by John H. Bracey Jr. and August Meier. Frederick, MD:
     University Publications of America, 1988. Microfilm.
*Black Nationalism and the Revolutionary Action Movement: The Papers of Muhammad Ahmad
     (Max Stanford).* Archives Unbound Series, Gale Cengage. www.gale.com/primary-sources/
     archives-unbound (subscription required).
The Black Power Movement. Part 1, *Amiri Baraka from Black Arts to Black Radicalism.* Edited
     by John H. Bracey Jr. and Sharon Harley. Bethesda, MD: University Publications of
     America, 2000. Microfilm.
The Black Power Movement. Part 2, *The Papers of Robert F. Williams.* Edited by John H.
     Bracey Jr. and Sharon Harley. Bethesda, MD: University Publications of America,
     2002. Microfilm.
The Black Power Movement. Part 3, *Papers of the Revolutionary Action Movement, 1962–1996.*
     Edited by John H. Bracey Jr. and Sharon Harley. Bethesda, MD: University Publica-
     tions of America, 2002. Microfilm.
Israel. Prime Ministry. Israel State Archives. www.archives.gov.il/en/.
The King Center. Online archives. Papers of Martin Luther King Jr. www.thekingcenter.org/
     archive.
The Papers of A. Philip Randolph. Edited by John H. Bracey Jr. and August Meier. Bethesda,
     MD: University Publications of America, 1990. Microfilm.
*Papers of the NAACP. Part 28. Special Subject Files, 1966–1970. Series A: "Africa" through "Poor
     People's Campaign."* Bethesda, MD: University Publications of America, 2001. Microfilm.
*Records of the American Committee on Africa. Part 1: ACOA Executive Committee Minutes and
     National Office Memoranda, 1952–1975.* Edited by John H. Bracey Jr. and August Meier.
     Bethesda, MD: University Publications of America, 1991.
*Records of the Southern Christian Leadership Conference, 1954–1970. Part 1: Records of the
     President's Office. Part 2: Records of the Executive Director and Treasurer.* Bethesda, MD:
     University Publications of America, 1995.
The Student Nonviolent Coordinating Committee Papers, 1959–1972. Sanford, NC: Microfilming
     Corporation of America, 1981. Microfilm.

Published and Microfilmed US Government Documents
Federal Bureau of Investigation. *FBI File on the Student Nonviolent Coordinating Committee
     (SNCC).* Wilmington, DE: Scholarly Resources, 1991.
———. *FBI Files on Black Extremist Organizations.* Part 1, *COINTELPRO Files on Black*

Hate Groups and Investigation of the Deacons for Defense and Justice. Edited by Robert E. Lester. A UPA Collection from LexisNexis, 2005.

———. "The Fedayeen Impact—Middle East and United States." June 1970. Governmentattic .org, www.governmentattic.org/2docs/FBI_Monograph_Fedayeen-Impact_1970.pdf.

———. *The Martin Luther King, Jr., FBI File.* Part 2, *The King-Levison File.* Edited by August Meier and John H. Bracey Jr. Frederick, MD: University Publications of America, 1987. Microfilm.

United States House of Representatives. *The Black Panther Party: Its Origins and Development as Reflected in Its Official Weekly Newspaper, "The Black Panther Black Community News Service."* Staff Study by the Committee on Internal Security, Oct. 6, 1970. Washington: US Government Printing Office, 1970.

———. *Congressional Record: Proceedings and Debates of the 94th Congress, 2nd Session.* Washington: Government Printing Office, 1976.

United States Senate Select Committee (Church Committee). *Final Report of the Select Committee to Investigate Governmental Operations with Respect to Intelligence Activities.* Washington: US Government Printing Office, 1976. https://archive.org/details/Church Committee_FullReport.

Interviews, Telephone Interviews, Personal Communications
Cleaver, Kathleen Neal
Cobb, Charles, Jr.
Cox, Courtland
Guerrero, Eugene
Hutchings, Philip
Kalbian, Vicken
Khaled, Leila
McReynolds, David
Medvecky, Nick
Schleifer, Abdallah
Simmons, Charles
Somburu, Kwame (formerly Paul Boutelle)
Spellman, Karen Edmonds
Zellner, Dorothy

UNPUBLISHED SECONDARY SOURCES
Brackman, Harold. "Jews, African-Americans, and Israel: The Ties That Bind." Unpublished manuscript for the Simon Wiesenthal Center/Museum of Tolerance, 2010.

Brenner, Lenni. "The Black Civil Rights Movement and Zionism." www.thestruggle.org/ blacks_civil_rights_zionism.htm.

Feldman, Keith P. "Racing the Question: Israel/Palestine and U.S. Imperial Culture." PhD diss., University of Washington, 2008.

Moore, Wilfred Arnett. "Wyatt Tee Walker: Theologian, Civil Rights Activist, and Former Chief of Staff to Martin Luther King, Jr." PhD diss., Fuller Theological Seminary, 2009.

Stanford, Maxwell C. "Revolutionary Action Movement (RAM): A Case Study of an Urban

Revolutionary Movement in Western Capitalist Society." Master's thesis, Atlanta University, 1986.

Wilkins, Fanon Che. "'In the Belly of the Beast': Black Power, Anti-Imperialism, and the African Liberation Solidarity Movement, 1968–1975." PhD diss., New York University, 2001.

PUBLISHED MATERIALS

Abu-Jamal, Mumia. *We Want Freedom: A Life in the Black Panther Party*. Cambridge, MA: South End, 2004.

Adams, Maurianne, and John Bracey, eds. *Strangers & Neighbors: Relations Between Blacks & Jews in the United States*. Introduction by Julian Bond. Amherst: University of Massachusetts Press, 1999.

Ahmad, Akbar Muhammad. "RAM: The Revolutionary Action Movement." In Jeffries, *Black Power*, 251–86.

———. *We Will Return in the Whirlwind: Black Radical Organizations, 1960–1975*. Introduction by John Bracey. Chicago: Charles H. Kerr, 2007.

Aidi, Hishaam. "Slavery, Genocide and the Politics of Outrage: Understanding the New Racial Olympics." *Middle East Report* 35 (Spring 2005): 40–56.

Allen, Robert. "A Historical Synthesis: Black Liberation and World Liberation." *Black Scholar* 3, no. 6 (1972): 7–23.

American Jewish Committee. *Arab Appeals to American Public Opinion*. New York: American Jewish Committee, Institute of Human Relations, 1969.

"An Appeal to Reason: A Message to the Negroes Who Support Israel." *Blacknews* 1, no. 18 (1970): 11–12.

Anderson, Charles. "Finger Pop'in." In *Black Fire: An Anthology of Afro-American Writing*, edited by Amiri Baraka and Larry Neal, 189–90. Baltimore: Black Classic Press, 2007. Originally published New York: Morrow, 1968.

Anti-Defamation League. "The Black Panthers." *Facts* 19, no. 2 (1970): 509–20.

"Anti-Semitism, White Racism." *Jewish Currents* 21, no. 9 (1967): 37.

Aronsfeld, C. C. "New Left Germans and El Fatah." *Jewish Frontier*, Oct. 1969, 21–23.

Aruri, Nasser, and Edmund Ghareeb, eds. *Enemy of the Sun: Poetry of Palestinian Resistance*. Washington: Drum and Spear, 1970.

Austin, Curtis J. *Up Against the Wall: Violence in the Making and Unmaking of the Black Panther Party*. Foreword by Elbert "Big Man" Howard. Fayetteville: University of Arkansas Press, 2006.

Axelrad, Albert S. *The Black Panthers, Jews and Israel*. New York: Jewish Currents, 1971.

Balagoon, Kuwasi. "Brink's Trial Opening Statement." Anarchist Library, http://theanarchist library.org/library/kuwasi-balagoon-brink-s-trial-opening-statement.

———. *Kuwasi Balagoon, a Soldier's Story: Writings by a Revolutionary New Afrikan Anarchist*. Montreal: Solidarity, 2001.

———. "Why Isn't the Whole World Dancin'?" In Balagoon, *Kuwasi Balagoon, a Soldier's Story*, 81–89.

Baldwin, James. "The Harlem Ghetto, Winter 1948: The Vicious Circle of Frustration and Prejudice." *Commentary*, Feb. 1948, 165–70.

———. "Negroes Are Anti-Semitic Because They Are Anti-White." *New York Times*, April 9, 1967.

Baldwin, Lewis V., and Amiri YaSin al-Hadid. *Between Cross and Crescent: Christian and Muslim Perspectives on Malcolm and Martin*. Gainesville: University Press of Florida, 2002.

Baraka, Amiri, ed. *African Congress: A Documentary of the First Modern Pan-African Congress*. New York: William Morrow, 1972.

———. "Confessions of a Former Anti-Semite." *Village Voice*, Dec. 17–23, 1980, 18–22.

Baraka, Amiri, and Larry Neal, eds. *Black Fire: An Anthology of African-Americans Writing*. New York: William Morrow, 1968.

Barbour, Floyd B., ed. *Black Power Revolt: A Collection of Essays*. Boston: Porter Sargent, 1968.

Baum, Phil, and Carol Weisbord. *Israel, Africa, Colonialism and Racism: A Reply to Certain Slanders*. New York: American Jewish Congress, Commission on International Affairs, 1967.

Berman, Paul, ed. *Blacks and Jews: Alliances and Arguments*. New York: Delacorte, 1994.

"Black Clergy Unites for Voice in Foreign Policy." *Jet*, Dec. 13, 1979, 18.

"The Black Panthers." *Facts* 19, no. 2 (1970). Published by the Anti-Defamation League of B'nai B'rith.

"To Blacks: Condemn P.L.O. Terrorism." *New York Times*, August 30, 1979.

Blackstock, Nelson. *COINTELPRO: The FBI's Secret War on Political Freedom*. Introduction by Noam Chomsky. New York: Pathfinder, 1988.

Bloom, Joshua, and Waldo E. Martin Jr. *Black Against Empire: The History and Politics of the Black Panther Party*. Berkeley: University of California Press, 2013.

Bond, Julian. "SNCC: What We Did." *Like the Dew: A Progressive Journal of Southern Culture and Politics*, (April 27, 2010). http://likethedew.com/2010/04/27/sncc-what-we-did.

Booker, Simeon. "Rep. Fauntroy Follows in Dr. M. L. King's Footsteps for Born-Again Politics." *Jet*, Nov. 1, 1979, 6–7.

"B.P.P. Position Paper Sent to World Leaders." *Black Panther*, June 1, 1974.

Breitman, George, ed. *Malcolm X Speaks: Selected Speeches and Statements*. New York: Grove, 1990.

Brenner, Lenni, and Matthew Quest. *Black Nationalism and Palestine Solidarity*. Atlanta: On Our Own Authority! 2013.

Brown, Elaine. *A Taste of Power: A Black Woman's Story*. New York: Pantheon, 1992.

Brown, H. Rap. *Die Nigger Die!* New York: Dial, 1969.

Brussell, Mae. "Why Was Patty Hearst Kidnapped?" *The Realist*, no. 98 (Feb. 1974): 1–40.

Buhle, Paul, and Robin D. G. Kelley. "Allies of a Different Sort: Jews and Blacks in the American Left." In *Struggle in the Promised Land: Toward a History of Black-Jewish Relations in the United States*, edited by Jack Salzman and Cornel West, 197–230. New York: Oxford University Press, 1997.

Bukhari, Safiya A. *Lest We Forget*. N.p.: n.p., n.d. Reprinted in Whitehorn, *Safiya Bukhari*, 135–55.

Burrough, Bryan. *Days of Rage: America's Radical Underground, the FBI, and the Forgotten Age of Revolutionary Violence*. New York: Penguin, 2015.

Carmichael, Stokely [Kwame Ture]. *Stokely Speaks: From Black Power to Pan Africanism.* Chicago: Lawrence Hill, 2007.

Carmichael, Stokely, and Charles V. Hamilton. *Black Power: The Politics of Liberation in America.* New York: Vintage, 1967.

Carmichael, Stokely, with Ekwueme Michael Thelwell. *Ready for Revolution: The Life and Times of Stokely Carmichael (Kwame Ture).* New York: Scribner, 2003.

Carson, Clayborne. "Black-Jewish Universalism in the Era of Identity Politics." In *Struggle in the Promised Land: Toward a History of Black-Jewish Relations in the United States,* edited by Jack Salzman and Cornel West, 177–96. New York: Oxford University Press, 1997.

———. "Blacks and Jews in the Civil Rights Movement: The Case of SNCC." In Adams and Bracey, *Strangers & Neighbors,* 574–89.

———. "Blacks and Jews in the Civil Rights Movement: The Case of SNCC." In *Bridges and Boundaries: African Americans and American Jews,* edited by Jack Salzman, Adina Back, and Gretchen Sullivan Sorin, 36–49. New York: George Braziller, in association with the Jewish Museum, 1992.

———. *In Struggle: SNCC and the Black Awakening of the 1960s.* Cambridge, MA: Harvard University Press, 1995.

———, ed. *The Papers of Martin Luther King, Jr.* Vol. 5, *Threshold of a New Decade, January 1959–December 1960.* Edited by Tenisha Armstrong, Susan Carson, Adrienne Clay, and Kieran Taylor. Berkeley: University of California Press, 2005.

———, ed. *The Papers of Martin Luther King, Jr.* Vol. 6, *Advocate of the Social Gospel, September 1948–March 1963.* Edited by Susan Carson, Susan Englander, Troy Jackson, and Gerald L. Smith. Berkeley: University of California Press, 2007.

Carter, Jimmy. *White House Diary.* New York: Farrar, Straus and Giroux, 2010.

Chapman, Abraham, ed. *New Black Voices: An Anthology of Contemporary Afro-American Literature.* New York: Penguin, 1972.

Cheatwood, Kiarri. "Stokely Speaks." *Black World/Negro Digest,* Nov. 1974, 76–83.

Chetrit, Sami Shalom. "The Black Panthers in Israel—The First and Last Social Intifada in Israel." *Manifesta Journal,* no. 15. www.manifestajournal.org/issues/i-forgot-remember-forget/black-panthers-israel-first-and-last-social-intifada-israel#.

———. *Intra-Jewish Conflict in Israel: White Jews, Black Jews.* London: Routledge, 2010.

———. "30 Years to the Black Panthers in Israel." www.authorsden.com/visit/viewArticle.asp?id=6831.

Christiansen, Samantha, and Zachary A. Scarlett, eds. *The Third World in the Global 1960s.* New York: Berghahn, 2013.

Christison, Kathleen. *Perceptions of Palestine: Their Influence on U.S. Middle East Policy.* Berkeley: University of California Press, 1999.

Churchill, Ward, and Jim Vander Wall. *Agents of Repression: The FBI's Secret Wars Against the Black Panther Party and the American Indian Movement.* Boston: South End, 1988.

Clay, William L. *Just Permanent Interests: Black Americans in Congress, 1870–1991.* New York: Harper Collins, 2000.

Cleaver, Eldridge. *Soul on Ice.* New York: Dell, 1978.

Cleaver, Eldridge, and Henry Louis Gates Jr. "Eldridge Cleaver on Ice." In "The Anniversary Issue: Selections from *Transition,* 1961–76." Special issue, *Transition* 75/76 (1997): 294–311.

Cleaver, Kathleen Neal. "Back to Africa: The Evolution of the International Section of the Black Panther Party (1969–1972)." In Jones, *The Black Panther Party [Reconsidered]*, 211–54.

———, ed. *Target Zero: A Life in Writing/Eldridge Cleaver*. New York: Palgrave Macmillan, 2006.

Cleaver, Kathleen Neal, and George Katsiaficas, eds. *Liberation, Imagination, and the Black Panther Party: A New Look at the Panthers and Their Legacy*. New York: Routledge, 2001.

Clemons, Michael L., and Charles E. Jones. "Global Solidarity: The Black Panther Party in the International Arena." *New Political Science* 21, no. 2 (1999): 177–203.

Cobb, William Jelani, ed. Foreword by Stanley Crouch. *The Essential Harold Cruse: A Reader*. New York: Palgrave, 2002.

Cohen, Shalom, and Kokhavi Shemesh. "The Origin and Development of the Israeli Black Panther Movement." *Middle East Research and Information Project (MERIP)*, no. 49 (July 1976): 21.

"Common Struggle of the Palestinian and African People: Interview with Stokeley [*sic*] Carmichael." *Palestine: P.L.O. Information Bulletin* 5, no. 16 (1979): www.newjerseysolidarity .net/plobulletin/vol5no16sep1979/stokeley_carmichael.shtml.

"Communiqué from the Revolutionary Armed Task Force of the Black Liberation Army." *Arm the Spirit*, no. 14 (1982): 16.

Cruse, Harold. *Rebellion or Revolution?* New York: William Morrow, 1968.

Curiel, Jonathan. "Newsmaker Profile: Agha Saeed." SFGate.com (Oct. 13, 2001).

Davis, Uri, and Norton Mezvinsky, eds. *Documents from Israel, 1967–1973: Readings for a Critique of Zionism*. London: Ithaca Press, 1975.

DeCaro, Louis A., Jr. *On the Side of My People: A Religious Life of Malcolm X*. New York: New York University Press, 1996.

Douglas, Emory. "On Revolutionary Culture." In Chapman, *New Black Voices*, 489–90.

Do You Know? Twenty Basic Questions About the Palestine Problem. Beirut: Palestine Liberation Organization Research Center, 1965.

Drabble, John. "Fighting Black Power–New Left Coalitions: Covert FBI Media Campaigns and American Cultural Discourse, 1967–1971." *European Journal of American Culture* 27, no. 2 (2008): 65–91.

"Drawing Lessons: H. Rap Brown and Stokely Carmichael Addresses at Newton Rally." Transcript of Feb. 17, 1968, speeches, based on "Pacifica Radio/UC Berkeley Social Activism Sound Recording Project." www.lib.berkeley.edu/MRC/carmichael.html.

Du Bois, Shirley Graham. "Confrontation in the Middle East." *Black Scholar*, Nov. 1973, 32–37.

Early, Gerald. "Muhammad Ali as Third-World Hero." *Ideas from the National Humanities Center* 9, no. 1 (2002): 5–15.

Essien-Udom, E. U. *Black Nationalism: A Search for an Identity in America*. 1962. Chicago: University of Chicago Press, 1995.

———. "From *Black Nationalism: A Search for Identity*." In *Racism: A Casebook*, edited by Frederick R. Lapides and David J. Burrows, 160–72. New York: Thomas Y. Crowell, 1971.

Evanzz, Karl. *The Messenger: The Rise and Fall of Elijah Muhammad*. New York: Pantheon, 1999.

"The Fall of Andy Young." *Time*, August 27, 1979.

Fanon, Frantz. *The Wretched of the Earth*. Translated by Constance Farrington. Preface by Jean-Paul Sartre. New York: Vintage, 1968.

Fateh, al-. "To Our African Brothers." *Black Panther*, Oct. 11, 1969.

————. "Toward a Democratic State." Statement Issued at the 2nd World Conference on Palestine. N.p.: n.p., 1970.

Feldman, Keith P. "Representing Permanent War: Black Power's Palestine and the End(s) of Civil Rights." *CR: The New Centennial Review* 8, no. 2 (2008): 193–231.

————. *A Shadow over Palestine: The Imperial Life of Race in America*. Minneapolis: University of Minnesota Press, 2015.

————. "Towards an Afro-Arab Diasporic Culture: The Translational Practices of David Graham Du Bois." *Alif* 31 (2011): 152–72.

Findley, Paul. *They Dare to Speak Out: People and Institutions Confront Israel's Lobby*. Westport, CT: Lawrence Hill, 1985.

"For Human Rights in the Middle East." *Black Panther*, May 25, 1974.

Forman, James. *The Making of Black Revolutionaries: A Personal Account*. New York: Macmillan, 1972.

————. *1967: High Tide of Black Resistance*. N.p.: n.p, n.d.

Forster, Arnold, and Benjamin R. Epstein. *The New Anti-Semitism*. New York: McGraw-Hill, 1974.

Frady, Marshall. *Jesse: The Life and Pilgrimage of Jesse Jackson*. New York: Random House, 1996; 1st pbk. ed. New York: Simon and Schuster, 2006.

Frankel, Oz. "The Black Panthers of Israel and the Politics of the Radical Analogy." In *Black Power Beyond Borders: The Global Dimensions of the Black Power Movement*, edited by Nico Slate, 81–106. New York: Palgrave Macmillan, 2012.

Freed, Rita. "Panthers: Vanguard Supporters of Arab Liberation." *Workers World*, May 1, 1970. Reprinted in *Free Palestine* 2, no. 2 (1970): n.p.

Friedman, Murray, with the assistance of Peter Binzen. *What Went Wrong? The Creation and Collapse of the Black-Jewish Alliance*. New York: Free Press, 1995.

Friedman, Robert I. "Confessions of an Israeli Press Officer." *Mother Jones* 12, no. 2 (1987): 20–35.

Fujino, Diane C. *Heartbeat of Struggle: The Revolutionary Life of Yuri Kochiyama*. Minneapolis: University of Minnesota Press, 2005.

Fuller, Hoyt T. "Algiers Journal." *Negro Digest/Black World*, Oct. 1969, 84.

————. "Oil, Pressure and Black Lives and Loyalties." *Negro Digest/Black World*, Feb. 1975, 79.

————. "Possible Israeli Attack on Africa?" *Negro Digest/Black World*, July 1973, 89.

Gershman, Carl. "The Andrew Young Affair." *Commentary*, Nov. 1, 1979. www.commentary magazine.com/article/the-andrew-young-affair/.

Goldstein, Eric L. *The Price of Whiteness: Jews, Race, and American Identity*. Princeton, NJ: Princeton University Press, 2006.

Greenberg, Cheryl Lynn. *Troubling the Waters: Black-Jewish Relations in the American Century*. Princeton, NJ: Princeton University Press, 2006.

Hall, Carla. "The Peaceful Preacher and the Palestinians: Joseph Lowery's Divine Mission to the Middle East." *Palestine Digest* 9, no. 6 (1979): 4–5.

Hall, Simon. "*On the Tail of the Panther*: Black Power and the 1967 Convention of the National Conference for New Politics." *Journal of American Studies* 37, no. 1 (2003): 59–78.

Hilliard, David, ed. *The Black Panther Intercommunal News Service, 1967–1980*. New York: Atria, 2007.

Hilliard, David, and Lewis Cole. *This Side of Glory: The Autobiography of David Hilliard and the Story of the Black Panther Party*. Boston: Little, Brown, 1993.

Horowitz, David. *Radical Son: A Generational Odyssey*. New York: Touchstone, 1998.

"How Racists, Black and White, Used Arab Propaganda Sources." *Facts* 17, no. 5 (1967): 421–32. Published by the Anti-Defamation League of B'nai B'rith.

"The Israeli Land Grab." *Jihad News* (volume and issue not indicated, but believed to be 1, no. 3 [Oct. 1973]).

"The Issue Is Not Territory: Black Panther Party Position Paper on the Middle East Conflict." *Black Panther*, May 25, 1974.

Jabaily, Annalisa. "How Estrangement and Alliances Between Blacks, Jews, and Arabs Shaped a Generation of Civil Rights Family Values." *Law and Inequality* 23 (Winter 2005): 197–237.

Jacobs, Paul. "Watts vs. Israel: Black Nationalists and an Israeli Diplomat." *Commonweal*, March 1, 1968, 649–51.

Jeffries, Judson L., ed. *Black Power in the Belly of the Beast*. Foreword by Tiyi M. Morris. Urbana: University of Illinois Press, 2006.

Jelinek, Don. "SNCC: Vietnam, Israel, & Violence," interview by Bruce Hartford, 2005, www.crmvet.org/nars/jelinek.htm#snccvietnam.

Jones, Bartlett C. *Flawed Triumphs: Andy Young at the United Nations*. Lanham, MD: University Press of America, 1996.

Jones, Charles E., ed., *The Black Panther Party [Reconsidered]*. Baltimore: Black Classic Press, 1998.

Jones, Junebug Jabo. "The Mid-East and the Liberal Reaction." *SNCC Newsletter* (Sept.-Oct. 1967): 5–6.

Joseph, Peniel E. *Stokely: A Life*. New York: Basic Civitas, 2014.

———. *Waiting 'til the Midnight Hour: A Narrative History of Black Power in America*. New York: Henry Holt, 2006.

Joyce, Donald F. *Black Book Publishers in the United States: A Historical Dictionary of the Presses, 1817–1990*. Westport, CT: Greenwood, 1991.

Kaufman, Jay. "Thou Shalt Surely Rebuke Thy Neighbor." *Black Anti-Semitism and Jewish Racism*. New York: Schocken, 1970.

Kaufman, Jonathan. *Broken Alliance: The Turbulent Times Between Blacks and Jews in America*. New York: Charles Scribner's Sons, 1988.

Kazarian, Richard, Jr. *Israel in the Black American Perspective*. Westport, CT: Greenwood, 1985.

Kiblawi, Fadi, and Will Youmans. "Desperation and Drastic Measures: The Use and Abuse of Martin Luther King Jr. by Israel's Apologists." *Counterpunch*, Jan. 17–18, 2004.

King, Casey, and Linda Barrett Osborne. *Oh, Freedom! Kids Talk About the Civil Rights Movement with the People Who Made It Happen*. Foreword by Rosa Parks. New York: Alfred A. Knopf, 1997.

King, Woodie. *The Impact of Race: Theater and Culture*. Foreword by Ossie Davis. New York: Applause Theatre and Cinema Books, 2003.

Klehr, Harvey. *Far Left of Center: The American Radical Left Today*. New Brunswick, NJ: Transaction, 1991.

Knee, Stuart. "The Impact of Zionism on Black and Arab Americans." *Patterns of Prejudice* 10, no. 2 (1976): 21–28.

Lapides, Frederick R., and David J. Burrows. *Racism: A Casebook*. New York: Thomas Y. Crowell, 1971.

Lens, Sid. "The New Politics Convention: Confusion and Promise." *New Politics* 6, no. 1 (1967): 9–12.

Levine, Daniel. *Bayard Rustin and the Civil Rights Movement*. New Brunswick, NJ: Rutgers University Press, 1999.

Lincoln, C. Eric. *The Black Muslims in America*. 3rd ed. Grand Rapids, MI: William B. Eerdmans; Trenton, NJ: Africa World Press, 1994. Originally published as *The Black Muslims in America*. Foreword by Gordon W. Allport. Boston: Beacon, 1961.

Lipset, Seymour. "The Socialism of Fools: The Left, the Jews, and Israel." *Encounter*, Dec. 1969, 24–35.

Lockwood, Lee. *Conversations with Eldridge Cleaver: Algiers*. New York: McGraw-Hill, 1970.

Logan, Jomo. "A Resolution by African-Americans Condemning the Appeal by So-called Black Leaders Calling for United States Support to Israel." *Black World* 19, no. 12 (1970): 39–42.

Long, Michael G., ed. *I Must Resist: Bayard Rustin's Life in Letters*. Foreword by Julian Bond. San Francisco: City Lights, 2012.

Lowery, Joseph. "All Children of Abraham." In Zogby and O'Dell, *Afro-Americans Stand Up*, 16–20.

Lubin, Alex. *Geographies of Liberation: The Making of an Afro-Arab Political Imaginary*. Chapel Hill: University of North Carolina Press, 2014.

Lynn, Frank. "New Left Rap Hits Israel, Viet War, Draft." *Newsday*, Sept. 5, 1967, 4, 59.

Madhubuti, Haki R. *Groundwork: New and Selected Poems of Don L. Lee/Haki R. Madhubuti from 1966–1996*. Foreword by Gwendolyn Brooks. Preface by Bakari Kitwana. Chicago: Third World Press, 1996.

Malcolm X. "Zionist Logic." *Egyptian Gazette*, Sept. 17, 1964.

Malcolm X, with the assistance of Alex Haley. *The Autobiography of Malcolm X*. Introduction by M. S. Handler. Epilogue by Alex Haley. New York: Ballantine, 1973.

Marable, Manning. *Malcolm X: A Life of Reinvention*. New York: Viking, 2011.

Marable, Manning, and Hishaam D. Aidi. *Black Routes to Islam*. New York: Palgrave Macmillan, 2009.

Masri, Bassem. "The Fascinating Story of How the Ferguson-Palestine Solidarity Movement Came Together." www.alternet.org/activism/frontline-ferguson-protester-and-palestinian -american-bassem-masri-how-ferguson2palestine.

Matthews, Connie. "Will Racism or International Proletarian Solidarity Conquer?" *Black Panther*, April 25, 1970.

McAlister, Melani. *Epic Encounters: Culture, Media, and U.S. Interests in the Middle East, 1945–2000*. Berkeley: University of California Press, 2001.

McCutcheon, Steve D. "Selections from a Panther Diary." In Jones, *The Black Panther Party [Reconsidered]*, 115–34.

McReynolds, David. "On Bayard Rustin and the Israel Question." *Left Letters*, August 8, 2006. www.barglow.com/aprildems/OnRustin.htm.

———. "A Thousand Coffins at the United Nations." *Women's World*, March 19, 2002. www.wworld.org/programs/middleEast.asp?ID=102.

Medvecky, Nick. "Revolution Until Victory—Palestine al-Fatah." *Inner City Voice* 2, no. 2 (1969): 5–6, 17.

"Message to the President on the Resignation of Ambassador Andrew Young and on United States Relations with the Middle East and Africa." In Zogby and O'Dell, *Afro-Americans Stand Up*, 35–39.

"The Middle East: An Editorial Comment." *Jihad News* (volume and issue not indicated, but believed to be 1, no. 3 [Oct. 1973]).

Miller, Alan W. "Black Anti-Semitism—Jewish Racism." *Black Anti-Semitism and Jewish Racism*. New York: Schocken, 1970.

Miller, Jake C. "Black Viewpoints on the Mid-East Conflict." *Journal of Palestine Studies* 10, no. 2 (1981): 37–49.

"NAACP Sponsors Black Leadership Meeting." *The Crisis*, Nov. 1979, 365–71.

National Committee to Defend New Afrikan Freedom Fighters. "Zionism Is Racism: Palestine Will Win! New Afrika and Palestine Linked in a Common Struggle." *Arm the Spirit*, no. 14 (1982): 10, 14.

Neal, Lawrence P. "Black Power in the International Context." In *Black Power Revolt: A Collection of Essays*, edited by Floyd B. Barbour, 136–42. Boston: Porter Sargent, 1968.

Nero, Ray. "An Appeal to Reason: A Message to the Negroes Who Support Israel." *Black News*, July 23, 1970.

Newby, Robert G. "Afro-Americans and Arabs: An Alliance in the Making?" *Journal of Palestine Studies* 10, no. 2 (1981): 50–58.

Newsome, Yvonne D. "International Issues and Domestic Ethnic Relations: African Americans, American Jews, and the Israel–South Africa Debate." *International Journal of Politics, Culture, and Society* 5, no. 1 (1991): 19–48.

———. "Transnationalism in Black-Jewish Conflict: A Study of Global Identification Among Established Americans." *Race and Society* 4 (2001): 89–107.

Newton, Huey P. *Revolutionary Suicide*. Introduction by Fredrika Newton. New York: Penguin, 2009.

———. *To Die for the People: The Writings of Huey P. Newton*. Introduction by Franz Schurmann. New York: Random House, 1972.

"No Easy Victories Interview: Robert Van Lierop." Interview by William Minter, New York, April 16, 2004. In *No Easy Victories: African Liberation and American Activists Over a Half Century, 1950–2000*, edited by William Minter, Gail Hovey, and Charles Cobb Jr. www.noeasyvictories.org/interviews/int07_vanlierop.php.

Oden, Robert Stanley. "A Comparison of the Political Thought of Huey P. Newton and Osama Bin Laden." *Black Scholar* 37, no. 2 (2007): 53–60.

Ogbar, Jeffrey O. G. *Black Power: Radical Politics and African American Identity*. Baltimore: Johns Hopkins University Press, 2004.

Olsson, Göran Hugo, dir. "The Black Power Mixtape, 1967–1975." Louverture Films, 2011. DVD.

Ongiri, Amy Abugo. *Spectacular Blackness: The Cultural Politics of the Black Power Movement and the Search for a Black Aesthetic*. Charlottesville: University of Virginia Press, 2010.

"The Palestine Liberation Organization and the Black Pastors' Conference." In Zogby and O'Dell, *Afro-Americans Stand Up*, 31–33.

"The Palestine Problem: Test Your Knowledge." *SNCC Newsletter* 1, no. 4 (1967): 4–5.

"Palestine Will Be Free! Zionism, White Supremacy and the Palestinian Revolution." *Breakthrough* 6, no. 1 (1982): 8–16.

"Paper Presented by Supporters of the Popular Front for the Liberation of Palestine." *Black Panther*, Jan. 24, 1970.

Pearson, Hugh. *The Shadow of the Panther: Huey Newton and the Price of Black Power in America*. Reading, MA: Addison-Wesley, 1994.

Pennock, Pamela. *The Rise of the Arab-American Left: Activists, Allies, and Their Fight Against Imperialism and Racism, 1960s–1980s*. Chapel Hill: University of North Carolina Press, 2017.

"Playboy Interview: Malcolm X." *Playboy*, May 1963, 53–63.

Podhoretz, Norman. "My Negro Problem—and Ours." *Commentary*, Feb. 1, 1963, 93–101.

Raab, David. *Terror in Black September: The First Eyewitness Account of the Infamous 1970 Hijackings*. New York: Palgrave Macmillan, 2007.

Rafalko, Frank J. *MH/CHAOS: The CIA's Campaign Against the Radical New Left and the Black Panthers*. Annapolis, MD: Naval Institute Press, 2011.

"Randa Khalidi on Palestinians, Black Panthers, and Dramaturgy." *Daily Star*, Feb. 16, 2013.

"A Reply to *Muhammad Speaks*," *African World*, July 1974.

"Resolution on Palestinian Rights and Middle East Peace." In Zogby and O'Dell, *Afro-Americans Stand Up*, 25–26.

Rout, Kathleen. *Eldridge Cleaver*. Boston: Twayne, 1991.

Rubin, Mike. *An Israeli Worker's Answer to M. S. Arnoni*. New York: Ad Hoc Committee on the Middle East, 1968.

Rustin, Bayard. "American Negroes and Israel." *The Crisis*, April 1974, 115–18. Reprinted in *Time on Two Crosses: The Collected Writings of Bayard Rustin*, edited by Devon W. Carrado and Donald Weise, 319–26. San Francisco: Cleis, 2003.

———. "Andrew Young, the PLO, and Black-Jewish Relations." *New Leader*, Sept. 10, 1979.

———. "Black Links to Israel." *Amsterdam News*, March 29, 1972.

———. "Black Power and Coalition Politics." *Commentary*, Sept. 1966, 35–40.

———. "Blacks and the PLO: Setting Back Peace and Civil Rights." *Washington Post*, Oct. 7, 1979.

———. "The PLO: Freedom Fighters or Terrorists?" *Miami Times*, Dec. 19, 1974.

Schanche, Don A. "Eldridge Cleaver Speaks from Exile. *True*, Jan. 1970, 34–37, 100–102.

Schneier, Rabbi Marc. "Remembering Martin Luther King's Ties to Israel." *Chicago Jewish News*, Jan. 15, 2010.

———. *Shared Dreams: Martin Luther King, Jr. and the Jewish Community*. Preface by Martin Luther King III. Woodstock, VT: Jewish Lights, 1999.

"SCLC Fact-Finding Mission to Lebanon." *Journal of Palestine Studies* 10, no. 2 (1981): 157–68.

"SCLC, PUSH Leaders Hit by Other Black Leaders for Meetings with PLO." *Jet*, Nov. 1, 1979.

Seale, Bobby. *Seize the Time: The Story of the Black Panther Party*. London: Arrow, 1970.

Sellers, Cleveland. *The River of No Return: The Autobiography of a Black Militant and the Life and Death of SNCC*. Jackson: University Press of Mississippi, 1990.

Selzer, Michael. *Israel as a Factor in Jewish-Gentile Relations in America: Observations in the Aftermath of the June, 1967 War*. Introduction by Rabbi Elmer Berger. New York: American Council for Judaism, 1968.

Sgt. Pepper. "Oy Veh." *Berkeley Barb*, Jan. 30–Feb. 6, 1970.

Shakur, Zayd Malik. "Zionist Attack on Harlem Office Foiled by Community." *Black Panther*, May 19, 1970.

Shemesh, Kokhavi. "This Is My Opinion," *Matzpen*, Jan. 1973. Reprinted in *Documents from Israel, 1967–1973: Readings for a Critique of Zionism*, ed. Uri Davis and Norton Mezvinsky, 15–16. London: Ithaca Press, 1975.

"The Silence Is Broken." *Freedomways* 23, no. 2 (1983): 67–69.

Singh, Nikhil Pal. *Climbin' Jacob's Ladder: The Black Freedom Movement Writings of Jack O'Dell*. Berkeley: University of California Press, 2010.

"The Sky's the Limit." *Black Panther*, Oct. 24, 1970.

Slate, Nico, ed. *Black Power Beyond Borders: The Global Dimensions of the Black Power Movement*. New York: Palgrave Macmillan, 2012.

Smethhurst, James Edward. *The Black Arts Movement: Literary Nationalism in the 1960s and 1970s*. Chapel Hill: University of North Carolina Press, 2006.

Stanford, Karin L. *Beyond the Boundaries: Reverend Jesse Jackson in International Affairs*. Foreword by Ronald W. Walters. Albany: State University of New York Press, 1997.

"Statement of David Gilbert." *Arm the Spirit*, no. 14 (Fall 1982): 9.

Staub, Michael E. *Torn at the Roots: The Crisis of Jewish Liberalism in Postwar America*. New York: Columbia University Press, 2002.

Stevens, Richard P. *Zionism, South Africa and Apartheid: The Paradoxical Triangle*. Beirut: PLO Research Center, 1969.

Sundquist, Eric J. *Strangers in the Land: Blacks, Jews, Post-Holocaust America*. Cambridge, MA: Belknap Press of Harvard University Press, 2005.

Tannous, Izzat. *The Enraging Story of Palestine and Its People*. New York: Palestine Liberation Organization, 1965.

Timmerman, Kenneth. *Shakedown: Exposing the Real Jesse Jackson*. Washington: Regnery, 2003.

Torregian, Sotère. "Poem for the Birthday of Huey P. Newton." In *New Black Voices: An Anthology of Contemporary Afro-American Literature*, edited by Abraham Chapman, 343–44. New York: Penguin, 1972.

Touré, Askia Muhammad. "A Song in Blood and Tears." *Negro Digest/Black World*, Nov. 1971, 20.

"Towards Peace in the Middle East." *Freedomways* 19, no. 3 (1979): 133–36.

Umoja, Akinyele O. "The Black Liberation Army and the Radical Legacy of the Black Panther Party." In Jeffries, *Black Power*, 224–51.

Van Deburg, William L. *Modern Black Nationalism: From Marcus Garvey to Louis Farrakhan*. New York: New York University Press, 1997.

———. *New Day in Babylon: The Black Power Movement and American Culture, 1965–1975*. Chicago: University of Chicago Press, 1992.

Vincent, Rickey. *Party Music: The Inside Story of the Black Panthers' Band and How Black Power Transformed Soul Music*. Chicago: Chicago Review Press, 2013.

Walker, Wyatt Tee. "Liberation Theology in the Middle East." *Freedomways* 23, no. 3 (1983): 147–52.

———. *A Prophet from Harlem Speaks: Sermons and Essays*. Foreword by W. Franklin Richardson. New York: Martin Luther King Fellows Press, 1997.

Walters, Ronald W. "The Black Initiatives in the Middle East." *Journal of Palestine Studies* 10, no. 2 (1981): 3–13.

———. "The Future of Pan-Africanism." *Black World/Negro Digest*, Oct. 1975, 4–18.

———. "The New Black Political Culture." *Black World/Negro Digest*, Oct. 1972, 4–17.

———. "The Resignation of Andrew Young: The Black Response." *New Directions: The Howard University Magazine*, Fall 1979, 7–15.

Warschawski, Michel. *On the Border*. Translated by Levi Laub. Cambridge, MA: South End, 2005.

Washington, James, ed. *A Testament of Hope: The Essential Writings and Speeches of Martin Luther King, Jr.* New York: HarperOne, 1990.

Watkins, Rychetta. *Black Power, Yellow Power, and the Making of Revolutionary Identities*. Jackson: University Press of Mississippi, 2012.

Watts, Jerry Gafio. *Amiri Baraka: The Politics and Art of a Black Intellectual*. New York: New York University Press, 2001.

Weisbord, Robert G. *Bittersweet Encounter: The Afro-Americans and the American Jews*. Foreword by C. Eric Lincoln. Westport, CT: Negro Universities Press, 1970.

Weisbord, Robert G., and Richard Kazarian Jr. *Israel in the Black American Perspective*. Westport, CT: Greenwood, 1985.

Weisbord, Robert G., and Arthur Stein. "Black Nationalism and the Arab-Israeli Conflict." *Patterns of Prejudice* 3 (Nov.-Dec. 1969): 1–9.

Whitehorn, Laura, ed. *Safiya Bukhari: The War Before: The True Life Story of Becoming a Black Panther, Keeping the Faith in Prison and Fighting for Those Left Behind*. Foreword by Angela Y. Davis. Afterword by Mumi Abu-Jamal. New York: Feminist Press, 2010.

"Why I Left America: Conversation: Ida Lewis and James Baldwin." In Chapman, *New Black Voices*, 409–19.

Williams, Michael W. "Pan-Africanism and Zionism: The Delusion of Comparability." *Journal of Black Studies* 21, no. 3 (1991): 348–71.

Williams, Yohuru R. "American Exported Black Nationalism: The Student Nonviolent Coordinating Committee, the Black Panther Party, and the Worldwide Freedom Struggle, 1967–1972." *Negro History Bulletin* 60 (July–Sept. 1997): 13–20.

Wilson, Ernest J. "Orientalism: A Black Perspective." *Journal of Palestine Studies* 10, no. 2 (1981): 59–69.

Winston, Henry M. "Black Americans and the Middle East Conflict." *World Marxist Review*, Nov. 1970, 18–23.

———. *Black Americans and the Middle East Conflict*. New York: New Outlook, 1970.

Yanker, Gary. *Prop Art: Over 1000 Contemporary Political Posters*. New York: Darien House, 1972.

Young, Andrew. *An Easy Burden: The Civil Rights Movement and the Transformation of America*. Foreword by Quincy Jones. Waco, TX: Baylor University Press, 2008.

Young, Cynthia A. *Soul Power: Culture, Radicalism, and the Making of a U.S. Third World Left*. Durham, NC: Duke University Press, 2006.

Young, Lewis. "American Blacks and the Arab-Israeli Conflict." *Journal of Palestine Studies* 2, no. 1 (1972): 70–85.

Zogby, James, and Jack O'Dell, eds. *Afro-Americans Stand Up for Middle East Peace*. Washington: Palestine Human Rights Campaign, 1980.

INDEX

Stanford Studies in

COMPARATIVE RACE AND ETHNICITY

Published in collaboration with the Center for Comparative Studies in Race and Ethnicity, Stanford University

SERIES EDITORS

Hazel Rose Markus
Paula M. L. Moya